American
Literary
History:
1607–1830

BORZOI
STUDIES IN HISTORY

Adviser:
EDWARD LURIE
Penn State University Medical School

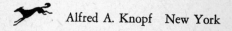 Alfred A. Knopf   New York

American Literary History:

1607–1830

RUSSEL B. NYE

Michigan State University

 *Prescript*

The aim of this book is to follow the development of the customary genres of American literature, using the term broadly, from the beginnings of colonization to the approach of the full tide of the American Romantic movement. It also involves an attempt to place the history of American literature during these years within the wider context of social, political, and cultural developments where such relationships seem relevant and where the connections seem meaningful.

For a relatively small book, this is a large topic, covering a long span of years. Obviously, all writers who ought to be mentioned cannot be. I have tried to include those who are representative of trends and ideas, those whose contributions to the literary tradition seem of more than minor importance, and those whose work, if not major or representative, provide some additional understanding of the life of their time and place. What this study is about, in essence, is the imaginative use that Americans made of their experience from the time of their arrival on the continent to the time of their unconscious but nonetheless valid conviction that they were *Americans,* a new and different kind of cultural entity.

The seventeenth-century immigrants to the New World were transplanted Englishmen and Europeans, who thought and wrote as their contemporaries at home, and whose writings reflected contemporary European and English issues, interests, and models. Yet the point is that they *were* transplanted, and what they thought and wrote existed in an American environment that modified and eventually transformed the cultural heritage they brought with them. The central purpose, therefore, of this study is to indicate, illustrate, and explain the naturalizing process as it applied to the American experience and as it appeared in the literature that experience produced.

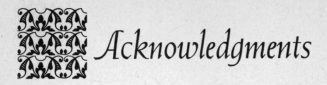 *Acknowledgments*

The author wishes to thank Edward Lurie, Richard Beale
Davis, and Norman Grabo, whose readings of the manuscript
measurably improved it. Thanks are also due to the staff of the
Michigan State University Library for cheerful, helpful co-
operation.

Contents

THE
GROWTH
OF
PROVINCIAL
CULTURE
1607–1730

 ONE

THE ENGLISH COLONIES
IN AMERICA

The Backgrounds of Colonization:
Renaissance and Reformation

Between 1607, when the London Company dispatched settlers for Virginia, and 1642, when civil war broke out in England, some 70,000 men, women, and children left the mother country for the American colonies. No one, of course, can determine exactly why they came, but they came from all parts of England and from all classes, though chiefly from the middle third of society. Some paid their way, others came under indenture. Some were (as legend has it) transplanted felons, debtors, vagrants, orphans, and others escaping from poverty and the law; the Virginia Company, for example, sent over one hundred children from the London slums in 1619 to swell the colony's population. A few were aristocrats like Thomas West, Lord De La Warre, who arrived at Chesapeake Bay in 1610; more often they were younger sons who had small hope at home of inheriting land and fortune. However, by far the greater majority of them were rather ordinary people—farmers, fishermen, tradesmen, artisans, coopers, sawyers, millers, and the like—from England's growing middle class.

Whoever they were and whatever their condition, New England Puritan and Virginia adventurer alike, they were Englishmen of the Renaissance, out of the age of Drake, Raleigh, and Marlowe. Shakespeare was at the height of his career when Jamestown was settled; Bacon's *Novum Organum* appeared the same year the Pilgrims landed at Plymouth; Massachusetts Bay was a flourishing colony when Milton published *Paradise Lost;*

3

Harvard College, in fact, was founded a year before Ben Jonson died.

In a manner of speaking, America itself was a Renaissance creation, discovered at the close of the fifteenth century when Europe was breaking out of its geographic shell. Though the Vikings settled in America almost 500 years earlier (and if colonists had followed the Vikings as they did Columbus and Cartier, North American civilization would have been something quite different), Europe was not sufficiently interested in the New World to explore it until the Renaissance displaced feudalism in European society and secularism replaced the theological spirit in the European mind.

Renaissance life pushed outward; men wanted to increase the scope of their experience, to see, hear, feel, know, and assimilate all knowledge that the universe held. Renaissance man hoped to find out everything about this world as well as the next and everything about himself as well as the Divine. Navigation and science revealed much to him about his world, literature and philosophy much about his own nature. Exploration turned Europe's eyes outward: Spain sent Columbus toward the Indies, he wrote, "so that I might see what they were like . . . and might seek out and know the nature of everything that is there," exactly as England sent Cabot westward in 1497, and as Portugal sent Vasco da Gama toward India in 1498. Humanism turned the eyes of Renaissance man inward, for the era of Galileo and Bacon was characterized by a consuming curiosity about the inward nature of man. When the colonists came to America, they brought with them the tremendous centrifugal energy of Elizabethan England and the great centripetal drive of Renaissance humanism.

The immigrants to America were also products of the Reformation as well as of the Renaissance. Beginning in the fifteenth century, powerful monarchs overthrew the authority of the Church and substituted their own, transferring temporal authority from Rome to throne, while cracks within the Church undermined its internal ecclesiastical and moral power. Magellan began his voyage around the world in 1519 (a voyage second in importance only to Columbus'), only two years after Luther nailed his theses to the door of the castle church at Wittenberg. In 1531, Henry VIII, for a variety of reasons, established the Church of England as a "protestant" move against Catholicism. By 1600, when England was ready to colonize America, it possessed not only a national Anglican Church but a strong tradition of religious dissent and diversity. Of the first four English Colonies, Virginia was Anglican; Plymouth, Separatist; Massachusetts Bay, Puritan; and Maryland, Catholic.

The spirit of American culture in the seventeenth and eighteenth centuries was thus overwhelmingly Protestant, whether it derived from Luther, Calvin, Cranmer, or George Fox. From the time of Henry VIII to that of William and Mary, England and Europe were in religious turmoil. The Stuarts rose and fell, as did Cromwell's Puritan Commonwealth, during the decades in which the American colonies were shaping their churches and governments. The settlers brought with them memories of plots, real and imagined; persecutions, wars, and bitter, endless disputes—another Reformation heritage kept fresh in American minds.

Not only England, but all of Europe shared in the colonization of the Americas. England, in fact, came late to the New World—more than a century after Columbus. Spanish explorers and settlers reached Florida, New Mexico, and California only a half-century after Columbus; Champlain founded Quebec before the Separatists arrived at Plymouth; there was a Dutch colony in America before Massachusetts Bay and a Swedish one less than a decade after.

But England, of course, furnished the great majority of settlers and the cultural, political, and social base on which American life was built; it was England that for 150 years ruled that part of the continent from which the United States emerged. "For better or worse," writes Louis Wright in describing the roots of American civilization, "we have inherited the fundamental qualities in our culture from the British. . . . We should not overlook other influences which have affected American life, influences from France, Holland, Spain, Germany, Scandinavia and the rest of Europe, and also influences from Asia and Europe. But we must always remember that such was the vigor of British culture that it assimilated all others. . . . We cannot escape an inheritance that has given us some of our sturdiest and most lasting qualities."

Those Who Came and Why

A knowledgeable, assertive, and independent middle class had grown up in England under Tudor rule, and the accession of James I in 1603 marked its emergence to power. By the time of the Stuarts, England was well on its way to becoming a nation of shopkeepers. James was a man of peace, stability, and bourgeois virtue, a "safe" monarch trusted by the middle class, and the mood and style of seventeenth-century colonial life was that of James' England. London, the focal point of English life, was controlled by an alert, vigorous middle class to whom the colonies meant trade, investment, and profit.

These people believed in work, self-help, caution, and thrift; the older idea of the gentleman, from the courtier's books of Elizabeth's time, was out of tune with their ideals. Noblemen still commanded respect and emulation, but rich and nonaristo-cratic men in trade and business commanded just as much in their own circles and often exercised considerably greater power. The English middle class believed that there was a relationship among virtue, property, work, and wealth. Defoe had Robinson Crusoe's father write to his son about the attractions of "the middle station of life," its "peace and plenty . . . temperance, moderation, quietness, health, society, all agreeable diversions and all desirable pleasures." From this diverse but substantial group came the bulk of American settlers.

They came for reasons as varied as the individuals themselves. There were, of course, zealots with visions, failures looking for another chance, fugitives fleeing justice, husbands leaving nagging wives, or speculators looking for quick wealth. The most impelling motive, undoubtedly, was the incentive to better one's self in the New World. The man who found insufficient outlet for his ambition and energy in the rather rigidly controlled English society of the times certainly must have hoped to find something better in the fluid and loosely regulated society of the Colonies.

England suffered a series of economic depressions over the first half of the seventeenth century, and English villages and cities were filled with desperate poor. Since land was held tightly in large estates, it was almost impossible for a poor farmer to own any or, if he owned some, to gain more; the prospect of owning one's own acres in America must have been a powerful lure. As John Winthrop asked, surveying his own village before leaving for America, "Why should we stand striving here . . . and in the meantime suffer a whole continent as fruitful and convenient for the use of man to be waste without any improvement?" "In Virginia land free and labor scarce," ran a saying in the 1640s, "in England land scarce and labor plenty." After 1492, whenever and wherever Europe lacked land and opportunity, men came to the New World to find them—this was as true of sixteenth-century Spain, England, and France as of nineteenth-century Ireland, Italy, or Germany.

There were naturally many other motives for coming to the New World beyond those of economic self-interest. Continuous conflicts between the Catholic Church and the Church of England and between the Church of England and its own dissenters sent some Englishmen to the Colonies in search of religious peace. If a man in England felt that he was not allowed to worship as he wished, it was only natural for him to go where the long arm of orthodoxy might not reach. Thus, Puritan Thomas Hooker, believing that in England "God is packing up the Gospel because nobody will buy His Wares," packed up too and left for New England.

Whereas emigration to America meant for an ambitious man a chance to get a fresh start, it represented to others—dissenters, Quakers, Catholics, Pietists—a chance for a pious man to live a godly life without interference. None can deny the powerful drive of economic self-interest in settling the Colonies, but it should also be remembered that six of the original settlements

(Plymouth, Massachusetts Bay, Maryland, Rhode Island, New Haven, and Pennsylvania) were founded by religious groups. There were those too, naturally, who conveniently combined the material and spiritual; as one Massachusetts settler put it bluntly, he came "to worship God and make money."

Patriotism brought some settlers to the New World; emigration offered the chance to plant England beyond the seas in order to make a stroke for God and King against the Spanish and French. John Donne, preaching a sermon to the Virginia Company in 1622, reminded prospective settlers that by emigrating they could "join all to that world that shall never grow old, the kingdom of heaven" and at the same time help to save the New World from Catholic Spain by "strengthening that plantation" in Virginia. Plain love of adventure brought others; what William Byrd of Virginia called the chance for "Quixotic adventure" appealed to those restless, adventurous men who, Sir Walter Raleigh wrote, must always "seek new worlds for gold, for praise, for glory." No doubt many a youth set sail to escape a humdrum life at home and to see what it was like in that strange new world beyond the sea.

The New World Vision

Many Englishmen accepted the chance to come to America for many different reasons; yet the early migrations could hardly be considered a mass movement. Compared to the number of Englishmen who preferred to stay at home regardless of conditions, the number who decided to leave for America was relatively small. Of the 70,000 or so who did migrate before the Cromwellian wars, more than half went to the West Indies, where living was easier and economic and social conditions more stable than in North America. Despite exposure to some of the most seductive propaganda ever penned, surprisingly few responded to the lure of "Come to America" promoters. The exact workings of the selective process that drew settlers to America must remain forever unknown, for in making his choice, each individual made his own private decision out of his own mixture of motives and dreams. "Intentions are secret," wrote settler John White. "Who can discover them?"

America epitomized, to those who decided to come to it, an idea into which men put faith, hope, and their vision of a fresh, new civilization. The idea of America appealed to the imagination as well as to the purse; it seemed a possible paradise where things could be better; "a land to be desired," Columbus called it, "and once seen, never to be left." Some of the emigrants found America to be this place and held to their vision through all the sicknesses, hardships, and loneliness that the land held for them. The first ordeal was the voyage to America across a treacherous sea in crowded, badly provisioned ships threatened by storms, disease, starvation, and pirates. The death rate would be high (out of 138 settlers in one Virginia-bound ship, 100 died), and nearly every immigrant in the early waves of settlement had a story of hardship to tell. They found a land blanketed with forests as Europe had not been for centuries; a "hideous and desolate wilderness," one of the Plymouth colonists wrote, "full of wilde beasts and wilde men."

Once the settlers confronted the hard facts of day-to-day survival, they tempered their enthusiasm and scaled down their expectations, for the effort of maintaining a new society was greater than that of exploration and settlement. The early colonist, John Smith said, faced "the furie of savages, famine, and all manner of mischiefs and inconveniences," as 1,000 deaths in Virginia by 1620 testified. Yet despite the disappointment that must have followed the first shock of reality, they seemed to believe that they had found a kind of Eden, which offered almost unlimited rewards. "This is as God made it," exclaimed Smith on viewing Virginia, "when he created the world."

The Transit of Calvinism

Martin Luther initiated the Reformation, but John Calvin had greater influence in bringing it to England. There, his *Institutes of the Christian Religion* (1536–1559) gained him a large following, as it had in France, Scotland, and

Holland. Calvin's doctrines were arranged in a tightly reasoned progression, beginning with the proposition that the chief end of man, as the Catechism phrased it, is "to glorify God and enjoy Him forever" in absolute dependence and obedience to His will. "Every action in a man's life that doth not serve this great end," wrote Samuel Willard of Massachusetts, "is a vain action." Man's power to serve God had been lost in Adam's fall; man's primary purpose since the fall was to strive for salvation so that he might regain that power.

In 1619, at the Synod of Dort in Holland, most of the differences over creed among Calvinists were resolved by agreement on five major points of doctrine: Man is inherently sinful and depraved, unable to choose good from evil; some men will be saved or "elected" by Christ's intervention; this salvation will come through God's "prevenient" and "irresistible" grace; the elect, once saved, "persevere" and remain saved; God is the absolute Sovereign of all things, and all things are governed by His providence.

In England, after Henry VIII, the clash between Catholic Church and Church of England was sharp and sometimes bloody. Elizabeth's Settlement Act of 1562, a compromise between Catholics and Anglicans, did not satisfy all her Calvinist subjects. Before long, those Calvinist dissidents who felt that the "purification" of the English Church had not gone far enough were generally called "Puritans." The Puritans believed that the Reformation in England was incomplete, that too many "Popish" elements survived in the church service—ornaments, vestments, swinging censers, rich music, prescribed forms of prayer and worship—and too much authority remained vested in the hierarchy of priests and bishops.

The Bible and the State

Theologically, the Puritans were in accord with most Church of England doctrines. Their great disagreement with the Anglican theologians centered on the importance and function of the Bible in worship and on the derivation and arrangement of authority in Church government. Available in English for only a century before the settlement of the American colonies, the Bible was to the Puritan the inexhaustible fountainhead of all knowledge. Church of England doctrine held that Scripture was a primary and infallible source of revelation, but not the only one; the writings of the Church fathers, the judgments of those in authority, and the accumulated knowledge of Church discipline were also important.

The Puritan, however, considered the Bible to be the sole revealed word of God, a complete body of laws and moral instructions so inclusive and sufficient that men could discover in it everything required for a Christian life. If God is infinite, he reasoned, it is inconceivable that anything worth knowing could exist outside His book, so therefore he rejected all Church discipline not specifically granted in the Bible. "All ecclesiastical actions invented and devised by man," wrote one of them, "are utterly to be excluded out of the exercise of religion," and nothing was to be accepted "without subordination under or dependence on" the Word as revealed in the Bible.

The English Puritan's revolt against royal and ecclesiastical authority took two directions. Some were willing to remain within the Church of England if allowed to reform it, especially in the matter of Church government. Refusing to acknowledge the jurisdiction of the Church hierarchy, they preferred to control themselves through "presbyters," or elders, appointed by each congregation and acknowledged no higher ecclesiastical office. Others (termed variously Independents, Separatists, or Congregationalists) withdrew from the Church of England to make each congregation into a separate, independent unit answerable to no one. While many Anglicans could accept and even admire the Puritan's theology (as reputedly King James did), neither Church nor Crown could tolerate his rejection of the episcopal system and his demand for presbyterian or congregational autonomy. "I shall make them conform themselves," James I said in 1604, "or I will harry them out of the land, or else I shall do worse," and with Archbishop Laud's help, he did.

Calvinism arrived in the American colonies during the second stage of its theological development, a few years after the Synod of Dort, when emphasis was less on the evolution of doctrine than on its exposition and application. The task of the Puritan colonists was not so much to develop their creed as to embody it in a government and a society. New England received from Old England both Presbyterians (as in Massachusetts Bay) and Separatists (as at Plymouth), as well as other dissident elements such as Quakers, Baptists, and individualists like Roger Williams and Anne Hutchinson, both of whom were shortly banished from Massachusetts.

To bring theological unity to the New England settlements, the leaders of Massachusetts Bay called a meeting which in 1648 adopted the Cambridge Platform of Church Discipline, approved by the Massachusetts General Court in 1651. Theologically, the Cambridge Platform followed the Westminster Confession (adopted two years earlier by the English Puritans), which differed little from the Dort agreement of 1619. However, the Cambridge group explicitly gave the state power to enforce obedience "in matters of godlinesse." With congregations determined to pursue "any corrupt way of their own," the Magistrate "is to put forth his coercive power as the matter shall require." From that point, although internal debate never lessened, New England Puritanism remained a relatively unified, self-regulating body of theology.

The Puritan Spirit

Puritanism dominated the life of New England for more than a century, and after its dominance was gone, continued to exert decisive influence on the shape of the American mind. As New Englanders moved westward, reinforced by other Calvinist migrants from England and Europe, they carried the Puritan faith and feel of life with them, impressing its distinctive mark on American manners, mores, and ideas. This much may be claimed, but it is also too easy to find the legacy of the Puritans in too many places and to use it to explain too many things. Many elements in the so-called American character conveniently attributed to the Puritan were also characteristic of other faiths in seventeenth-century life. The New England Puritans have been called pious, sober, self-disciplined, self-reliant, pragmatic, idealistic, narrow, self-righteous, hypocritical, and many other things. They undoubtedly were all of these, but so too, at one time or another, were Catholics, Anglicans, Quakers, Dutch Reformed, Lutherans, and almost every other religious group in the Colonies, England, or Europe. The Puritans had no monopoly on any of those qualities customarily called "puritanical" in their own or later times.

Since the word is still loaded with a variety of connotations, one must be careful to distinguish between Puritanism as a body of theological doctrine and church polity and "puritanism" as a set of attitudes and a way of life deriving from that theology. At bottom, puritanism involves first an acceptance of the fundamental imperfection of human nature and all its creations, an acceptance of the fact that neither man nor his society is perfect, and that life on earth is permanently flawed, though possibly pleasurable. Second, it takes a morally idealistic stance toward this fact. The puritan personality is convinced that his and life's imperfections can be repaired, and that it is the individual's duty and responsibility to do so with God's help. Truly, the world is blemished, but it can be made better; man is defective, but he *is* man, and he can make himself a little lower than the angels.

Third, puritanism was always intensely earnest, and seventeenth-century Calvinism gave short shrift to the tender minded. "You must not think to go to heaven on a feather-bed," one New England minister warned his flock. "If you will be Christ's disciple you must take up His Cross and it will make you sweet." "God sent you *not* in this world as a Play-house," said another, "but a Work-house." To be Puritan demanded self-discipline, self-trial, self-denial. Fourth, puritanism was individualistic. Salvation depended for the Puritan on himself; the Bible, the church, good works, and good intentions might help, but in the end he faced God alone.

Fifth, the experience of conversion and salvation set the Puritan apart, gave him special obligations and privileges, and instilled in him a sense of specialty. Puritanism contained the assurance that one *can* be saved; sometimes, unfortunately, this assurance turned puritanism into self-righteousness unless one tempered it with humility. Sixth, puritanism gave life an ethical bias, that rigid obedience to moral standards was important, that men were personally accountable for the consequences of their actions. In its totality, this "puritanical" set of mind could lead to intolerance, self-righteousness, single-minded narrowness, perhaps hypocrisy. It could also lead toward activism, self-faith, energy, hope for the future, and joy in accomplishment.

The Colonial Cultural Setting

The literature of the first American century accurately reflected the time and place that produced it. The point is not that it was scarce, but rather that considering the conditions under which it was written, there was such a considerable amount of it. The colonists were plain people set down in the middle of a blank land, and the task of making homes and communities where none existed left little time for the politer arts. Simply to survive in the new settlements was a serious effort, for during the first half-century or so there was scant opportunity for the leisurely contemplation of the world that literature needed.

Yet the difficulties of establishing the cultural amenities on the first frontiers should not be overemphasized. The colonists were middle-class people concerned with making a viable, civilized society as quickly as possible, but they also respected learning as one of its necessities. Settlers in all the Colonies quickly set up schools and kept their cultural ties with England as close as possible—George Sandys, for example, in the midst of Jamestown's miasmic swamps, kept working on his translation of Ovid. Massachusetts had a press a year before Glasgow did and a hundred years before Liverpool; Winthrop, Mather, and a dozen other New Englanders belonged to the Royal Society.

Ships from London and Bristol always carried books to America along with their cargoes. In homes North and South there were good libraries, which, like those in England, included More, Raleigh, Sidney, Bacon, Burton, Browne, and the classics. William Brewster owned 400 books; even Captain Miles Standish, who was no scholar, owned 50. By the eighteenth century such scholars as Cotton Mather, William Byrd of Virginia, or Penn's secretary James Logan owned 3,000 or more volumes—respectable libraries even by English standards.

Colonial life, once the initial phase of settlement had passed, was not a barren intellectual wasteland—provincial and isolated, perhaps, but never separated from the mainstream of English and European thought. The kind of society in which arts and letters flourished came later, but this did not mean that the early colonists wrote nothing. They wrote in surprising quantities and with remarkable vitality. They constantly recorded what they saw and felt, using chiefly those forms that to them had public value—sermons, tracts, journals, histories, moralistic verse—and that best fitted and expressed the aims and needs of their society.

Colonial literature was derivative rather than native or original, a combination of American experience and English tradition. Since the colonial writer usually considered himself an Englishman who merely happened not to be in England, much of what he wrote was for English consumption; he wrote, therefore, according to standards that would be approved at home, in forms whose purpose was primarily utilitarian.

Literary Beginnings

Three facts influenced American colonial writing over most of its first century. First, it represented the viewpoint of the middle-class Englishman whose major interest was the advancement of his material welfare (illustrated by the first book to come from Virginia, Captain John Smith's *True Relation* of 1608) and his soul's salvation (illustrated by the second, the Reverend Alexander Whitaker's *Good News From Virginia* of 1613). Industrious, moralistic, and energetic, these authors were practical men concerned with subduing and exploiting a new land. Suspicious of the imagination, essentially conservative in taste and pragmatic in temperament, the colonists believed literature should be purposeful as well as attractive. The motive that induced most colonial Americans to put pen to paper was practicality, and they valued writing that was done, as New England's Thomas Hooker said, with "plainnesse and perspicuity, both of matter and manner of expression." Literature and the fine arts did not occupy a large part in the colonists' lives, for they considered such things to be only handmaidens to learning and theology.

Second, American colonial writing derived directly in form and content from contemporary (or earlier) English and European writing. Crossing the ocean by no means severed the colonist's connections with his literary heritage. Spenser, Sidney, Herbert, and Quarles echoed through the poetry of the period; the language and pattern of Elizabethan travel books appeared in New England and Virginia accounts of exploration and settlement; the Cambridge scholars' imprint was clear on the sermons and commentaries of the clergy.

Being Protestants, and usually dissenters, colonial writers found the Bible, in both the Genevan and King James versions, a rich storehouse of language, symbol, imagery, and fact, and they used it in their own poetry and prose. This was especially true, of course, in New England; in probably no other society has Biblical knowledge been so widely diffused and deeply ingrained. While the Bible lent tremendous weight and resonance to colonial writing, it was also a constricting influence, a handy source of language and example which sometimes came too readily to mind.

Colonial culture was vigorously classical, too, and like educated men everywhere, American writers leaned heavily on Greek and Roman literature and learning, although they sometimes found some embarrassing conflicts among Rome, Athens, and Jerusalem. Michael Wigglesworth thought that the classics contained "a deal of Blasphemy and Heathenish Impiety," but Cotton Mather, on the other hand, advised young ministers to study Homer, Virgil, and Horace for good as well as pleasure. Whatever their misgivings, colonial writers found inspiration in the classical tradition second only to what they gained from the Bible itself. Nor were they provincial—William Brewster owned Machiavelli's *Prince;* Samuel Lee, the works of Descartes; Jonathan Mitchell, Montaigne's; Cotton Mather knew Rabelais and Cervantes.

Third, the impact of Calvinism on colonial culture lent American writing a distinctive tone of its own—plain, purposeful, direct, and centered on moralism and theology. Calvinism was never confined solely to New England. The German Lutherans, Reformed Dutch, French Huguenots, Scottish and Scotch-Irish Presbyterians, and Methodists and Baptists (whose creed contained strong "puritanical" elements) later augmented and deepened the Calvinistic influence introduced into America by the Separatists and Puritans. Since most of the formal writing and thinking in the seventeenth century was done by religiously minded men, the Calvinistic view of life tended to dominate their art. It was not that the English Calvinists who settled the Colonies lacked imagination or exclusively kept their eyes turned heavenward, for they were well aware of the beauty of the world and fully appreciative of the pleasures of life in it, however probationary and perilous living might be. It was, rather, that as Calvinists they believed that all intellectual and imaginative activity was purposeful, to be put to use in finding God and glorifying Him. The highly codified cultural and theological system in which the Calvinist lived controlled the way he used his experience, artistically and otherwise.

Society North and South

Four colonies—Virginia, Massachusetts, New York, and Pennsylvania—dominated the intellectual life of the seventeenth century; the other nine were either offshoots of these four or dependent in some way on their leadership. Massachusetts and Virginia, settled first, evolved distinctive societies earliest; however, New York, taken from the Dutch in 1664, and Pennsylvania, settled in 1681, soon also developed their own. New York and Virginia were basically Anglican and aristocratic, their social and cultural organization determined by their inheritance from Dutch patroons and English country gentry. Massachusetts and Pennsylvania, settled by dissenters, were organized somewhat more on nonconformist, middle-class lines. The literature produced during the seventeenth century tended to polarize around New England and the seaboard South because colonization came sooner to these areas, allowing social organization to be achieved earlier than in the other colonies.

The Southern colonies lacked population and trade centers such as Boston and New York. Distances were great, settlement sparse, roads poor, and travel difficult. A planter's life tended to be isolated, and his interests centered in London or Bristol, where his credit came from and where he sold his tobacco. However, the dominant class held to the cultured and gentlemanly tradition of English country families, who combined business and gracious living, trade and learning in aristocratic proportions. Well-to-do Southern families owned good libraries, educated their children by tutors at home or in English schools, and cultivated the arts, as Englishmen of their class did in England. The Reverend Hugh Jones thought his Virginia parishioners too often "diverted by Business or Inclination from profound Study and prying into the Depths of Things," but the evidence belies his judgment. The society of Virginia and Maryland, no less than that of Massachusetts or Pennsylvania, was a society in which educated men were trained to read, write, and think, one in which writing and reading were the marks of a gentleman. John Pory, first speaker of the Virginia House of Burgesses, was typical of his class in his resolve "to have some good book always in store, being in solitude the best and cleverest company." Robert Carter, who held 300,000 acres of good Virginia land in his estate, Corotoman, also held an excellent personal library; read Greek and Latin; was soundly grounded in law, history, philosophy, science, religion, and music; and played several instruments. Though wealthier than most of his neighbors, he was not unrepresentative of their interest in things of the mind.

As Louis Wright has explained and documented, similarities between the literary tastes of colonial New Englanders and

Southerners were as striking as their differences. Surveys of book collections and library lists show a surprisingly large number of titles common to collections of both sections; nor were their intellectual interests and attainments so different as earlier estimates assumed. Theologically minded Southerners read Milton, Calvin, and Richard Baxter as New Englanders did; Bunyan was as much a favorite in Virginia as in Massachusetts. Intelligent, educated men, North and South, were products of the same English system and looked across the Atlantic to the same models.

New England developed a literary life of its own more quickly than the Southern colonies, for it was more tightly organized and more compact geographically. It also had better roads and waterways. The Puritan colonists founded their faith on the individual's ability to read the Scriptures and to hear them expounded; illiteracy was therefore a real threat to society and the soul's salvation.

Southern writers had fewer places to publish what they wrote and a less geographically unified reading public. A great deal of early colonial Southern writing, like New England's, dealt with public experience and was contained in journals, addresses, letters, laws, and proclamations. Since a substantial proportion of Southern political writing was done in opposition to governmental policies, much of it could not be printed on government-controlled presses but appeared in newspapers or was circulated in manuscripts (as poetry often was); when published in these forms, it failed to survive. A large body of Southern writing did not survive, or else remained in manuscript collections for generations. The three wars that occurred in Virginia before 1815 no doubt destroyed other materials. Thousands of letters and journals that never reached print certainly existed in the South. An impressive body of Southern literary expression, therefore, has never been revealed for study. Richard Beale Davis' edition of William Fitzhugh's letters is an excellent example of the rich resources still to be made available for the study of Southern Colonial culture.

As might be expected, then, the majority of published writing in the seventeenth century in America appeared in New England. Massachusetts established a college in 1636 and two years later a printing press, which issued nearly 200 items over the next fifty years. An unusually high proportion of the settlers in both Northern and Southern colonies were university-trained men (despite legend, there was probably as high a proportion in Virginia as in Massachusetts and Connecticut), and the literacy rate was as high in Maryland, Virginia, and South Carolina as anywhere else in the Colonies. Virginia, in fact, established a college in 1620 (destroyed by Indian massacre in 1622), and William and Mary (1643) was only seven years younger than Harvard. The difference was that the South had few presses, a loosely organized and scattered semirural society, and no urban centers of trade and learning.

Faith and Art in New England

New Englanders took writing as a public expression of their ideas and wrote with conviction, occasionally with inspiration. They wrote about things that concerned them directly, for they believed that since they were involved in the most crucial experiment in history—to build God's Kingdom in this green, new land—what they said, did, and felt was worth remembering. The New England Puritan was not hostile to literature or neglectful of it; he simply believed that artistic expression had a higher purpose than pleasure alone.

New England's writing therefore, was divinely centered— "from God and to glorify God." God's sovereignty, the conviction that God is the ultimate authority and final measure, provided an ever-present theme in Puritan writing—"Man saith," wrote Urian Oakes, "he will do this and that, but he must ask God leave first." Art was purposeful, useful, insofar as it shaped man's life and spirit to understand and worship his Maker and celebrate His sovereignty.

The Puritan was not alone in blending aesthetics and theology or in claiming art for religious purposes. The concept of poetry as moral philosophy flourished in contemporary England; the example of John Milton came somewhat too late to have great effect on colonial verse, but colonial writers knew George Herbert and Francis Quarles and agreed with Abraham Cowley that "he who can write a *prophane poem well,* may write a *Divine one* better." The art they produced was prevailingly austere, moralistic, and directed to religious ends. Since they were not so much concerned with precision of form as with conviction of content, Puritan writing was remarkably varied and individualistic. They regarded boundaries between genres as fluid and indeterminate—Cotton Mather's incredibly inclusive *Magnalia Christi Americana,* published in London in 1702, contained about all the literary types popular in the seventeenth century, which were combined with a fine disregard for consistency.

New England, however, distrusted fiction and drama (by which the imagination might make human error too attractive) or any literature, Cotton Mather said, that "might tempt men away from truth to fables"; he preferred that "Words of Wisdom" should rule always over "Wisdom of Words." The function of poetry, of which the Puritans produced a good deal, was to move "the hearts and minds of men to righteousness," but this did not mean that they interpreted this injunction narrowly. They knew and imitated Spenser, Sidney, and Du Bartas and admired the English metaphysicals, finding in them an ethical and moral strain congruent to their needs; they were well aware of poetry's powerful aesthetic appeal and respected it as an effective means of expressing one's worship of God.

In prose the Puritan chose to write in a style stripped of Elizabethan circumlocutions and decorations, attending, as the *Bay Psalm Book* said, to "Conscience rather than Eloquence," or in William Bradford's definition, "a plaine style, with singular regard for the simple truth." The "plain style," however, did not mean that it was written without art. It meant, rather, that it was not the ornate pulpit style of the Anglican preachers, which the Puritans wished to avoid as they avoided stained-glass windows or gold-laced vestments and for the same reasons. Puritan prose reflected the disciplined restraint of men thoroughly trained in the art of discourse, who valued the apt word and the clear elucidation of knotty ideas. Good writing, wrote Thomas Hooker, should not "dazzle, but direct the apprehension," and his own sermon, "Repentant Sinners," exemplified this:

Sound contrition and brokenness of heart brings a strange and a sudden alteration into the world, varies the price and value of things and persons beyond imagination, turns the market upside down, makes the things appear as they be, and the persons to be honored and respected as they are in truth, that look what the truth determines, reason approves, and conscience witnesseth. That account is current in the hearts and apprehensions of those whose hearts have been pierced with godly sorrow for their sins. Because such judge not by outward appearance as it is the guise of men of corrupt minds, but upon experience, that which they have found and felt in their own hearts, what they have seen and judged in their own spirits, they cannot but see so and judge so of others. Those who were mocked as "men full of new wine" are now the precious servants of the Lord; flouted to their faces not long since, now they attend them, honor and reverence them—yea, fall at their very feet. It was before men and drunkards, now men and brethren; the world you see is well amended, but strangely altered. It was said of John Baptist, the forerunner of our savior, and the scope of whose doctrine was mainly to prepare the way for the Lord—it's said of him that Elias is come and hath reformed all, set a new face and frame in the profession of the Gospel: (Matt. 17. 11) "Turned the disobedient to the wisdom of the just men, the hearts of children to the fathers." That though they were so degenerate that Abraham would not own them had he been alive, yet when the ministry of John had hammered and melted them for the work of our savior, they became to be wholly altered, their judgments altered and their carriage also. For in truth, the reason why men see not the loathsomeness of other men's sins, or else have not courage to pass a righteous sentence upon them, it is because they were never convinced to see the plague sore of their own corruptions.

Prose: Discovering the Land

The colonial writer used the literary forms he brought with him, for he had no reason to try to create a literature of his own or to reject his literary heritage. His writing was concerned with three major themes, two public and one private: discovering and settling his land; building his society; exploring his inward, private life.

Books of exploration and settlement came first. There was already a vast and complex body of travel literature in Scandinavian, English, Dutch, Spanish, and French. Hakluyt's *Divers Voyages* (1582) and *Principal Navigations* (1589), Thomas Hariot's *Briefe and True Report* (1588), Samuel Purchas' *Purchas His Pilgrimes* (1625), and others were easily familiar to the American colonists. The traveler's first contact with America gave him much to write about, for he came to a whole new fascinating world where savages, woods, and previously unknown plants and animals were in prolific abundance. England and Europe wanted "reports of newes" about the new country and could hardly get enough of it.

John Smith's *A True Relation of . . . Virginia Since the First Planting of That Collony* (1608), his *Map of Virginia* (1612), his *The General Historie of Virginia, New England, and the Summer Isles* (1624), and his charming, untrustworthy *The True Travels, Adventures, and Observations of Captaine John Smith* (1630) comprised the most substantial body of travel literature done on America during the early years of colonization. William Bradford's *Of Plymouth Plantation* (begun about 1630), John Hammond's *Leah and Rachel, or the Two Fruitful Sisters, Virginia and Maryland* (1656), George Alsop's *Character of the Province of Maryland* (1666), and Gabriel Thomas' *Historical and Geographical Account of . . . Pennsylvania* (1698) were similar exploratory accounts.

Written by explorers, traders, promoters, and administrators, these books supplied a great deal of specific information, recording routes, events, crops, weather, geography, and other such things for those who were interested. However, a few were more than straightforward travel accounts, as they reflected something of the personalities who wrote them and something too of the headiness that came with discovery. George Alsop, who spent four years in Maryland as an indentured servant, admitted that

his witty, burlesque book was sometimes "wild and confused
. . . because I am so myself; and the world, so far as I can
perceive, is not much out of the same trim." Alsop's prose, too,
filled with Elizabethan ornamentation and wordplay, showed his
familiarity with Lyly and the court writers.

John Josselyn's *New England's Rarities* contained rumors, tall
tales, adventures, and a happy little poem to the Indian girls,
"plump as Partridges," whom he loved. Nobody in the era, of
course, matched John Smith for sheer adventurous narrative. A
hardy colonial favorite, the seventeenth-century travel book
eventually included social commentary, personal observations,
character sketches, and various bits of information, as in Madam
Sarah Kemble Knight's chatty record of her trip from Boston to
New York and back in 1704–1705 or William Byrd's famous
surveying tour of the dividing line between Virginia and North
Carolina in 1728.

Allied to the travel narrative and serving somewhat similar
purposes was a large body of descriptive writing designed to
attract investors and settlers to the new country and to describe
it to those who stayed at home. In Smith's *Description of New
England* (1616), he proposed to speak, he said, of "the estate of
the Sea, the Ayre, the Land, the Fruites, the Rocks, the People,
the Government, Religion, Territories and Limitations, Friends
and Foes" of the new country. William Wood, in *New England's
Prospect* (1634), carefully described the terrain, plants, and animals of New England and then gave over half his book to a
study of its Indians; his book displayed the same fascination
with the new land as Francis Higginson's *New England's Plantation* (1630) and Daniel Denton's *Brief Description of New
York* (1670). Wood reported that New England weather was so
healthful that "it is strange to hear a man sneeze or cough as
ordinarily they do in England," and Higginson (who soon died
of tuberculosis) thought that "a Sup of New England's air is
better than a whole draught of Old England's ale." To the South,
John Lederer, a German who may have been the first to look
across the Appalachian Mountains into the West, wrote a book
in Latin that, when translated into English, became *The Discov-*

*eries of John Lederer in Three Several Marches from Virginia to
the West of Carolina* (1677).

These descriptive travel books were relatively formal presen-
tations, written for a book-reading public. There was also a large
amount of frankly promotional "Come to America" propaganda
intended to attract settlers to the company colonies that badly
needed them. As Smith described it, America was an unspoiled
Paradise filled with fruits, game, and fertile lands, where one by
his "labour may live exceeding well" and "quickly growe riche"
to "the incredible benefit of King and Countrey, Master and
Servant." Over the years, writers rang Smith's theme in various
mutations in dozens of pamphlets, books, and letters home, explaining that America offered a fresh start and "prospects of
great richnesse" to "those which Fortune hath frown'd upon in
England."

Prose: Building a Society

The most extensive body of colonial writing was
that concerned with the construction of a stable, unified, civilized society where none had existed. This task required the colonist's greatest concentrated effort and elicited his most significant writing. Sermons bulked largest of all, for the church stood
at the center of community intellectual life, and its chief vehicle
of communication was the sermon. Since the minister was the
chief interpreter of God's word to the community and the authority for all churchly affairs, what he said from the pulpit was
of vital importance. "Whatsoever any faithful minister shall
speak out of The Word," wrote Thomas Hooker, "That is also
the voice of Christ"; no minister took this responsibility lightly.

Sermons in the seventeenth century were given not only at
Sunday worship, but for holidays, ordinations, elections, militia
days, fast days, the installation of magistrates, court days, funerals, midweek lectures, marriages, and any other public occasion
that warranted celebration or exhortation. Next to the Bible itself, the sermon was the most crucial element of the Protestant
faith, providing not only its doctrine but also much of its poetic

and imaginative life. Preaching involved more than exposition and admonition; it furnished the congregation with anecdotes and tales, character sketches, exempla, and analyses of current events. Sermons by preachers prominent and obscure appeared in literally thousands of pamphlets, books, and collections, and the colonists found them good reading, not only for their learning and messages, but for their coverage of every phase of contemporary life.

The colonial sermon was a highly developed kind of writing, organized in a recognized homiletic pattern consisting of the choice from a scriptural text, explications of principles derived from the text, their justification, and, finally, an "application" of these principles to life. Complex and intricate variations within this pattern gave ample opportunities to the preacher for the creation of his personal sermonic style—Thomas Shepard once preached 200 sermons on the meanings and applications of a single Biblical passage. Some ministers, like Thomas Hooker, followed the Puritan "plain style," thought it to be "the chiefest part of judicious learning to make a hard point easy and familiar in explication." Later seventeenth-century divines sometimes preferred the richer, heavier, Stuart-Anglican style, which was more involved and allusive.

Whatever his style, the Puritan minister knew that he faced a congregation that followed him closely; some listeners took notes on the sermon to review its logic and reflect on its message. He preached to an audience of ordinary people—fishermen, farmers, merchants, artisans, sailors—who were literate and critical, so his sermon had to be couched in terms that gave them the message they came to hear, in a manner neither cheap nor meretricious. Ministers did not hesitate to use learned allusions, but they also drew their metaphors from areas of experience meaningful to the audience. Hooker talked of "meditation" as

not the flourishing of a man's wit, but hath a set bout as the search of the truth, beats his brain as we use to say, hammers out a business, as the Goldsmith with his mettal, he beats it and beats it, turns it on this side and then on that, fashions it on both that he might frame it to his mind.

John Cotton's earthy analogy made his point with a jolt:

And so an Huswife that takes her linen, she Sopes it, and bedawbs it, and it may be defiled it with dung, so as it neither looks nor smells well, and when she hath done, she rubs it, and buckes it, and wrings it, and in the end all this is but to make it cleane and white; and truly so it is here, when as Tyrants most of all insult over God's people and scoure them and lay them in Lee, or Dung, so the very name of them stinks, yet what is this but to purge them and to make them white, and it is a great service they doe to the people of God in so doing.

In addition to the sermon, the Colonies developed a considerable literature of disputation, at first theologically centered, later expanded to include political and social issues as well. The colonists lived in a society of perpetual discussion, and as they evolved or adapted the necessary institutions of society, they faced a constant need for decision. Their disagreements and arguments, usually published in pamphlets or tracts, took various forms—a series of questions and answers, a "letter to a friend" explaining one person's position and refuting another's, the "discourse" or straight argument giving one side of a debate. Thomas Shepard's *Sincere Convert* (1641), an elucidation of the basic points of Calvinism, went through twenty editions; John Davenport's *Discourse About Civil Government in a New Plantation Whose Design Is Religion* (1663) told New England what theocratic government should be.

The matter of putting church and state into proper relationship produced a large body of ecclesiastical-political writing hammered out on the anvil of pamphleteering prose—Richard Mather's *Church Government* (1643), John Cotton's *Keyes of the Kingdom of Heaven* (1644), Thomas Hooker's *Survey of the Summe of Church Discipline* (1648), among many others. The argument between Roger Williams and Massachusetts Bay

produced a lively literature of its own, including Williams'
Bloody Tenent of Persecution (1644), John Cotton's *Bloody
Tenent Washed* (1647), William's *Bloody Tenent Yet More
Bloody* (1652), and so on. The seventeenth century was an age
of prolific debate over theological and civil questions in which
almost every prominent figure took some part.

The revolutionaries of the next century found this well-
developed tradition of disputation a particularly useful tool in
their contest with Parliament and Crown. How this kind of
American writing adapted itself to secular use may be illustrated
by a sample sequence: This literary tradition developed from
John Cotton's religious *Way of the Churches of Christ* (1645)
to Samuel Sewall's humanitarian tract against slavery, *The Selling of Joseph* (1700), to Benjamin Franklin's political *Paper
Currency* (1729) to James Otis' *Rights of the British Colonies*
(1764), one of the opening guns of revolution.

The Reverend Nathaniel Ward's book *The Simple Cobler of
Aggawam in America* (1647) did not quite belong with the
theological literature of Shepard and others. Ward, a peppery
man who came to New England in 1634 as pastor of the church
at Ipswich, Massachusetts (or "Aggawam" as the Indians called
it), proposed to mend "with honest stiches" the "lamentably tat-
tered . . . upper leather and sole" of a backslid New England.
He returned to England in 1646, possibly because of ill health,
and published *The Simple Cobler* under the pseudonym of
"Theodore de la Guard." It was a loosely organized book pleading for unity among the New England churches and containing
digressions on various issues in which Ward was interested. He
wrote a lively, mannered prose somewhat removed from the
"plain style," as illustrated in his remarks on the necessity of
unity:

Civil commotions make room for uncivil practices; religious mutations, for irreligious opinions; change of air discovers corrupt bodies; reformation of religion, unsound minds. He that has any well-
faced fancy in his crown and does not vent it now, fears the pride
of his own heart will dub him dunce forever. Such a one will

trouble the whole Israel of God with his most untimely births, though he makes the bones of his vanity stick up, to the view and grief of all that are godly wise. The devil desires no better sport than to see light heads handle their heels and fetch their careers in a time when the roof of liberty stands open.

Or, as in his opinion of women's clothes, a wildly inventive prose after the extreme Elizabethan fashion:

It is known more than enough that I am neither niggard nor cynic to the due bravery of the true gentry; if any man mislikes a bulli-mong drassock more than I, let him take her for his labor; I honor the woman that can honor herself with her attire; a good text always deserves a fair margin; I am not much offended if I see a trim far trimmer than she that wears it; in a word, whatever Christianity or civility will allow, I can afford with London measure. But when I hear a nugiperous gentledame inquire what dress the Queen is in this week, what the nudiustertian fashion of the court, with edge to be in it in all haste, whatever it be; I look at her as the very gizzard of a trifle, the product of a quarter of a cipher, the epitome of noth-ing, fitter to be kicked, if she were of a kickable substance, than either honored or humored.

Prose: The Meaning of the Past

The most vigorous and readable body of colonial writing consisted of histories, not only because these constituted an invaluable chronicle of the events of early American life, but because they recorded so much of its stir, sense, and temper. In general, Europeans of the seventeenth century were history-conscious; the colonists, acutely aware of their separation from the homeland, were especially so. Having left behind the prece-dents and records of their English past, they hoped to supply their new society with its own history, reestablishing on American soil the feeling of tradition and continuity needed for stability and order.

This desire to establish a strong tradition was especially char-acteristic of New England, for the Puritans, conscious of their importance as a chosen people carrying out God's plan for a new

Jerusalem, were certain that what happened to their experiment held great meaning for the world. Convinced (in the oft-quoted words of John Winthrop) that "wee shall be as a Citty upon a Hill, the eyes of all People uppon us," they believed it imperative to chronicle the workings of the Divine will in New England and to keep the record of their commonwealth for the inspiration of future generations. William Bradford said that he kept his record of the Plymouth settlers so "that their children may see with what difficulties their fathers wrastled in going through these things in their first beginnings, and how God brougt them along notwithstanding all their weaknesses and infirmities. And allso that some use may be made hereof in after times by others in shuch like weightie imployments."

Two generally accepted principles governed historical writing in New England. First, since God controls all events, all have meaning and must be noted. All "undertakings and affairs" are determined, said the Reverend Urian Oakes, "by the counsel and Providence of God ordering and governing time and chance according to His own good pleasure." History therefore was a concrete, specific, detailed record of everything, great and small, that God had willed to happen. Second, since God controls all events to some purpose, the historian must therefore try to discover in the meaning of events some suggestion of what His purposes may be. Edward Johnson, in his account of New England, noted that when the Puritans were hungry, "Christ caused abundance of very good Fish to come to their Nets and Hookes," and that when hostile Indians threatened the settlements, a smallpox epidemic decimated the savages like "a wondrous worke of the Great Jehovah."

History in New England was a detailed account of difficulties surmounted, providences granted, temptations resisted, and evils overcome; a linear timetable of events stretching in chronological order from Creation to the present and projected into the future to Christ's return. This view of history was not confined to the Puritans, for seventeenth-century historians in general believed that since human nature was the same in all ages and places, one could use the past as example, learn from it, and discover a plan in it; to the Puritan, that plan was God's.

This theory of history lay beneath William Bradford's *Of Plymouth Plantation* (1620–1647), John Winthrop's *History of New England* (originally kept as a journal, 1630–1649), Edward Johnson's *Wonder-Working Providence of Sion's Saviour in New England* (1653), and Nathaniel Morton's *New England's Memoriall* (1669, based on Bradford's manuscript and Edward Winslow's journal), which was officially printed by Plymouth at a cost of twenty pounds of corn and a barrel of beef. Not all Puritan histories were alike, of course. Some, especially the earlier, tended to be "annalistic," that is, they represented a somewhat indiscriminate year-by-year reporting of events; others, later and more sophisticated, displayed greater awareness of the allegorical possibilities of events and allowed more latitude in interpreting them. Thomas Morton of "Merrymount," a settlement between Boston and Plymouth, left a quite different kind of historical record in his *New English Canaan* (1637), written after the Plymouth colony had twice thrown him out of New England for general roistering and selling rum, guns, and powder to the Indians.

For models the Puritans drew from the Bible, the Greeks and Romans, and the medieval ecclesiastical historians. They were familiar with "annalistic" history, which was a form of writing common in the sixteenth century and which they knew from Holinshed's *Chronicles* and especially from Sir Walter Raleigh's popular *History of the World* (1614). Bradford's library included Livy, Virgil, and Plutarch, in addition to the usual church histories; Cotton Mather, powerful scholar that he was, could cite Thucydides, Xenophon, Tacitus, Sallust, and Suetonius, all in one passage.

To the Puritan, biography, like history, was an unusually useful form of writing. Although he knew that no two persons ever reached grace by the same road, he also felt, as Plutarch taught, that the lives of great and saintly men were worth studying and imitating, as they helped to disclose something of the meaning of the past. The "character," or brief descriptive sketch that was a favorite literary form in seventeenth-century England, furnished a convenient model for longer, more formal biographical studies; since sermons often employed "characters" for purposes of illustration, the seventeenth-century colonist was quite familiar with the uses of this form.

Funeral sermons often turned into biographies of some length, while historical chronicles usually contained accounts of the lives of prominent men. John Norton's *Abel Being Dead Yet Speaketh* (1658), whose subject was John Cotton, was one of the earliest formal biographies written in the Colonies. Increase Mather's life of his father Richard, published in 1670, was well-known and widely read, and Cotton's *Magnalia* (1702) included brief lives of governors, magistrates, famous Harvard graduates, and sixty great ministers. Increase Mather showed how the biographer might use the virtues of his subject as examples for his readers to follow; in this case, he wrote of his father's humility, a trait much emphasized by the Puritans:

Notwithstanding those rare gifts and graces wherewith the Lord had adorned him, he was exceeding low and little in his own eyes. Some have thought that his greatest error was that he did not magnify his office, as he might and sometimes should have done. If a man must err, it is good erring on that hand. "Humble enough, and good enough," was the frequent saying of a great divine. And another observeth, "That every man hath just as much and no more truth in him, as he hath humility." Austin, being asked which was the most excellent grace, answered "Humility," and which was the next, answered "Humility;" and which was the third, replied again "Humility." That indeed is comprehensively all, being of great price in the sight of God. And if so, Mr. Mather was a man of much real worth.

Prose: The Inward Life

Although it is difficult to estimate proportions, a great deal of colonial writing was done for private consumption, rarely published nor intended to be. The seventeenth century had its introspective, inward side, especially important to theologically minded New Englanders, for the great drama of Puritanism occurred within each individual. Conversion was a private problem, and men often kept records, in one fashion or another, of their search for it. Keeping a diary or journal was common English practice, since it provided an account of family or business affairs, plantings and harvests, weather, community events, and the trivia of daily life. Quite often the keeper might also record his attempts to live a godly life, not only for his own purposes, but for the edification of others. Roger Clap's *Memoirs,* written about 1676, were intended for the use of his family; Anne Bradstreet left her diary to her children; Samuel Sewall's classic *Diary* (written 1674–1729) was, among other things, an interpretation of Biblical prophecy and current events.

The journal was a valuable instrument in the individual's struggle for self-improvement. The Puritan kept a journal because he needed a record of how God dealt with him, and he with God, so that as the final judgment drew near he might assess the relationship; and so he could leave his children something of benefit to them in arranging their own lives. Thomas Shepard, the "soul-melting preacher" of Cambridge, who wrote his journal about 1636–1638, explained how important it was for him to take down his experience:

My chiefe meditation was about the evill of sin, the terrour of God's wrath, day of death, bewty of Christ, the deceiptfulness of the hart . . . and this I remember I never went out to meditate in the feelds, but I did find the Lord teaching me somewhat of myselfe or himselfe or the vanity of the woorld, I never saw before; and hence I tooke out a little booke I have every day into the feelds and writ down what God taught me least I should forget them.

Shepard's entry in his journal on the occasion of his wife's death, something never intended for publication, is a moving, restrained, and beautifully written literary document:

But the Lord hath not been wont to let me live long without some affliction or other, and yet ever mixt with some mercy; and there-

fore April the second, 1646, as He gave me another son, John, so
He took away my most dear, precious, meek and loving wife, in
childbed, after three weeks' lying in, having left behind her two
hopeful branches, my dear children, Samuel and John. This affliction was very heavy to me, for in it the Lord seemed to withdraw
His tender care for me and mine. . . . This loss was very great:
she was a woman of incomparable meekness of spirit, toward myself especially, and very loving; of great prudence to take care for
and order my family affairs, being neither too lavish nor sordid in
anything, so that I knew not what was under her hands. She had an
excellency to reprove for sin and discerned the evils of men; she
loved God's people dearly, and studious to profit by their fellowship, and therefore loved their company. She loved God's word
exceedingly, and hence was glad she could read my notes, which
she had to muse on every week. She had a spirit of prayer beyond
ordinary of her time and experience; she was fit to die long before
she did die, even after the death of her first-born, which was a
great affliction to her: but her work not being done then, she lived
almost nine years with me, and was the comfort of my life to me,
and the last sacrament before her lying in seemed to be full of
Christ and thereby fitted for heaven. She did oft say she should not
outlive this child; when her fever first began (by taking some
cold), she told me so, that we should love exceedingly together
because we should not live long together. Her fever took away her
sleep, want of sleep wrought much distemper in her head, and filled
it with fantasies and distractions but without raging; the night before she died, she had about six hours unquiet sleep, but that so
cooled and settled her head that when she knew none else so as to
speak to them, yet she knew Jesus Christ and could speak to him.
Therefore, as soon as she awakened out of sleep, she broke out into
a most heavenly heartbreaking prayer after Christ, her dear redeemer, for the sparing of life, and so continued praying until the
last hour of her death; "Lord, though I unworthy, Lord, one word,
one word," etc., and so gave up the ghost. Thus God hath visited
and scourged me for my sins, and sought to wean me from this
world; but I have ever found it a difficult thing to profit ever but
a little by the sorest and sharpest afflictions.

Done with dignity and seriousness and often with great sensitivity and unconscious art, these accounts of daily personal life

formed an important undercurrent in colonial writing. Later journals developed a rudimentary pattern of conflict between the individual as he was and ought to be, between his picture of himself and the image of what God intended him to be. The events of one's life supplied the material of tension between ideal and real, resembling somewhat the old medieval dialogues between body and soul. They continued to be written well into the eighteenth century, both as personal records, like Jonathan Edwards' *Personal Narrative,* and as formalized autobiographies, like Benjamin Franklin's, written (as was Clap's) to show his son what in his father's life might "be fit to be imitated."

Allied to the journal was the meditation, an essay-like genre long popular among the Puritans and written to a more consciously interpretive pattern than the diary. A strenuous intellectual discipline and inward exploration, the meditation was, as Thomas Hooker defined it, "a serious intention of the mind whereby we come to search out the truth, and settle it effectively on the heart." As Norman Grabo has pointed out, the meditation was, for the Puritan, "basically a method for channelling emotion into verbal structures" and therefore was, in a sense, a poetic form—a way of treating affective experience, a vital and significant literary genre for the seventeenth-century artist. Anne Bradstreet's meditation, written in 1664 and addressed to her son Simon, recorded, she said, those times "when my soul hath been refreshed with consolations which the world knows not," as two illustrate:

He that is to sail into a far country, although the ship, cabin, and provision be all convenient and comfortable for him, yet he hath no desire to make that his place of residence, but longs to put in at that port where his business lies. A Christian is sailing through this world unto his heavenly country, and here he hath many conveniences and comforts; but he must beware of desiring to make this the place of his abode, lest he meet with such tossings that may cause him to long for shore before he sees land. We must, therefore, be here as strangers and pilgrims, that we may plainly declare that we seek a city above, and wait all the days of our appointed time till our change shall come.

. . .

As man is called the little world, so his heart may be called the little commonwealth: his more fixed and resolved thoughts are like to inhabitants; his slight and flitting thoughts are like passengers that travel to and fro continually. Here is also the great court of justice erected, which is always kept by conscience, who is both accuser, excuser, witness and judge, whom no bribes can pervert, nor flattery cause to favor; but as he finds the evidence, so he absolves or condemns. Yea, so absolute is this court of judicature that there is no appeal from it—no, not to the court of heaven itself. For if our conscience condemn us, He also, who is greater than our conscience, will do it much more. But he that would have the boldness to go to the throne of grace to be accepted there must be sure to carry a certificate from the court of conscience, that he stands right there.

Other meditations, more formal and structured, accompanied sermons and were (as in the prose-poem meditations of Edward Taylor and the great prose of Jonathan Edwards) among the finest products of seventeenth-century prose. Some collections were published—Charles Morton's *Spirit of Man,* and Shepard's *Meditations and Spiritual Experiences*—but publication was not usually the writer's primary aim.

Puritanism and Poetry

Poetry to the Calvinist was a useful branch of rhetoric but by no means the most important one. The Puritan was not hostile to poetry, for he knew and admired the great classical, medieval, and Renaissance poets; like other men of his time he agreed that while poetry was a decorative and stimulating form of art, its chief aim was to persuade and instruct. Poetry could be, as Cotton Mather called it, "a meer Playing and Fiddling upon Words," but the Puritan also appreciated its influence on the soul when directed toward proper ends. "There is something of Heaven in Holy Poetry," wrote English Puritan Richard Baxter. "It charmeth Souls into loving harmony and concord." Much of the seventeenth-century colonists' creative energy was channeled into theology and government and into other forms of writing better adapted to their needs. Though they produced nothing remotely resembling the achievements of their English and European contemporaries, they wrote a great deal of poetry, or at least verse, not unworthy of literary consideration.

Colonial verse was of two varieties: public and private. The colonists wrote public poetry dealing with current or historical events, theological arguments, commemorations, funerals, ordinations, and the like, whose aim was expository and instructive. *The Whole Booke of Psalmes Faithfully Translated into English Metre,* published at Cambridge in 1640 and better known as the "Bay Psalm Book," was exactly such poetry, intended to turn the Psalms into metrical versions suited to singing by the church congregation. Since it was necessary neither to obscure nor change the literal Biblical meaning in translating from the Hebrew, the editors strove "for conscience rather than elegance, fidelity rather than poetry." Within this requirement they succeeded rather well, and in instances such as John Cotton's rendition of the Twenty-Third Psalm with more than a little art:

The Lord to me a shepherd is,
Want therefore shall not I.
He in the folds of tender grass,
Doth cause me down to lie:
To waters calm me gently leads
Restore my soul doth He:
He doth in paths of righteousness:
For His name's sake lead me.
Yea though in valley of death's shade
I walk, none ill I'll fear:
Because Thou are with me, Thy rod,
And staff my comfort are.
For me a table Thou hast spread,
In presence of my foes:
Thou dost anoint my head with oil,
My cup it overflows.

Goodness and mercy surely shall
  All my days follow me:
And in the Lord's house I shall dwell
  So long as days shall be.

Michael Wigglesworth explained and justified Puritanism in his *Day of Doom* (1662) and his interminable *Meat out of the Eater* . . . (1670). His aim, like that of the "Bay Psalm Book," was more sermonic than poetic. He was not writing artistic poetry, but rather putting Calvinist doctrine into an easily understood and easily memorized ballad meter familiar to everyone. He was willing "to play the fool this once for Christ" by writing poetry, he told his readers, "if this my foolishness help thee to be more wise." The first edition of 1,800 copies sold out within a year (not one survives), and the poem went through ten more editions by 1775. A man of some culture and attainments, Wigglesworth occasionally captured in his jigging verse something more than simple doctrinal exposition. His picture of Judgment Day arriving suddenly on a surprised and sinful world is an effective one:

Still was the night, serene and bright,
  when all men sleeping lay;
Calm was the season, and carnal reason
  thought so 't would last for aye.
"Soul, take thine ease, let sorrow cease,
  much good thou hast in store":
This was their song, their cups among,
  the evening before. . . .

They put away the evil day,
  and drowned their cares and fears,
Till drowned were they, and swept away
  by vengeance unawares;
So at the last, whilst men sleep fast
  in their security,
Surprised they are in such a snare
  as cometh suddenly.

For at midnight brake forth a light,
  which turned the night to day,
And speedily an hideous cry
  did all the world dismay.
Sinners awake, their hearts do ache,
  trembling their loins surpriseth;
Amazed with fear, by what they hear,
  each one of them ariseth.

They rush from beds with giddy heads,
  and to their windows run,
Viewing this light, which shines more bright
  than doth the noon-day sun.
Straightway appears (they see't with tears)
  the Son of God most dread;
Who with his train comes on amain
  to judge both quick and dead. . . .

Despite the steady thumping of his stanzas, Wigglesworth was not devoid of the poetic touch, and in his verse, as in *The Day of Doom*, there appeared unexpected flashes of imagery, such as his comment on mankind's brief, restless existence in this life:

A restless Wave o'th' troubled Ocean,
A Dream, a lifeless Picture finely drest,
A Wind, a Flower, a Vapour and a Bubble,
A Wheel that stands not still, a trembling Reed,
A Rolling Stone, dry Dust, light Chaff, and Stubble,
A Shadow of something, but nought indeed.

Benjamin Tompson's *New England's Crisis* and *New England's Teares* and Peter Folger's *Looking Glass for the Times*, which all appeared in 1676, were rimed attempts to illustrate the larger meaning of King Philip's War and other recent disasters, which to them represented God's visitation of punishment on a recreant New England. A great deal of Puritan poetry was written for such "edification," but in addition there was an amazing amount of occasional verse, written purely for enjoyment—anagrams, epigrams, ditties, acrostics, riddles, and allegories—scattered through histories, biographies, sermons, broadsides, almanacs, letters, journals, and so on, resembling English verse of the same kind. Solemn old Nathaniel Ward actually inserted more verse in his *Simple Cobler* than scapegrace Thomas Morton put into his *New English Canaan*. Samuel Danforth's riddle, for example, in the *Almanack* for 1647, suggested that the four New England colonies should aid the "hive" (Harvard College) by raising funds through a fishing tax so that serious students would be protected from Satanic diversions, and the useless driven out:

Four heads should meet and counsell have,
The chickens from the kite to save,
The idle drones away to drive,
The little Bees to keep i' th' hive.
How honey may be brought to these
By making fish to dance on trees.

The elegy, another common type of public verse, was especially popular because it not only commemorated the lives of prominent and obscure, but drew lessons from them for survivors to emulate. This form was used in John Cotton's elegy for Hooker (1647), Urian Oakes' for the Reverend Thomas Shepard (1677), or John Rogers' moving memorial to Mistress Anne Bradstreet in 1678. Death and what came after were of great interest to the Puritan, and the elegy allowed the poet to speculate not only on the meaning of the life just ended but on the great adventure with God just begun. Elegy writing was not unique to New England. Nathaniel Bacon's revolt in Virginia in 1676 elicited a curious double elegy, found in a manuscript collection two centuries later and ascribed to a planter named John Cotton. "Bacon's Epitaph, by His Man," the better of the two pieces, expressed a view diametrically opposed to that of its companion; together they formed a kind of debate or dialogue written by someone who knew Jonson, Donne, and the English metaphysical poets rather well. Cotton's poem, if it is his; is not especially distinguished verse, but its existence leads one to wonder how many other manuscript poems might have existed in the colonial South, since practically nothing of this kind has survived.

The majority of colonial poetry, however, was not written for publication at all. Many writers considered poetry to be substantially private self-expression, an intimate conversation between the writer and God, not something written for others to read. A large amount of poetry circulated in manuscript for the enjoyment of the poet's friends, but it was rarely preserved and even more rarely published during the poet's lifetime. John Cotton himself wrote poetry in his almanac, using the Greek alphabet for concealment of such worldly recreation. Samuel Sewall wrote poetry, apparently, that he liked to read aloud to his family, and so did Cotton Mather; Thomas Dudley, the first deputy-governor of Massachusetts Bay, had one of his own poems in his pocket when he died. Anne Bradstreet's brother-in-law, without her knowledge, published her first poems in London in 1650. Edward Taylor's poetry, the most distinguished written in colonial America, remained unpublished for two and a half centuries, until 1939. Young Philip Pain's friends published his verse in England in 1668, a year or so after he was drowned in a shipwreck.

Poetry: Mistress Bradstreet's World

Out of the surprisingly large amount of verse produced in seventeenth-century New England, that of Anne Bradstreet and Edward Taylor stands eminent. Mistress Bradstreet, Governor Thomas Dudley's daughter, lived near Andover, Massachusetts, and wrote of her domestic and religious experiences with considerable skill and charm. Born in England in 1612, she married Simon Bradstreet at sixteen and sailed to Massachusetts Bay in 1630. For the next forty years, while "rearing eight children, lying frequently sick, keeping house at the edge of the wilderness," she wrote poetry. Though much of her work was done before she had the eight children, she kept revising until her death and produced a few of her longer poems in later life.

Mistress Bradstreet wrote of her husband, of her children, and of the trials and pleasures of family life in verse that bore the marks of a woman of charm, wit, and strength. Her verse to her "Dear and Loving Husband" is as delicately restrained and emotionally valid as any written in any century:

If ever two were one, then surely we.
If ever man were lov'd by wife, then thee;
If ever wife was happy in a man,
Compare with me ye women if you can.
I prize thy love more than whole Mines of gold,
Or all the riches that the East doth hold.
My love is such that Rivers cannot quench,
Nor ought but love from thee, give recompence.
Thy love is such I can no way repay,
The heavens reward thee manifold I pray.
Then while we live, in love let's so persever,
That when we live no more, we may live ever.

Domesticity, however, was a subject of marginal interest to her, and in her collection *The Tenth Muse Lately Sprung up in America* (1650, with an expanded posthumous edition in 1678) she placed greater emphasis on her erudite, formalized, religious poetry fashioned after Spenser, Herbert, Du Bartas, and a bevy of minor Elizabethans. Sylvester's translation of the French Calvinist poet Du Bartas deeply influenced her, as it did many other poets in England and the Colonies, by its combination of "profound learning" and "grave divinity." Her description of Heaven, from her medievalized debate between *The Flesh and the Spirit,* illustrated her consciously formal manner and her debt to Du Bartas and the English poets.

The City where I hope to dwell,
There's none on Earth can parallel;
The stately Walls both high and strong,

Are made of pretious Jasper stone;
The Gates of Pearl, both rich and clear,
And Angels are for Porters there;
The Streets thereof transparent gold,
Such as no Eye did e're behold,
A Chrystal River there doth run,
Which doth proceed from the Lambs Throne:
Of Life, there are the waters sure,
Which shall remain for ever pure,
Nor Sun, nor Moon, they have no need,
For glory doth from God proceed:
No Candle there, nor yet Torch light,
For there shall be no darksome night.
From sickness and infirmity,
For evermore they shall be free,
Nor withering age shall e're come there,
But beauty shall be bright and clear;
This City pure is not for thee,
For things unclean there shall not be:
If I of Heaven may have my fill,
Take thou the world, and all that will.

Poetry: Edward Taylor and his God

Edward Taylor, the most gifted of the New England poets, wrung his intricate, intense poetry out of his soul's struggle with doubt and his achingly passionate pursuit of God. A minister and physician in rural Massachusetts, Taylor wrote a large body of brilliantly learned sermons, but he also left more than 400 manuscript pages of poetry that he instructed his heirs never to publish, for as a devout Puritan, his inward life was not for public display. Strongly affected by the English metaphysical poets, he wrote meditations, elegies, versified theology, and strikingly original reflective religious poems written between the 1680s and his death in 1729.

Twisted, difficult, intellectualized, and charged with tremendous emotion, Taylor's poetry, though it echoes Donne and Herbert at times, had its own powerfully individualized force. His "Preface," written about 1682, speaks of the majesty of God, building up tension in a series of striking images toward the final metaphor of man's once-diamond-bright virtue turned into coal-black stone:

Infinity, when all things it beheld,
In nothing, and of nothing all did build,
Upon what base was fixed the lathe wherein
He turned this globe and riggaled it so trim?
Who blew the bellows of His furnace vast? 5
Or held the mould wherein the world was cast?
Who laid its corner-stone? Or whose command?
Where stand the pillars upon which it stands?
Who laced and filleted the earth so fine
With rivers like green ribbons smaragdine? 10
Who made the seas its selvedge, and it locks
Like a quilt ball within a silver box?
Who spread its canopy? Or curtains spun?
Who in this bowling alley bowled the sun?
Who made it always when it rises, set: 15
To go at once both down and up to get?
Who the curtain rods made for this tapestry?
Who hung the twinkling lanthorns in the sky?
Who? who did this? or who is he? Why, know
It's only Might Almighty this did do. 20
His hand hath made this noble work which stands
His glorious handiwork not made by hands.
Who spake all things from nothing; and with ease
Can speak all things to nothing, if He please.
Whose little finger at His pleasure can 25
Out mete ten thousand worlds with half a span.
Whose might almighty can by half a look
Root up the rocks and rock the hills by th' roots.
Can take this mighty world up in His hand
And shake it like a squitchen or a wand. 30
Whose single frown will make the heavens shake

Like as an aspen leaf the wind makes quake.
Oh! what a might is this! Whose single frown
Doth shake the world as it would shake it down?
Which all from nothing fet, from nothing all;   35
Hath all on nothing set, lets nothing fall.
Gave all to nothing man indeed, whereby
Through nothing man all might Him glorify.
In nothing is embossed the brightest gem
More precious than all preciousness in them.   40
But nothing man did throw down all by sin,
And darkened that lightsome gem in him,
*   That now His brightest diamond is grown*
*   Darker by far than any coal-pit stone.*

The Perils of Drama

Not surprisingly, neither fiction nor drama appears in seventeenth-century American literature, for both were as deeply distrusted in the Colonies as in England. The novel was still a relatively undeveloped form, and the attacks on the English stage by William Prynne in 1632 and Jeremy Collier in 1698 said exactly what the colonists felt about the moral dangers of this form of imaginative art. Plays and actors were viewed with deep distrust by Northern and Southern colonists alike; in seventeenth-century Connecticut, a person who "set up . . . common plays, interludes, and other crafty science" risked fifteen lashes on the back. New England Calvinists, New York Dutch, Pennsylvania Quakers, and Virginia Anglicans agreed that the theater was likely to encourage habits of idleness and immorality. Cotton Mather, who spoke against "the Passionate and Measured Pages" of poetry in his book of instructions for young divinity students, *Manuductio ad Ministerium* (1726), warned them that "the powers of Darkness have a library among us" and concluded that "most of the Modern Plays, as well as the Romances and Novels, and Fictions, which are a sort of poem, do belong to the Catalogue of this cursed Library."

Plays seldom appeared in colonial libraries; of the four folio editions of Shakespeare published in the seventeenth century, apparently not one copy came to New England before 1700. Plays were perhaps presented at a few places in the early eighteenth century, but although Williamsburg built a theater in 1716, it is doubtful any plays were actually produced for some years. Thomas Godfrey's *Prince of Parthia,* conveniently called the first American play, was written in 1759 but not produced until 1767. (By contrast, the French at Port Royal had presented a water-pageant in 1606 and in 1694 were playing Molière at Quebec.) Certainly the Bible itself was a great quarry of dramatic narrative, and the struggle between God and Satan, good and evil, Hell and salvation, was all the drama the Puritan needed.

Folklore and the Popular Mind

Poems, histories, meditations, sermons, and other formal literary productions were written for an educated public, to recognized standards. There also existed in the Colonies a tremendous body of popular material, which supplied the normal human demand for adventure, excitement, and interest, and which also provided literary substance for American writers over the next three centuries. The settlers brought with them the great fund of British and European folktale and folklore, which they grafted to the new environment and adapted to their new experiences.

The virgin country filled with innumerable marvels and wonders furnished fresh matter for the old legends—the land, its strange plants and animals; Indians, first savages Englishmen had ever seen at first hand; the hazards and adventures of life in the wilderness. Early "relations," "reports of news," chronicles, and journals comprised storehouses of materials, containing tales of Indians, shipwrecks, pirates, "providences," earthquakes, floods, wars, captivities and escapes, and nearly everything else. John Josselyn, for example, picked up within few months of his arrival in 1638 tales of a mysterious lion, a sea-serpent, and a merman, as well as reports of a witches' revel, a spectral voice, a strange flame above the trees, and "the birth of a monster at Boston." Josselyn was only one of many such reporters.

The settlers also brought with them an oral storytelling tradition that reached the Colonies in undiminished strength. Since books were few, and there was much to tell, the storyteller became a familiar figure in colonial communities. Everyone who kept a journal wrote down the stories he heard; sermons and chronicles recorded events and tales as remarkable and suspenseful as anything in the Bible, Hakluyt, or Defoe. Though he may have distrusted fiction, Cotton Mather advised ministers in his *Manuductio* that they ought to have "an Inexhaustible Store of Stories" and "the Skill of telling them Handsomely" if they were to be successful in their profession. Many of these were ancient folktales put into an American setting. Mermaids, St. Elmo's fire, ghostly appearances, heavenly displays, spectral ships, and dozens of other familiar motifs common to European folklore for centuries appeared in colonial diaries and journals, and were recorded by Winthrop, Morton, Wood, Josselyn, and the Mathers.

Stories about unfamiliar animals and plants naturally bulked large, constituting a kind of American bestiary. These tales were usually variants of British originals and included whale, bear, snake, alligator, wolf, and many other kinds of stories. John Lawson reported a horn snake in Carolina with a poisonous spur in its tail; James Kenny told of wild horses so large they slept leaning on tall trees; Cotton Mather sent a letter to the Royal Society describing a rattlesnake that bit a chunk out of a broadax. Lawson heard of a tulip tree so large that a man moved his furniture into it and lived inside; Beverley described a "love flower" of startlingly phallic appearance; he also told how chewing "Jamestown weed" (which survives as "jimson weed") sent men out of their minds.

Specters appeared very early in the Colonies and continued to do so, beginning a long tradition of ghost sightings that still provides material for American writers. Reports appeared in diaries, histories, and oral tales, and later in newspapers and magazines, literally by the hundreds. A spectral ship visited New Haven harbor in 1647, and Sir Walter Raleigh's vessel was observed on the Carolina coast as late as 1709. Cavendish, Vermont, had a local ghost seen several times over a span of years from 1680 to 1790, and the ghost of a girl murdered by pirates in Marblehead Harbor screamed in terror on the anniversary of her death for 150 consecutive years.

Spectral appearances were very real, very much a part of the colonial, imaginative experience. The account left by a bereaved father in his journal could have been duplicated a dozen times in any decade of the seventeenth or eighteenth century:

Thursday 29 (1735) of october my wife went into a chambur that was lock to seek candels that was in a half bushel under a bed and as shee kneled down and tock her candels and laid them on the beed and as shee thrust back the half bushel there came out a childs hand she saw the fingers the hand a striped boys cife or sleve and upon shurch there was no child in the chamber on thursday a fort nite aftar my stepen son henery died. The next thursday Ebenezar died the next monday morning his eldest son Stephen died.

Witches, Devils, and Providences

The great witchraft delusions that swept England, Europe, and the Colonies in the seventeenth century created a body of witch and devil literature that persisted for 300 years. The devil appeared very early in America and never left it. Settlers found his hoofprints on rocks all over the Colonies, and reports of his appearances were common. He was in Plymouth at the beginning, Bradford believed, and certainly at Merrymount with Morton. He drank with a crony at Plymouth in 1670, knocked off a minister's hat in Hopkinton in 1767, and stole Mr. Brainerd's ax at Braintree in 1771. He visited an elderly gentleman in Connecticut on a stormy night in 1732, but the old man fortunately saw the tail beneath his coat and drove him out.

Since the existence of workers in the black arts was unhesitatingly accepted among learned and ignorant alike, stories of the exposure, capture, and trial of witches were regarded as no different from those of pirates, murderers, or other criminals.

The Colonies were filled with these stories; the first historians began recording them in the early days of settlement and never stopped. Susannah Trimmings of Piscataqua, New Hampshire, for example, swore under oath in April 1685 that

ON LORD'S day 30th of March, at night, going home with Goodwife Barton, she separated from her at the freshet next her house. On her return, between Goodman Evens's and Robert Davis's she heard a rustling in the woods, which she at first thought was occasioned by swine, and presently after there did appear to her a woman whom she apprehended to be old Goodwife Walford.

She asked me where my consort was. I answered, I had none. She said, Thy consort is at home by this time. Lend me a pound of cotton.

I told her I had but two pounds in the house, and I would not spare any to my mother. She said I had better have done it; that my sorrow was great already, and it should be greater—for I was going a great journey, but should never come there. She then left me, and I was struck as with a clap of fire on the back, and she vanished toward the waterside, in my apprehension in the shape of a cat. She had on her head a white linen hood tied under her chin, and her waistcoat and petticoat were red, with an old green apron and a black hat upon her head.

At the death of the celebrated witch, Moll Piccher (not to be confused with Revolutionary heroine Molly Pitcher), at Lynn, Massachusetts, in 1813, newspapers printed long obituaries with accounts of her prophecies and sorceries; so too at the death of Simeon Smith, a famous practitioner of the black arts who lived at Wentworth, New Hampshire. Accounts of witchcraft investigations and trials appeared in profusion, especially in the latter decades of the seventeenth century. Some were frankly sensational, others were more seriously done, such as Cotton Mather's *Wonders of the Invisible World* (1693), Robert Calef's *More Wonders of the Invisible World* (1702), and the Reverend John Hale's *A Modest Inquiry into the Nature of Witchcraft* (1702). The devil tale and the witch tale were driven deep into the American consciousness before the eighteenth century.

So too were "providences," remarkable happenings, which, because of their unusual character, were assumed to have some significant message or meaning. Providences were, of course, as old as folklore itself, but for the Puritan, who felt God's direction keenly, they were especially important. If God controlled all, then any deviation from the usual course of events ought to be analyzed and interpreted carefully. The colonists recognized three varieties within the providential framework—those reflecting God's wrath and punishments, His prophecies and forewarnings, and His rewards and "deliverances." An Indian attack, a sick calf, a sudden plague of disease, a lost crop, a bolt of lightning, the death of a blasphemer—these were clearly judgments. In 1640, John Winthrop told how God handled certain "profane scoffers":

JULY 27, 1640. Being the second day of the week, the *Mary Rose,* a ship of Bristol, of about two hundred tons, lying before Charlestown, was blown in pieces with her own powder, being twenty-one barrels; wherein the judgment of God appeared. For the master and company were many of them profane scoffers at us, and at the ordinances of religion here; so as our churches keeping a fast for our native country they kept aboard at their common service, when all the rest of the masters came to our assemblies; likewise the Lord's day following. And a friend of his going aboard next day and asking him why he came not on shore to our meetings, his answer was that he had a family of his own, and they had as good service aboard as we had on shore. Within two hours after this (being about dinner time) the powder took fire (no man knows how) and blew all up, viz., the captain and nine or ten of his men, and some four or five strangers.

God struck infidels of a century later equally as hard, as a report from New York State showed in 1767:

Another strange Report has also been current for some Time past, and we imagine of equal Truth with the above, viz. That a Man near Albany, contrary to the Advice and Entreaties of his Friends, lately went out to Work in his Field on the Lord's Day with a Pair of Oxen, and were all turn'd into Statues where 'tis said they remain immoveably fixed as Examples of God's Judgment against Sabbath breakers.

A blazing comet, a strange dream, a spectral vision, a rain of frogs—these were considered portents, as in the report by workmen in Connectitcut in the 1760s:

A report prevails that some unaccountable noises were lately heard near Hartford; and 'tis said, via Derby, that a few men being lately at work in a wood they were terrified with an extraordinary Voice, commanding them to read the seventh chp. of Ezekiel.

Mather reported that a red snow once preceded an Indian attack, allowing the colonists time to prepare a defense, and the Massachusetts militia refused to march in King Philip's War during a partial eclipse of the moon. A school of fish at starving-time, a miraculous cure from illness, a smallpox epidemic that decimated hostile Indian tribes—these were obviously God's deliverances. Increase Mather's compilation of 1684, *Illustrious Providences,* still remains one of the best of all such accounts. The belief that events had symbolic value was deeply ingrained in the colonial mind from the start, to appear later throughout American poetry, novel, and drama.

Satan and the Red Man

The largest body of potentially usable literary materials, however, was that which concerned the Indian. The English had had few contacts with primitive peoples, and they found the red savages strange, puzzling, dangerous, and absolutely fascinating. Every journal keeper, diarist, sermonizer, explorer, and historian who had any contact with Indians seemed to have written of it. They recorded customs, dress, manners, language, society, and appearances, and speculated endlessly about their origins and history; they killed them indiscriminately and were killed in turn. The colonists eagerly adopted their legends (the country is still dotted with cliffs from which maidens were sacrificed, lovers leaped, and heroic braves jumped rather than surrender), used their herb remedies, took some of their words, and copied their hunting methods and some of their cookery.

In a world dominated by witchcraft, providences, and supernaturalism, since the Indian was assumed to be in league with the Devil or one himself, the Indian shaman, or sorcerer, commanded much interest. Historians gathered many tales of Indian magic, rituals, and transformations; even sophisticated William Byrd reported the success of an Indian rainmaker who brought a shower to one of his fields in exchange for two bottles of whiskey. Passaconaway, an actual Penacook "pawaw," or shaman, whose deeds were noted by both Wood and Morton, became a legendary figure who appeared in journals, newspapers, and historical accounts until the nineteenth century. At the same time, the spectacle of the Indian's confrontation with the apparatus of an advanced society led to the creation of stories of an Indian booby, a redskinned comic who put gunpowder in the fire, looked down pistol barrels, and ran away in fright when an Englishman took off his wig. A good many of these folktales later were transferred to the Negro.

But as witches were Satan's emissaries, so were Indians, whose depredations brought fear and sorrow to the settlements; Mather called them "miserable Salvages" whom "probably the Devil decoy'd hither" to destroy New England's Christian society. The seventeenth-century Indian wars produced a substantial body of writing, for these small conflicts were bitter and bloody reminders of the perils of frontier life. King Philip's War took the life of one of every sixteen New England males and destroyed thirty settlements; stories of the colonists part in this war were told in such narratives as William Hubbard's *Narrative of the Troubles with the Indians* (1677), Cotton Mather's *Decennium Latuosum* (1699), and Thomas Prince's *History of King Philip's War* (1716).

Indian Captivities and Deliverances

Quite early, the tale of Indian captivity took on some of the qualities of the sermon, the novel, and of the adventure story. Captain John Smith, in his story of Powhatan and Pocahontas, wrote the original of them all, but in its later manifestations the type took a different cast. The point of the captivity narrative was neither excitement nor terror alone, but rather the struggle waged between the red servants of Satan and the captive Christian for his soul; it was a story of trial and victory, of suffering and martyrdom, and came complete with sentimentality, moralizing, psychological probings, and exciting narrative. Such captivity stories—the first authentically native American novels—mixed fact and fancy, religion and sensationalism, in highly satisfactory fashion. An ex-captive was virtually assured of a reading public; 500 such accounts were published during the colonial period, and one, Mary Rowlandson's, ran through thirty-one editions. John Gyles of Maine, who spent the years 1689–1698 in captivity, authored one of the best-known; John Williams of Deerfield, Massachusetts (whose daughter chose to stay with her Indian husband), wrote another in 1707; Elizabeth Harris' (1725) was a best seller. By far the most popular was *The Sovereignty and Goodness of God, Together with the Faithfulness of His Promises Displayed; Being a Narrative of the Captivity and Restoration of Mrs. Mary Rowlandson,* an account of her capture during King Philip's War, published in its second edition in 1682.

"No one can imagine," Mrs. Rowlandson said, "what it is to be captivated and enslaved to such atheistical, proud, wild, cruel, barbarous, brutish (in one word) diabolicall creatures as these, the worst of heathen. . . ." She treated her captivity as a test of her faith, "for whom the Lord loveth he chasteneth," and instilled into her reader the values of high Christian ideals and faith in God. She also had an unerring sense of the right detail and a swift rushing style that never slowed the narrative pace. Her opening description of the raid, evoking all the terror and shock of its sudden savagery, still retains all its effectiveness after nearly three hundred years:

On the tenth of February 1675, Came the Indians with great numbers upon Lancaster: Their first coming was about Sunrising; hearing the noise of some Guns, we looked out; several Houses were burning, and the Smoke ascending to Heaven. There were five persons taken in one house, the Father, and the Mother and a sucking Child, they knockt on the head; the other two they took and carried away alive. Their were two others, who being out of their Garison upon some occasion were set upon; one was knockt on the head, the other escaped: Another their was who running along was shot and wounded, and fell down; he begged of them his life, promising them Money (as they told me) but they would not hearken to him but knockt him in head, and stript him naked, and split open his Bowels. Another seeing many of the Indians about his Barn, ventured and went out, but was quickly shot down. There were three others belonging to the same Garison who were killed; the Indians getting up upon the roof of the Barn, had advantage to shoot down upon them over their Fortification. Thus these murtherous wretches went on, burning, and destroying before them.

At length they came and beset our own house, and quickly it was the dolefullest day that ever mine eyes saw. The House stood upon the edg of a hill; some of the Indians got behind the hill, others into the Barn, and others behind any thing that could shelter them; from all which places they shot against the House, so that the Bullets seemed to fly like hail; and quickly they wounded one man among us, then another, and then a third, About two hours (according to my observation, in that amazing time) they had been about the house before they prevailed to fire it (which they did with Flax and Hemp, which they brought out of the Barn, and there being no defence about the House, only two Flankers at two opposite corners and one of them not finished) they fired it once and one ventured out and quenched it, but they quickly fired it again, and that took. Now is the dreadful hour come, that I have often heard of (in time of War, as it was the case of others) but now mine eyes see it. Some in our house were fighting for their lives, others wallowing in their blood, the House on fire over our heads, and the bloody Heathen ready to knock us on the head, if we stirred out. Now might we hear Mothers and Children crying out for themselves, and one another, Lord, What shall we do? Then I took my Children (and one of my sisters, hers) to go forth and leave the house: but as soon as we came to the dore and appeared, the Indians shot so thick that the bulletts rattled against the House, as if one had taken an handfull of stones and threw them, so that we were fain to give back. We had six stout Dogs belonging to our Garrison, but none of them would stir, though another time, if any Indian had come to the door, they were ready to fly upon him and tear him down. The Lord hereby would make us the more to acknowledge his hand, and to see that our help is always in him. But out we must go, the fire increasing, and coming along behind us, roaring, and the Indians gaping before us with their Guns, Spears and Hatchets to devour us.

These tales of captivity, witchcraft, and danger furnished in America a base for the Gothic novel, the romance of sensibility, the frontier Indian novel, and the folk tale, and marked as well the beginnings of a native literary tradition which would eventually come to include Charles Brockden Brown, Poe, Cooper, Hawthorne, and Melville.

The Seventeenth-Century Achievement

No one can reasonably claim any Donnes, Marvells, or Miltons for the American Colonies. The greater amount of seventeenth-century American writing, compared to the rich, exuberant, and brilliant English literature of the late Renaissance, may seem didactic and pious, obsessed by matters of Bible and salvation, indifferent to the beauty and sweetness of life that the Renaissance so enjoyed. Yet what the colonist wrote ought not to be dismissed out of hand, for he created a literature valid for himself and his place and time. If the Puritan's writing seems heavily moralistic, it is because of his will to live in unison with God; if he seems always to return to the Bible for inspiration, it was because he found there the sum of God's truth on which all depended; if he overlooked beauty here on earth, he was moved by his tremendous vision of it in God's heaven.

Colonial American literature, Puritan as well as non-Puritan, was not inconsequential. The men who wrote it were engaged directly and totally with their new life, and the intensity of their involvement shows through in the records they left behind. What they wrote still preserves much of the curiosity and excitement of discovery of the new land; what they wrote about themselves still retains much of the appeal and wonder of their discovery of themselves.

Here, in seventeenth-century colonial America, American literature began. Some of what the colonial American wrote can stand as art on its own merit; beyond that, an understanding of colonial American literature as a whole is prerequisite to any understanding of the subsequent development of American life and literature. There is no break in the stream; later American prose and poetry continues many of the themes and reflects many of the qualities of colonial writing. American prose, as Robert Spiller has pointed out, has been recognizably and permanently marked by the directness of language, the closeness to fact, and the vigor and energy of expression that characterized seventeenth-century style.

What the early colonists wrote was realistic, rarely sentimental; they were at grips with problems of life, death, and duty, and their books and poems grew out of their immediate needs and interests, out of the emergencies of life in a strange world. The necessity to confront daily foes in both the physical and spiritual worlds gave their writing distinctive toughness; as their outlook on life was free of gaudiness and irrelevance, so their literature was one of strength. The major themes of colonial writing—its awareness of the doubleness of life, its ethical earnestness, its preoccupation with the exploration of self, its sense of conflict between past and present—appear and reappear in American literature, in Emerson, Hawthorne, and Melville, in Emily Dickinson, Whitman, Robinson, Frost, and Eliot. The Puritans' awareness of the emblematic, metaphoric quality of experience, blended with the more sophisticated Romanticism of England and Europe, helped to create the richly symbolic literature of the American Renaissance. To the Puritan, as to Melville's Ahab, life was a chain of "linked analogies"; to Mather, as to Emerson, life was double, made up of This and Other, of the world here and the world beyond. Thomas Hooker's awareness of "the inconceivable hainousness of the hellish nature of sin" is Hawthorne's major theme; Emily Dickinson's probings of death resemble terse Puritan gravestone epitaphs; William Faulkner's *Bear* records a search for the meaning of primitive wilderness that began with John Lawson and William Wood. The red thread of morality and guilt, of virtue and anguish, that runs through the pattern of American writing from Mather to Hawthorne to Faulkner was shaped in these earliest days. American literature began with the sermons, narratives, journals, poetry, tales, and legends of the seventeenth century.

TWO

FROM COLONIES TO PROVINCES

The Provincial Mood

The years that stretched from about 1680 to about 1730 marked a subtle alteration in the mood and rhythm of colonial life. During this deceptively quiet half-century in which nothing decisive seemed to happen, people in the Colonies stopped being Englishmen living away from home and somehow became Americans. Changes in society, shifts in internal balances of power, the growing complexity of life—these and other factors operative in these decades of transit made the American Colonies a different place from what they originally had been.

By the 1730s the American Colonies hardly could have been called uniform or unified. There were economic, racial, and cultural differences among them as great as those between Massachusetts, settled in 1620, and Georgia, still unsettled by 1720. Even in 1765, when the first Continental Congress assembled in New York, delegates from different sections sometimes seemed like strangers to one another. Yet at the same time these disparate colonial societies had many bonds of union—language, culture, trade, proximity—to tie them together. They were all strongly Protestant, all dependent on England, all common enemies of the French and Indians. In a broad sense, they were all in the process of becoming Americanized.

For one thing, most of the early eighteenth-century colonists were second-generation Americans, who knew England only through its laws, the presence of Crown officials, or from already fading parental memories. The population of the Colonies, too, was rapidly increasing. In 1690 there were about 200,000 people in England's North American possessions; by 1710 the number doubled; by 1720 it quadrupled; in 1763, at the close of the French and Indian Wars, there were. 2 million colonists, two-thirds of them American-born.

For another thing, this colonial population was not only larger, but different. London tried to control the flow of migration to the Colonies in the seventeenth century, even forbidding by law the departure of certain skilled craftsmen while encouraging the exit of convicts, unemployed, and poor. But in spite of the laws, more Englishmen came to America than the homeland wanted to lose. The Dutch and Scandinavian settlements established in the seventeenth century attracted new arrivals; sizeable groups of French Huguenots (carrying such well-known names as Revere, Faneuil, Vassar, Jay, and Delano) came after the revocation of the Edict of Nantes in 1685, settling in towns with names like New Rochelle and New Bordeaux.

These ripples of non-English migration became a flood. After the signing of the Peace of Utrecht gave Europe peace for the first time in two generations, thousands of war-weary emigrants turned toward America. The German states, ravaged by marauding armies, sent more than 100,000 to the Colonies before 1770, putting names on the map like Germantown, Rhinebeck, Mecklenburg, and Hagerstown. The Scotch-Irish (who were not Irish but Scots from Ulster with names like Jackson and Calhoun) and Scots from Scotland numbered nearly a quarter of a million before the Revolution. Some Jews, a few Portuguese, and a sprinkling of arrivals from elsewhere came in this first stirring of the melting pot.

Colonies and Cities

New England after 1700 was no longer the same focal point for colonial life that it had been over the previous half-century. Much of the flood of immigration funneled into the Middle Colonies; these were not dominated by a single theological system like New England was and were not politically ruled by planters nor economically ruled by tobacco, as was the South. New York, taken from the Dutch in 1664, retaken by the Dutch in 1673, and returned to English rule a year later, became a royal province only in 1685. Pennsylvania was not settled until 1681; Delaware, although settled by Swedes, was claimed by Penn and Baltimore in 1684. New Jersey, settled in 1666, was annexed to New England, restored to its proprietors in 1692, and made a royal province in 1702.

Once stabilized, the Middle Colonies grew and prospered. With ample natural resources, good land, extensive forests, and convenient waterways, they soon developed a wealthy, balanced, relatively stable economy of trade, agriculture, and manufacturing. Much more diverse in character than either New England or the South, they drew Dutch, German, French, and Welsh settlers as well as English and Catholics, Jews, and Quakers as well as Calvinists and Anglicans. Middle Colony society, partly because of newness and partly because of diversity, remained much more open than that of New England or the South. Significantly, when young Franklin left Boston at seventeen to seek his fortune, he went first to New York and then to Philadelphia.

In the colonial society of 1680–1730, the city began to occupy an increasingly important role. Population, commerce, and wealth all added up to growing cities—Boston, New York, Philadelphia, Baltimore, Charleston, as well as to smaller ones such as Hartford, Trenton, Wilmington, and Annapolis. Urban life brought a much more complicated society, more sharply differentiated economic classes and more specialized occupations. It also marked the rise to influence of city shopkeepers, traders, artisans, and mechanics (called by Franklin "leather-apron men"), who soon became a powerful force in city and colonial affairs.

In 1730, government in the expanding Colonies was much more complex at every level. Cities required services, taxes, protection, financing; colonial legislatures had to raise troops, levy taxes, make civil and criminal law, deal with Parliament and King. Economic life was more intricate. On the way toward becoming a prospering merchant people, the colonists traded all over the world in such lucrative raw materials as furs, tobacco, fish, lumber, and products like rum, glass, hardware, paper, and furniture. By the opening of the eighteenth century, the American Colonies displayed much of the apparatus of a settled civilization—schools, libraries, courts, societies, trade centers, currency, and everything else needed for a life now more complicated and more culturally mature.

Secularization and Colonial Life

Beginning in the latter decades of the seventeenth century, the most singular change in the cultural life of the Colonies was its gradual secularization. Over the span of the first century of American settlement, Kepler and Galileo, along with Newton, Locke, and Descartes changed the nature of the universe, shifting its center from heaven toward earth, from divinity to humanity, from salvation toward knowledge. In the colonies, as elsewhere in the Western world, Howard Mumford Jones wrote:

The theocratic Utopia, by insensible degrees, merged into the mercantile state, a mundane spirit appeared in letters, questions of science were debated by the dilettanti, the almanacs were advocating the doctrines of Newton, invigorating winds were blowing through the musty clerical libraries.

Within this secular society, the colonists began to prosper. In particular, colonial New Englanders began to amass great wealth, which was distributed in a fashion that seemed to bear no particular relation to the recipient's sanctity. Puritans had long agreed that each man had two "callings," as Cotton Mather explained in *A Christian and His Calling* (1701)—a "general calling" to pursue salvation in Heaven and a "personal calling" to do as well as he could for himself on earth.

Colonial America was growing rich. The theocentric piety of an older Calvinism seemed to have small relevance to the facts of life in an expanding mercantile society, which soon would be deeply concerned with natural rights, social contracts, and Acts of Trade. The Puritan preoccupation with the state of the soul and the next world did not fit the New Yorker's or the Bostonian's interest in the state of his pocketbook and the pleasures of this world, which impressed him as a rather good one. As Franklin said, "after the first Cares for the Necessaries of Life are over," Americans had time "to think of the Embellishments."

The successful development and maturing of a wealthy, American society in the early eighteenth century seemed to have little relationship to either Calvinist or Anglican doctrine, and a growing number of Americans tended to ignore theology as being of small consequence for practical living. The book that replaced Wigglesworth's *Day of Doom* as a best seller in the early eighteenth century was Franklin's manual for the ambitious, *The Way to Wealth;* it is symbolic that when Franklin planned his academy for general learning, he left religion to be studied chiefly for its "usefulness to the public" and for "the advantage of a religious character."

Evidences of increased secularism were to be seen in all aspects of American life after 1700. The Colonies often seemed to be half in and half out of the eighteenth century as the tide of British and European Enlightenment washed against the walls of older, Reformation-rooted ways of life. Thus Cotton Mather, who believed the witchcraft witnesses in 1692, a few years later fought and won the battle for smallpox inoculation over the bitter objections of conservative Boston. Jonathan Edwards and Benjamin Franklin were born into Calvinist New England homes within three years of each other; Edwards hoped to spend his life, he said, "wrapt and swallowed up in God," while Franklin hoped to spend his in the laboratory. By 1725, Cotton Mather had preached at the ordination of a Baptist; Samuel Sewall had confessed to the errors of the Salem trials; Franklin had published his first deist tract; and Boston booksellers were selling fiction. Dr. Alexander Hamilton of Annapolis, who attended a book auction in Boston in 1744, reported that among the better sellers were Samuel Richardson's sentimental novel *Pamela,* Ovid's *Art of Love,* and a sermon collection called *The Marrow of Divinity.*

Science and Reason: Newton and Locke

To a large extent, the reason for the change from religions to secular priorities was the influence of the scientific rationalism of the Age of Reason. Descartes and Galileo suggested that if a person wished to understand Nature, he could best do so through Mathematics and Astronomy rather than Scripture. The universe that the new Science postulated was a great and infinitely perfect machine, operating in rational harmony by uniform and undeviating laws; Kepler viewed it as "something like a clockwork in which a single weight drives all the gears." How the world worked depended less on God's providence, perhaps, than on mathematical principles; the world was less a prelude to Heaven than an intricate structure that man could study and imitate in his society.

Isaac Newton's *Principia Mathematica* (1687), published only two years before Cotton Mather was made a Fellow at Harvard, provided the details of this novel and fascinating concept of a fixed universe, which was created perfect by a Supreme God, and was discoverable only by Reason through Science. "Nature and Nature's laws lay hid in night," wrote Alexander Pope, "God said *Let Newton be!* and all was light." What Science and Reason had to say to an age divided by religious controversy, split with political unrest, and racked with intermittent war was highly encouraging. The American colonists, like men everywhere, welcomed the Newtonian world view and eagerly took it as their model.

John Locke's *Essay Concerning Human Understanding,* which appeared in 1690, three years after Newton's book, changed man's picture of his own mind as drastically as Newton had altered his picture of the universe. Whatever knowledge man might obtain, Locke suggested, originated in his senses. At birth the mind was a blank tablet; experiences of the external world, gained through the senses, made impressions on it. Ideas, then, according to Locke, were the result of combining and shaping experiences.

Locke's view of knowledge required a thorough reconsideration of both the source and the nature of man's knowledge of God. If one could know God from experience, theologians argued, religion was not wholly a matter of faith. And if man were born with nothing at all on his mind, he could not be born with ideas of sin or good, which must be acquired from outside. The *New England Primer*'s lesson that "In Adam's Fall we sinned all" no longer had the same meaning, and neither Puritan nor Anglican could provide satisfactory explanations for it.

"The Old Spirit of New England," Cotton Mather wrote in 1702, "hath been sensibly going out of the world, as the old saints in whom it hath gone; and instead the return of *the spirit of the world* with a lamentable lack of strict piety has crept in upon the rising generation." What Mather said of New England applied as well to other Colonies, where religion was becoming relaxed, easy, and accommodating. The old-fashioned Calvinist doctrines of depravity and election did not hold up under the scrutiny of the rationalists nor did the old beliefs seem to square with common sense. "Christianity is a rational religion," said the Reverend Samuel Quincy, "and those who deny it can, or ought to be maintained upon rational principles, do in effect give it up."

Doctrines preached in church were likely to be left there during the week. It was difficult for a churchgoer to accept the idea on Sunday that his prosperous neighbor was really, beneath his moral mask, a confirmed sinner possibly condemned to hell. Nor did the doctrine of election, another keystone of the Puritan edifice, find much confirmation from daily observation. In the fluid society of the eighteenth century, the ability of a man to win spiritual election was assumed to be a corollary of his right to win economic or political distinction.

New Arrivals: Pietists and Quakers

The heavy migrations of the turn-of-the-century years brought into the Colonies many whose religion was not of the New England variety of Puritanism. A few immigrants were Jews; a sizeable number were Catholics, especially among the Highland Scots; an increasing number were Baptists, that is, Calvinists who had revived the early practice of baptismal immersion. Germans and Swiss sometimes belonged to such individualistic sects as Mennonites, Amish, Dunkards, and Moravians, or to branches of Reformed or Lutheran churches. The religious diversity of the populous Middle Colonies helped to counterbalance some of the influence of monolithic New England Calvinism; for that matter, few of the refugees who fled Europe's holy wars wanted anything more to do with state churches or religious disorders. One group of immigrants in particular, the Quakers, who began to arrive in the Colonies from Britain in 1656, by 1720 exerted an influence in American life far out of proportion to their numbers.

Quakerism in England was to a great extent the result of the efforts and example of George Fox, who in 1647 began preaching a radically individualized kind of faith. Known as the Society of Friends ("Quaker" was a name applied in derision, for Friends actually trembled or "quaked" at the Word of God), Fox and his converts spread their ideas throughout Britain, the Continent, and the American Colonies. Quakers claimed that each man was possessed of an "inner light," a source of direct inspiration from God, which served him as a guide for conduct and belief. William Penn defined it as "the Light of Christ in your Conscience, by which . . . you may clearly see if your Deeds, ay and your Words and Thoughts too, are wrought in God or not." Because of the sufficiency of the Inner Light, Quakers saw no need for church, ministry, sermons, or creeds; they refused to honor such accepted customs as the sanctity of the Sabbath, military service, class distinctions, the authority of magistrates, or the taking of oaths.

Imprisoned and persecuted by Puritan and Anglican alike in England and in the Colonies (Massachusetts hanged four of them), the Quakers nevertheless persisted. When Fox visited the Colonies from 1671 to 1673, he found Quakers in every Colony; Rhode Island had the greatest number until 1681, when the King granted Pennsylvania to the sect's most influential convert, William Penn, who opened Pennsylvania as a haven for any persecuted sect. Left to themselves, the Quakers became a stable, peaceful, and particularly prosperous people in control of one of the largest American Colonies and possessed of considerable power in others.

The "Great Awakening" of Religion

The decline of religious interest bewailed by Mather actually had begun a quarter of a century or more before he wrote. By 1659, church membership in New England had slacked off sharply, and after long argument the New England churches accepted, in 1662, a so-called "Half-Way Covenant," which allowed the children of church members to join the church without the usual required testimony of conversion. Although intended to encourage church membership, the Covenant did not succeed in strengthening the churches, and Calvinist congregations continued to decline in numbers and influence.

For the next forty years, sermons ceaselessly lamented the sinfulness of the times. Historians and biographers recalled the glories of the Church in the past; ministers found in every public disaster or personal misfortune an illustration of God's disapproval of a morally declining New England. When clergymen like Solomon Stoddard of Northampton adopted some of the techniques and principles of evangelism in an attempt to reinvigorate their congregations, they were soundly censured by their orthodox brethren. The Mathers and their followers fought "Stoddardism" and other such deviations from the New England way by pamphlet and sermon, but by 1730 their cause seemed lost. By then most of the old leaders—Increase and Cotton Mather, Samuel Willard, Edward Taylor, and many more—were gone.

The "Great Awakening," the name given to the wave of religious revivals that swept over the Colonies between 1730 and 1750, furnished both rebuttal to and replacement for a fading Puritanism. In 1720, a Dutch Reformed minister in New Jersey, Theodore Freylinghuysen, began preaching the necessity of a "personal experience of regeneration"; revival meetings sprang up in New Jersey, and preachers in other Colonies took up the theme. Jonathan Edwards, Gilbert Tennent, James Davenport, Samuel Davies, Devereux Jarratt, all famous evangelistic preachers, gave impassioned sermons warning of the agonies of hellfire and the joys of repentance to audiences of thousands. The Reverend George Whitefield, a young English evangelist, left a trail of fervent converts throughout the Colonies on his tour from 1740 to 1741. Harvard theologians called him a "deluder of the people"; nevertheless, he eventually made six more highly successful tours.

The intention of Great Awakening theology was simple. It personalized religion by maintaining that each man found his own salvation through his own sense of inward, personal conversion without the aid or approval of a church or minister. A minister might assist in bringing to each sinner consciousness of his sin and, therefore, the possibility of his salvation, but otherwise each man was his own judge. Evangelism "awakened" the individual; it started an inward process that ended in his spiritual conversion.

No one can calculate the numbers who heard the evangelical messages preached during the period of the Awakening, for famous exhorters like Whitefield preached in open fields to crowds of thousands. The religious enthusiasm evangelism generated swept through all the churches, although it struck with special force in Baptist, Methodist, and frontier Presbyterian communities. Nor was the American experience unique, for similar religious emotionalism swept England and Europe, including some of the Catholic countries, at the same time.

In its later stages, the Awakening's emotional excesses produced reactions against it. Ministers like Charles Chauncy protested that the evangelists stirred people's "passions into a ferment" and subverted "reasonable religious feeling." It was true that some of them encouraged mass hysteria and employed methods far beyond the boundaries of taste. James Davenport, an obviously unbalanced man, sometimes tore off his clothes in public, provoked fights, and supervised book burnings of the works of rival divines. Gilbert Tennent was given to violent personal attacks on respected local clergymen, and he and other extremists did irreparable damage to what was originally a sincere crusade for religious conversions. As an Anglican clergyman described them:

They strive with all their might to raise in their hearers what they call *Convictions,* which is thus performed. . . . They thunder out in awful words and new coin'd phrases what they call the terrors of the law, cursing and scolding, calling the old people Grayhair'd Devils, and all promiscuously Dam'd and Double Dam'd, whose souls are in hell though they are alive on earth, Lumps of Hellfire, incarnate devils, 1000 times worse than devils, etc., and all the while the preacher exalts his voice, puts himself in violent agitation, stamping and beating his desk unmercifully until the weaker sort of his hearers being scared cry out, fall down, and work like people in convulsion fits . . . These things are extoll'd by the preacher as the mighty power of God's grace in their hearts, and they who thus cry out and fall down are caressed and commended as the only penitent souls who come to Christ, whils't they who don't are often condemned by the lump as hardened wretches almost beyond the reach of mercy. . . .

Excess brought revulsion; overheated emotions cooled; and during the 1740s the Awakening receded, leaving a permanent print on the American religious mind.

The Great Awakening is significant in American history as more than a religious movement, for it marked a shift of attitudes and values in American life. It disturbed society deeply (it was in a real sense a class movement) and introduced new ideas, which, as Perry Miller has noted, "American society, having been shaken by this experience, was henceforth consciously to observe." Evangelism remained the dominant force in the American religious tradition; the emotional approach to religious experience is permanently ingrained in the American heritage. (A century later, in fact, Methodists and Baptists accounted for 70 percent of American Protestant church membership.)

By emphasizing the individual's ability to improve himself and his responsibility to do so, the Awakening reinforced the individualistic strain in American thought, and by fostering the "missionary spirit" it contributed much of the American sense of social responsibility. Perhaps more important than anything else, the revivalism of the Great Awakening helped make religion native. The Awakening showed Americans acting like Americans, not Englishmen, in reacting to their own spiritual experiences. They were "discovering," Miller wrote, "especially on the frontier where life was toughest, that they rejected imported European philosophies of society."

Jonathan Edwards

The turmoil and excitement of the Great Awakening drew from Jonathan Edwards the most brilliant theological writing of the eighteenth century. A precocious boy, who graduated at seventeen from Yale, Edwards joined his grandfather Solomon Stoddard as colleague-minister at Northampton, Massachusetts, and soon made his own reputation as preacher and writer. During the 1730s, before revivalism was fully under way in New England, Edwards tested out some of its ideas by leading an "awakening" of some proportions in his own parish. "People do not need to have their heads stored," he said, "so much as their hearts touched." The psychology of conversion particularly interested him; the Church must accept as valid that "sense of God" brought by the emotional experience of conversion even though such uncorroborated evidence of salvation was highly suspect under orthodox Calvinistic rules.

Familiar with what Locke, Berkeley, and others said about knowledge, Edwards concluded that true faith and spiritual grace came to the individual by an intuitive process through his emotions or "affections," as they were called in current terminology. "God has given to mankind affections," he said, "for the same purpose he has given all the faculties and principles of the human soul for *viz.,* that they might be subservient to man's chief end, and the great business for which God created him, that is, the business of religion." Disagreements with his congregation led to his resignation from his Northampton pulpit in 1750, but he already had written three important studies of emotionalism in religion—*A Faithful Narrative of the Surprising Works of God* (1737), *Thoughts Concerning the Present Revival of Religion* (1742), and *A Treatise Concerning Religious Affections* (1746)—which together constitute perhaps the most searching exploration of religious psychology written in America.

Serving a small congregation of Indians in the backcountry village of Stockbridge, Massachusetts, after he left Northampton, gave Edwards the time and opportunity to pursue his speculations wherever they led him. What he wanted to do was to strip away the nonessentials of the current argument, expose the fundamental issues, and reestablish once and for all the basic doctrines of Calvinism—free will, sin, the nature of virtue, election. *The Freedom of the Will,* his study of the first, appeared in 1754. However, Edwards died suddenly of smallpox in 1757, leaving behind the manuscripts of *Original Sin Defended* (published in 1758) and *Two Dissertations: The Nature of True Virtue and the End for Which God Created the World,* which was finally published in 1765. These three works contained Edwards' restructuring of the Calvinistic system; they represented the most cogently and closely argued body of theology produced during Puritanism's American existence, but they came too late to save it.

Edwards' religious beliefs derived from his own personal conversion through a mystic experience in his youth and from his conviction that the primary principle of faith was the absolute sovereignty of God. In the Great Awakening he saw a way to validate his faith as well as the chance to redeem a fading Calvinism. His revivalist sermons, including the famous "Sinners in the Hands of an Angry God," represented neither his theology nor his temperament. Edwards' hellfire sermons served a specific purpose at a specific time, in that they were preached to arouse in his congregation the realization of personal sinfulness that all ministers regarded as the first step toward conversion. The contours of his mind and heart were much more clearly delineated in his *Personal Narrative,* the journal he began writing about 1740, which was published after his death.

The *Personal Narrative* is Edwards' private record of his spiritual life—mystic, introspective, poetic, emotional—and one of the most compelling autobiographical accounts ever penned. Written in clear and flowing style, free of pedantry, it shines with illumination. Thus Edwards speaks of his youthful "sweet inward sense" of union with God:

From about that time, I began to have a new kind of apprehensions and ideas of Christ, and the work of redemption, and the glorious way of salvation by him. An inward, sweet sense of these things, at time, came into my heart; and my soul was led away in pleasant views and contemplations of them. . . .

After this my sense of divine things gradually increased, and became more and more lively, and had more of that inward sweetness. The appearance of every thing was altered; there seemed to be, as it were, a calm, sweet, cast, or appearance of divine glory, in almost every thing. God's excellency, his wisdom, his purity and love, seemed to appear in every thing; in the sun, moon, and stars; in the clouds and blue sky; in the grass, flowers, trees; in the water and all nature; which used greatly to fix my mind. I often used to sit and view the moon for continuance; and in the day, spent much time in viewing the clouds and sky, to behold the sweet glory of God in these things; in the meantime, singing forth, with a low voice, my contemplations of the Creator and Redeemer. And scarce any thing, among all the works of nature, was so sweet to me as thunder and lightning; formerly, nothing had been so terrible to me. Before, I used to be uncommonly terrified with thunder, and to be struck with terror when I saw a thunder-storm rising; but now, on the contrary, it rejoiced me. I felt God, if I may so speak, at the first appearance of a thunder-storm; and used to take the opportunity, at such times, to fix myself in order to view the clouds, and see the lightnings play, and hear the majestic and awful voice of God's thunder, which oftentimes was exceedingly entertaining, leading me to sweet contemplations of my great and glorious God. While thus engaged, it always seemed natural to me to sing, or chant forth my meditations; or, to speak my thoughts in soliloquies with a singing voice.

Edwards' sense of personally perceived salvation was not Puritan, but mystic. Calvinism had a strong introspective element, but Edwards projected his inward awareness of God's grace far beyond its usual Puritan boundaries. This sets Edwards' thought apart from that of his fellow Calvinists and helps to explain the contradictions in his thought that make it difficult to place him in the theological categories of the times. Edwards followed his own way, sometimes leaning toward the aggressive evangelism of the Great Awakening, sometimes toward the stubborn dogmatism of old-fashioned Puritanism. Meanwhile, within himself, he followed the still older path of the mystic.

Edwards' literary importance lies not in the fact that he developed or embraced any particular system of theology. It lies rather in his acceptance of human imperfection, God's sovereignty, and the risks of life. He caught a glimpse—as only a few great artists and philosophers have—of man's tragic predicament, held over a fiery pit by an angry God, or joyfully finding union with his loving God in a thunderstorm. "Dear children," he told his congregation, as he might have spoken to all his fellowmen, "I leave you in an evil world, that is full of snares and temptations. God only knows what will become of you."

The Secular Spirit in Prose

Colonial writing of the later seventeenth and early eighteenth centuries reflected the effects of secularization just as American society itself did. The older forms persisted—sermons, meditations, devotional verse, historical narratives in prose and verse, pamphlets—but there were also essays, satires, songs, debates, and a great deal of writing on topics of strictly secular and popular interest, from witchcraft to statecraft, science to fashion, war to earthquakes. People still kept journals; travel accounts sold well; and almanacs began to appear in profusion in the late seventeenth century. (The second printed piece in America, in fact, was an almanac issued at Cambridge in 1639.)

Along with the weather, calendars, astronomical calculations, and astrological prophecies, almanac editors added scraps of other things—verse, history, biography, proverbs, jests, riddles—anything of value or interest. Not merely collections of casual information, they were often edited by men of learning and served, as Franklin said, as "vehicles for conveying instruction among the common people." The almanac, hung from a nail on the wall, was probably the only printed material besides the Bible in many colonial households. Nathaniel Ames of Massachusetts began his famous series in 1725 (he reprinted, incidentally, Addison, Pope, Milton, Dryden, and Butler, among others), and Franklin began *Poor Richard* in 1733.

The essay was a relatively new form to the Colonies, and it grew steadily in importance along with the growth of newspapers and magazines, just as it had in England. Modeling themselves closely on the great British writers, American essayists imitated Addison, Steele, and Swift with varying degrees of skill and success. Franklin quite consciously patterned his work after Addison in his "Silence Dogood" essays for his brother's paper in 1722; in fact, Franklin taught himself to write, as almost every fledgling author in the Colonies did, by copying *The Spectator*.

With a few exceptions, colonial writing during the late seventeenth and early eighteenth centuries was not particularly distinguished. The clergy still supplied volumes of sermons to a wide public, but tastes in sermonic style altered with changes in theology. The current ministerial generation had little concern for minute explications of texts and (except for the overheated evangelists) was not at all interested in frightening its congregations into conversion. The prevailing eighteenth-century sermonic style emphasized generality, urbanity, grace, and even sentimentality. Mather Byles, for example, who spent forty-three years as pastor of Boston's Hollis Street Church, said that a minister must display "graceful deportment, elegant address, and fluent utterance," and that his sermons should be in "an easy style, expressive diction, and tuneful cadences."

Byles represented the "new style," smooth divine to whom thunder and lightning in the pulpit was long outmoded. His sermon to the congregation on the prospects of death, with its "graveyard school" vocabulary and Gothic overtones, might have caused delicious shivers in his audience, but it carried little of the urgent force of a Thomas Hooker or Urian Oakes:

Is this the Face we once gaz'd upon with so much Pleasure? Are these the Cheeks that glow'd so fresh, and bloom'd so lovely? Are these the Lips that smil'd so graceful, and pour'd out such a gliding Stream of Eloquence and Musick? Where's the tuneful Voice that once held the listening Ear, and rais'd the attentive Eye? Where are the proportioned Limbs, the supple Joints, the vigorous Pulses, the beating Heart, the working Brain, and the breathing Breast? Lo, the Body is laid in the Dust, and the Worms cover it. Polluted Vermine crawl over every Part of the elegant Form, and the beautious Face. It is folded in a winding Sheet, it is nailed in a black Coffin, and it is deposited in a silent Vault, amidst Shades and Solitude. The Skin breaks and moulders away; the Flesh drops in Dust from the Bones; the Bones are covered with black Mould, and Worms twist about them. The Coffins break, and the Graves sink in, and the disjointed Skelliton strows the lonely Vault. This shapely Fabrick must leave its Ruins among the Graves; lie neglected and forgot; moulder away without a Name, and scatter among the Elements. "And were these Bones once living like ours? and must ours be as they"? This hideous Skull, the frightful Jaw fallen, and the black Teeth naked to the Eye, was it once a thinking Frame, covered with a beauteous Skin? Strange Alteration made by Death!

As might be expected, Byles wrote fashionable poetry and enjoyed a wide reputation as a punster and wit that neither Richard Mather nor John Cotton could conceivably have welcomed. (Byles once said that Rhode Islanders went to Heaven by way of Providence, and he remarked to an old lady during the famous eclipse of 1780, "Madam, I am as much in the dark about this as you are.")

Of the hundreds of collections of sermons published during the years from 1660 to 1730, several attained wide popularity. Benjamin Colman's were polished Addisonian performances; John Barnard's intellectualized preaching read like a lawyer's brief. However, there were still collections written in the old style; Samuel Willard's *Complete Body of Divinity* (1726), the largest book yet printed on an American press, was a literary mammoth of 250 sermons, all peculiarly devoid of vigor. Willard's volume, already an anachronism when it appeared, represented the last of the old tradition. Pastor of Old South Church in Boston, Willard (who died in 1707) had intended his book to be the definitive exposition of the orthodox Calvinism of his era, a theological parallel to Mather's *Magnalia* and like it a foundation on which the next generation could build. On Tuesday afternoons for nineteen years Willard lectured on systematic theology, aiming to move step by step, he said, "around the whole circle of religion."

The Reverend James Blair, who served for fifty years as president of William and Mary College, published four volumes of sermons in 1722 that represented the best prose and the most learned theology in the South—the equal of any published elsewhere during the period. An exception to the blandness of the prevailing style was John Wise's *Vindication of the Government of New England Churches* (1717), a blast against theocracy produced during his earlier battle with the Mathers over New England church polity. Wise's prose, like his ideas, was new—a precise and convincing forensic style that looked ahead to the political prose of the Revolution and *The Federalist.*

The Encyclopedic Dr. Mather

Cotton Mather, who produced a few specimens of almost every form of writing practiced in the Colonies, dominated contemporary prose by bulk if not by talent. Son of Increase Mather, grandson of Richard Mather and John Cotton, Cotton Mather represented the cumulative intellectual endowment of three Puritan generations. Graduate of Harvard at fifteen, he served as minister of Old North Church in Boston for his entire life (until 1728). A fearsomely learned man and owner of the largest library in New England (he owned about as many books as Harvard), he handled seven languages and even wrote sermons in one of the Indian tongues. His bibliography of published items totaled several hundred separate pieces; he wrote sermons, essays, histories, biographies, letters, journals, meditations, pamphlets, scientific papers, textbooks, and dozens of unclassifiable works. In one year, according to his records, Mather published fourteen items, kept twenty vigils, and observed sixty fasts.

Mather's interests ranged over all contemporary fields of learning, but he devoted much of his life to preserving the traditional New England way, trying desperately to strengthen the position of Puritanism in a society growing less pious and more worldly. Himself the product of a century of Puritan culture, he could not believe that its influence might be fading, or that it had any less to contribute to his world than to his grandfather's. Of his multitude of productions, his *Magnalia Christi Americana* (1702) probably represented his best effort. A book of vast erudition, the *Magnalia* was designed to check the rising forces of liberalism and worldliness by arousing New England's pride in its past and by guiding the next generation to an equally glorious Puritan future. His *Christian Philosopher* (1721) intended to show that the new science was not a threat to faith, "but a mighty and wondrous Incentive to Religion." (Others were not so sanguine. Samuel Sewall, noting in his diary for December 23, 1714, that Dr. Mather's sermon that day spoke of the sun being in the center of the universe, added uneasily, "I think it inconvenient to assert such problems.")

Bonifacius (1710), or "Essays to Do Good," a little book stressing the humanitarian side of Puritanism, influenced thousands of readers toward a sense of social responsibility—including Franklin, who named it as one of the books that most affected him as a youth. *Manuductio ad Ministerium* (1726), Mather's handbook for divinity students, is still a charming and valuable record of what people of the eighteenth century believed a minister should be and do.

Mather's influence on the mind and culture of his times was very great. By no means universally loved, he was nonetheless for forty years the acknowledged leader of New England theology, the man to whom the greater portion of the public looked for guidance in things churchly and non-churchly. Because of his part in the witchcraft affairs he came to be a symbol of Puritan bigotry, although he was not a bigot; and because of his lifelong struggle to preserve the old orthodoxy, he became a symbol of Puritan reaction, although he was by no means an instinctive conservative.

Mather was not a deep thinker, but he had an inquisitive, logical, and above all a well-ordered and vastly stocked mind. Much of his writing was second hand, hasty hackwork, for he was eager to write anything publishable if it would provide somebody with advice or information. His prose style tended to be elaborate and overly pedantic. With almost every sentence pivoting on a learned allusion, a page of Matherian prose sometimes turned into a jungle of twisting prolixities. But he also wrote to suit his purpose and audience; *Bonifacius,* aimed at the ordinary reader, was much plainer and more direct than his customary hortatory style. In contrast to his plain style, in the *Magnalia,* when he tried to explain that the discovery of America had been prophesied in the Bible, he couched it in practically impenetrable prose:

It is the Opinion of some, though 'tis but an Opinion, and but of some Learned Men, That when the Sacred Oracles of Heaven assure us, The Things under the Earth are some of those, whose Knees are to bow in the Name of Jesus, by those Things are meant the Inhabitants of America, who are Antipodes to those of the other Hemisphere. I would not Quote any words of Lactantius, tho' there are some to Countenance this Interpretation, because of their being so Ungeographical; Nor would I go to strengthen the Interpretation by reciting the Words of the Indians to the First White Invaders of their Territories, We hear you are come from under the World, to take our World from us. But granting the uncertainty of such an Exposition, I shall yet give the Church of God a certain Account of those Things, which in America have been Believing and Adoring the glorious name of Jesus, and of that Country in America, where those Things have attended with Circumstances most remarkable.

But in *Bonifacius* his language took on an ease and flexibility comparable to that of Franklin, the urbane style of the eighteenth-century essay:

Our opportunities to do good are our talents. An awful account must be rendered to the great God concerning the use of the talents with which he has intrusted us in these precious opportunities. Frequently we do not use our opportunities, because we do not consider them; they lie by unnoticed and unimproved. We read of a thing which we deride as often we behold it. "There is that maketh himself poor, and yet hath great riches." This is too frequently exemplified in our opportunities to do good, which are some of our most valuable riches. Many a man seems to reckon himself destitute of these talents, as if there were nothing for him to do; he pretends that he is not in a condition to do any good. Alas, poor man, what can *he* do? My friend, think again; think frequently; inquire what your opportunities are; you will certainly find them to be more than you were aware of. "Plain men dwelling in tents," persons of ordinary rank in life, may, by their eminent piety, prove persons of extraordinary usefulness.

History and Travel: Beverley's Virginia, Madame Knight's Journey

The aims of historical writing underwent a similar secularistic shift toward the close of the seventeenth century. Usually written by doctors, planters, businessmen, lawyers, colonial officials, or gentlemen, rather than the clergy, these histories (excepting Cotton Mather's) did little either to justify the ways of God to Americans or to recount the workings of providence. Instead the chroniclers wrote of government, resources, conflicts with royal officials, scientific observations, and other mundane matters. New England continued to produce most of the current historical writing, much of which was relatively mediocre and bloodless.

Daniel Neal, a dissenting English clergyman, published a two-volume *History of New England* in 1720, drawing heavily on Morton, Wood, and especially on the *Magnalia*. Thomas Prince, whose scholarship Mather praised, published the first part of his *Chonological History of New England* in 1730; it was less a history, he said, than "a Register, comprising only Facts in a Chronological Epitome, to enlighten the Understanding." Since

Prince began his chronology with Adam, he never got beyond 1633 in the first part of his work; he never finished the second, which he issued in pamphlets over the next twenty years. John Callender's *Historical Discourse* (1739), dealing with Rhode Island, was not much better; William Douglass, a Scottish physician, published *A Summary, Historical and Political of . . . the British Settlements* (1748–1752), which was highly personalized and eccentric. Essentially a journalist and pamphleteer, he spent his space on what interested him the most, with the result that he limited the history of Virginia to ten pages and gave twenty to a history of smallpox.

Thomas Hutchinson, a descendant of Anne and Governor of Massachusetts in his own right, published the first volume of his *History of the Colony of Massachusetts Bay* in 1764. His second appeared in 1767, when royal officials were not popular, and when he was suspected of Tory sympathies, a mob sacked his home, destroyed his library and manuscripts, and drove him into exile. The third volume of his history, which did not appear until 1828, long after his death, was quite understandably biased. In New York, William Smith, a lawyer and colonial official, published a two-volume *History of the Province of New York* in 1757, concentrating on its political history and providing a model for other provincial histories soon to appear. Cadwallader Colden, a Scottish physician and scientist who came to America in 1710, wrote *A History of the Five Indian Nations* (1727) chiefly as a warning, he said, of the danger of a French-Indian alliance against the frontier settlements; but it constitued one of the first serious historical treatments of the Indian in that century.

The best historical writing of the period appeared in the South, primarily because of the decision of Robert Beverley of Virginia to write a history of his Colony to correct the errors he found in a Britisher's manuscript given to him by a London publisher. Beverley was a planter of wealth and importance, an intelligent and well-read man. His *History and Present State of Virginia* appeared in 1705—it was a literate, personalized view of Virginia history, and included sketches of men he liked or disliked, British merchants who bilked colonial planters, his opinions of certain royal governors and officials, and other matters put together "with no other Design than the Gratification of my own Inquisitive Mind."

For all his eccentricities, Beverley wrote good sound prose, and had an eye for detail, a sense of humor, and a pervasive love of his Virginia home—"the best poor Man's Country in the world." He spoke with contempt of English visitors who

go sweltering about in their thick clothes all summer . . . greedily devour the green fruit and unripe trash they met with, and so fell into fluxes, fevers, and the bellyache and then, they in their tarpaulin language cry, God d-n this country.

He also explained Virginia hospitality:

The inhabitants are very courteous to Travellers, who need no other Recommendation, but being human Creatures. A stranger has no more to do, but to inquire upon the Road, where any Gentleman, or good House-keeper, lives, and there he may depend upon being received with Hospitality. This good Nature is so general among their people that the Gentry, when they go abroad, order their principal Servant to entertain all Visitors, with every thing that the Plantation affords. And the poor Planters, who have but one Bed, will very often sit up or lie upon a Form or Couch all Night to make room for a weary Traveller to repose himself after his Journey. If there happens to be a Churl, that either out of Covetousness, or Ill-nature, won't comply with this generous Custom, he has a Mark of Infamy set upon him, and is abhorr'd by all.

Since his outspokenness offended influential persons both in London and at home, Beverley omitted or softened some of the critical passages for his second edition of 1722, providing for greater acceptance but making it less readable.

Beverley's work, an interesting reflection of an interesting man, remains a minor classic. Other Southern histories were less notable. Hugh Jones, a clergyman who served as rector to the Virginia House of Burgesses, wrote *The Present State of Virginia* in 1724—a careful scrutiny of the Colony's society, manners, and politics. William Stith's *History of the First Settlement and Discovery of Virginia* (1747) covered only the years to 1624 and showed the author's admiration for Tacitus and Suetonius; according to Thomas Jefferson, this book displayed a prose style that was "inelegant and often too minute to be tolerable." A curious book, not quite classifiable as history, was *A True and Historical Narrative of the Colony of Georgia,* "by Patrick Tailfer, M.D., Hugh Anderson, M.A., David Douglas, and Others," published in London in 1741. Done by three Scotsmen who were evicted from Georgia, it apparently was, as one of its Georgia critics called it, "a narrative founded in lies and misrepresentations." It also was a salty piece of Swiftian satire done with more than average skill, demonstrated in the dedication to Governor Oglethorpe who, the author mockingly writes, has discovered that the "usual liberties" granted colonists "pamper the body and introduce a long variety of evils." Oglethorpe, therefore, has

afforded us the opportunity of arriving at the integrity of primitive times, by entailing a more than primitive poverty on us. . . . As we have no properties to feed vainglory and beget contention . . . the valuable virtue of humility is secured to us . . . and that we might fully receive the spiritual benefit of those wholesome austerities, you have wisely denied us the use of such spirituous liquors as might in the least divert our minds from the contemplation of our happy circumstances.

Eighteenth-century colonists continued to write travel books in much the same form and manner as before. John Lawson's *New Voyage to Carolina* (1709) the best travel book published in the colonial South, was written chiefly to attract prospective settlers. Nevertheless, it was an observant account of what he saw in a thousand miles of travel through the Carolinas and especially described the Indian tribes of the region—who later killed him. Dr. Alexander Hamilton, a Scots physician who practiced in Annapolis, kept a journal (not published until the nineteenth century) of his trip to New York and New England. The classic travel book of the eighteenth century, however, was Madam Sarah Kemble Knight's journal of her trip from Boston to New York by way of Rhode Island and Connecticut; her trip extended from October 2, 1704, to March 3, 1705. Mrs. Knight, wife of a ship captain and a widow at forty, supported herself and her daughter by teaching school (possibly to young Ben Franklin), running a boarding house, keeping a shop, and copying legal documents. In 1704 she set out for New York to settle an estate, making notes at the end of each day's travel; these she later revised into a continuous narrative. Her manuscript, titled "The Private Journal of a Journey from Boston to New York," remained unpublished until 1825.

Madam Knight, an independent and resourceful woman, sprinkled her account with verse, epigrams, witty illustrations, and commonsense judgments. Her journal provided a superb picture of the still half-primitive backwoods settlements and their sharp contrast with the emergent urban societies of the early eighteenth century, while her own shrewd comments lent spice to the story. Her picture of New York as it looked in 1704 is still vivid:

The Cittie of New York is a pleasant, well compacted place, situated on a Commodius River which is a fine harbour for shipping. The Buildings Brick Generaly, very stately and high, though not altogether like ours in Boston. The Bricks in some of the Houses are of divers Coullers and laid in Checkers, being glazed look very agreeable. The inside of them are neat to admiration, the wooden work, for only the walls are plasterd, and the Sumers and Gist[1] are plained and kept very white scowr'd as so is all the partitions if made of Bords. The fire places have no Jambs (as ours have) But the Backs run flush with the walls, and the Hearth is of Tyles and is as farr out into the Room at the Ends as before the fire, which is Generally Five foot in the Low'r rooms, and the peice over which the mantle tree should be is made as ours with Joyners work, and as I suppose is fasten'd to iron rodds inside. The House where the Vendue[2] was, had Chimney Corners like ours, and they and the hearths were laid with the finest tile that I ever see, and the stair cases laid all with white tile which is ever clean, and so are the walls

[1] Beams and joists
[2] Auction

of the Kitchen which had a Brick floor. They were making Great preparations to Receive their Govenor, Lord Cornbury from the Jerseys, and for that End raised the militia to Gard him on shore to the fort.

They are Generaly of the Church of England and have a New England Gentleman for their minister, and a very fine church set out with all Customary requisites. There are also a Dutch and Divers Conventicles as they call them, viz. Baptist, Quakers, &c. They are not strict in keeping the Sabbath as in Boston and other places where I had bin, But seem to deal with great exactness as farr as I see or Deall with. They are sociable to one another and Curteos and Civill to strangers and fare well in their houses. The English go very fasheonable in their dress. But the Dutch, especially the middling sort, differ from our women, in their habitt go loose, were French muches which are like a Capp and a head band in one, leaving their ears bare, which are sett out with Jewells of a large size and many in number. And their fingers hoop't with Rings, some with large stones in them of many Coullers as were their pendants in their ears, which You see very old women wear as well as Young.

They have Vendues very frequently and make their Earnings very well by them, for they treat with good Liquor Liberally, and Generally pay for't as well, by paying for that which they Bidd up Briskly for, after the sack has gone plentifully about, tho' sometimes good penny worths are got there.

The Inner Light: John Woolman's Journal

Three great journals that are among the most important productions in American literary history belong to the early eighteenth century: John Woolman's, reflecting the gentle, introspective world of the Quaker; Samuel Sewall's, reflecting the secular, workaday world of the New England man of affairs; William Byrd's, reflecting the contrasts between the elitist society of the plantation South and the crude backcountry of the poor white.

The Quaker, whose faith was inward and experiential, wrote much in his diary; the journal was for him a characteristic literary form, rarely written for publication. William Penn, an exception, wrote energetically on a variety of topics, coined proverbs and maxims, and left a volume of essays, *Some Fruits of Solitude* (1693). Quakers, like the Puritans, kept journals as records of spiritual progress and wrote as plainly as they dressed and lived. "Use plainness of speech and plain words," George Fox wrote, and Penn agreed that "Truest Elegance is Plainest." Quaker prose tended sometimes to be overly simple and to fall easily into cliché, but journals left by Friends could also contain sensitive and illuminating writing.

Woolman's was one of these. Born in New Jersey, Woolman was so successful as a merchant that he gave up business, lest wealth taint his conscience, to become an itinerant preacher. For thirty years he traveled by foot and horseback through the Colonies, keeping a journal of his worldly and spiritual experiences. He observed in his travels the growth of what he called a "Spirit of Fierceness"—of egotism, materialism, and competitiveness that seemed to him the cause of many of society's troubles. Against this he preached the Quaker doctrine of humanitarianism, humility, and helpfulness, "convinced in mind," he said,

that true Religion consisted in an inward life, wherein the Heart doth love and reverence God the Creator, and learns to exercise true Justice and Goodness, not only toward all Men, but also toward the brute Creatures—that as the Mind was moved, by an inward principle, to love God as an invisible incomprehensible Being, by the same Principle it was moved to love him in all his Manifestations in the visible World.

Woolman's journal was published first in 1774, two years after his death, and was reprinted later more than thirty times. John Greenleaf Whittier, who edited it in the nineteenth century, rightly called it "a classic of the inner life." Built around two themes—his sense of intimate communion with God and his quiet desire to live life in accord with the "inner light"— the *Journal* is written in simple and unaffected prose with strong Biblical overtones. Woolman distrusted "superfluity of workmanship," he said, and rewrote his manuscript twice to make it plain and sincere. The result was a pure and functional English of great effectiveness, demonstrated in his remarks on his business life:

Until this Year, 1756, I continued to retail Goods, besides following my Trade as a Taylor; about which Time, I grew uneasy on Account of my Business growing too cumbersome: I had begun with selling Trimmings for Garments, and from thence proceeded to sell Cloths and Linens; and, at length, having got a considerable Shop of Goods, my Trade increased every Year, and the Road to large Business appeared open; but I felt a Stop in my Mind. . . .

The Increase of Business became my Burthen; for, though my natural Inclination was toward Merchandize, yet I believed Truth required me to live more free from outward Cumbers: and there was now a Strife in my Mind between the two; and in this Exercise my Prayers were put up to the Lord, who graciously heard me, and gave me a Heart resigned to his holy Will: Then I lessened my outward Business; and, as I had Opportunity, told my Customers of my Intention, that they might consider what Shop to turn to: And, in a while, wholly laid down Merchandize, following my Trade, as a Taylor, myself only, having no Apprentice. I also had a Nursery of Appletrees; in which I employed some of my Time in hoeing, grafting, trimming, and inoculating. In Merchandize it is the Custom, where I lived, to sell chiefly on Credit, and poor People often get in Debt; and when Payment is expected, not having wherewith to pay, their Creditors often sue for it at Law. Having often observed Occurrences of this Kind, I found it good for me to advise poor People to take such Goods as were most useful and not costly. . . .

Or in his moving account of his youthful struggles with his conscience:

Thus time passed on: my heart was replenished with mirth and wantonness, and pleasing scenes of vanity were presented to my imagination, till I attained the age of eighteen years; near which time I felt the judgments of God, in my soul, like a consuming fire; and, looking over my past life, the prospect was moving.—I was often sad, and longed to be delivered from those vanities; then again, my heart was strongly inclined to them, and there was in me a sore conflict: at times I turned to folly, and then again, sorrow and confusion took hold of me. In a while, I resolved totally to leave off some of my vanities; but there was a secret reserve, in my heart, of the more refined part of them, and I was not low enough to find true peace. Thus, for some months, I had great troubles; there remaining in me an unsubjected will, which rendered my labours fruitless, till at length, through the merciful continuance of heavenly visitations, I was made to bow down in spirit before the Lord. I remember one evening I had spent some time in reading a pious author; and walking out alone, I humbly prayed to the Lord for his help, that I might be delivered from all those vanities which so ensnared me. Thus, being brought low, he helped me; and, as I learned to bear the cross, I felt refreshment to come from his presence; but, not keeping in that strength which gave victory, I lost ground again; the sense of which great affected me: and I sought desarts and lonely places, and there, with tears, did confess my sins to God, and humbly craved help of him. And I may say, with reverence, he was near to me in my troubles, and in those times of humiliation opened my ear to discipline. I was now led to look seriously at the means by which I was drawn from the pure truth, and learned this, that, if I would live in the life which the faithful servants of God lived in, I must not go into company as heretofore in my own will; but all the cravings of sense must be governed by a divine principle. In times of sorrow and abasement these instructions were sealed upon me, and I felt the power of Christ prevail over selfish desires, so that I was preserved in a good degree of steadiness; and, being young, and believing at that time that a single life was best for me, I was strengthened to keep from such company as had often been a snare to me.

The New England Temper: Samuel Sewall's Journal

Samuel Sewall's *Diary* came from an entirely different kind of America. Brought to Massachusetts from England at the age of nine in 1661, Sewall was trained as a minister but instead entered business and politics to become signally successful at both. He spent thirty-six years as judge of the Massachusetts Supreme Court and served at the witchcraft trials, for which he made public confession of error—something no other judge felt constrained to do. Sewall began keeping his journal in 1673 and continued until 1729, a year before his death; it was published (except for a missing record book for 1677–1685) in 1878–1882. In 1692, during his lifetime, he published an odd book called *Phaenomena Quaedam Apocalyptica* explaining his somewhat eccentric theory of Biblical prophecies, but he had neither literary nor historical ambitions.

Sewall wrote his journal wholly without pretense or self-consciousness; a man absolutely honest with himself, he simply put down everything he deemed worth remembering. Curious about everything going on about him, he possessed a gift for the fleeting picture, the evocative incident, the sudden flash of feeling. Like his Puritan forebears, he had the habit of seeing events as emblems and often moralized out of them. Watching his chickens feed suggested to him man's need for spiritual grain, or a wineglass spilled at table reminded him of life's brief mortality. At the same time, he noted with pleasure the return of the swallows in spring, the bursting flowers in his garden, the taste of good food and wine, the sweet anxieties of courtship. He entered the facts of his public apology for his part in the Salem trials with simple dignity:

Oct. 12. Jn⁰ Cunable finishes the Stairs out of the wooden house to the top of the Brick House. Little Mary grows a little better after very sore illness. Copy of the Bill I put up on the Fast day; giving it to Mr. Willard as he pass'd by, and standing up at the reading of it, and bowing when finished; in the Afternoon.

Samuel Sewall, sensible of the reiterated strokes of God upon himself and family; and being sensible, that as to the Guilt Contracted upon the opening of the late Comission of Oyer and Terminer at Salem (to which the order for this Day relates) he is, upon many accounts, more concerned than any that he knows of, Desires to take the Blame and shame of it, Asking pardon of men, And especially desiring prayers that God, who has an Unlimited Authority, would pardon that sin and all other his sins; personal and Relative: And according to his infinitive Benignity, and Sovereignty, Not Visit the sin of him, or of any other, upon himself or any of his, nor upon the Land: But that He would powerfully defend him against all Temptations to Sin, for the future; and vouch-safe him the efficacious, saving Conduct of his Word and Spirit.

The shrill, faraway cry of women brings back with sudden clarity the shock of a public hanging in 1704:

Feria Sexta, Junij, 30. After Dinner, about 3. p.m. I went to see the Execution. . . . Many were the people that saw upon Broughton's Hill. But when I came to see how the River was cover'd with People, I was amazed: Some say there were 100 Boats. 150 Boats and Canoes, saith Cousin Moody of York. He told them. Mr. Cotton Mather came with Capt. Quelch and six others for Execution from the Prison to Scarlet's Wharf, and from thence in the Boat to the place of Execution about the mid-way between Hanson's point and Broughton's Warehouse. Mr. Bridge was there also. When the scaffold was hoisted to a due height, the seven Malefactors went up; Mr. Mather pray'd for them standing upon the Boat. Ropes were all fasten'd to the Gallows (save King, who was Repriev'd) When the Scaffold was let to sink, there was such a Screech of the Women that my wife heard it sitting in our Entry next the Orchard, and was much surprised at it; yet the wind was sou-west. Our house is a full mile from the place.

His record of the Widow Winthrop's final refusal of a lonely old man's proposal of marriage, as she lets the fire in the hearth die and speeds his departure with a glass of wine, is superb storytelling:

Monday, Novr 7th. I went to Mad. Winthrop; found her rocking her little Katee in the Cradle. I excus'd my Coming so late (near Eight). She set me an arm'd Chair and Cusheon; and so the Cradle was between her arm'd Chair and mine. Gave her the remnant of my Almonds; She did not eat of them as before; but laid them away; I said I came to enquire whether she had alter'd her mind since Friday, or remained of the same mind still. She said, Thereabouts. I told her I loved her, and was so fond as to think that she loved me: She said had a great respect for me. I told her, I had made her an offer, without asking any advice; she had so many to advise with, that twas a hindrance. The Fire was come to one short Brand besides the Block, which Brand was set up in end; at last it fell to pieces, and no Recruit was made: She gave me a Glass of Wine. I think I repeated again that I would go home and bewail my Rashness in making more haste than good Speed. I would endeavor to contain myself, and not go on to sollicit her to do that which she could not Consent to. Took leave of her. As came down the steps she bid me have a Care. Treated me Courteously. Told her she had enter'd the 4th year of her Widowhood. I had given her the News-Letter before: I did not bid her draw off her glove as sometime I had done. Her dress was not so clean as sometime it had been. Jehovah jireh!

Sewall personified the Puritan Yankee. A man of sincere religious convictions, he was also very much a virile, energetic participant in affairs of the world. His diary described a society moving from the Reformation toward the Age of Reason—a prosperous, comfortable, and increasingly worldly society quite capable of taking care of itself here and less concerned about the hereafter.

Sewall's New England was still a powerfully religious community—his entries list fasts, prayers, sermons, weddings, funerals, ordinations, christenings, and other church-centered events in great abundance. Yet it was also a sophisticated and secularized society, for his journal mentions dancing, drinking, courtships, roistering sailors, riots, hangings, trials, and all the evidences of an energetic and worldly way of life.

The Disposition of Virginia: William Byrd's Journal

William Byrd's Virginia had little in common with Woolman's Quaker Jersey or Sewall's Boston. Byrd's world was centered on the estate of the landed aristocrat, in the urbane, civilized, self-assured society of country gentry—a society which did little soul-searching and in which, a contemporary said, "A man might be a Christian in any church, but a gentleman only in the Church of England." Born into a powerful and wealthy planter family, Byrd was educated in London and spent much of his youth there as a well-known man about town and avid theatergoer. Owner of some 180,000 acres and of Westover, a magnificent estate on the James River, Byrd surrounded himself, between trips to London, with the finest furniture, the best company, and the largest collection of books in the South. A member of the House of Burgesses and the Council (the aristocratic group that virtually ran Virginia), he was one of the Colony's influential citizens.

William Byrd, however, was no mere fox-hunting squire, but a businessman, public official, and scholar who read seven languages. He considered himself a gentleman, whether at Queen Anne's court or in Virginia, and he spent his life being one. He dabbled in literature; wrote light verse, dramatic criticism, satire, "characters," and translations such as gentlemen did; and sent scientific reports to the Royal Society, to which he belonged. His writings, bound and preserved for his descendants in the Southern fashion (including *A Progress to the Mines* and *Journey to the Land of Eden,* reports of trips taken in 1732 and 1733 to inspect property on the frontier), remained unpublished until 1841, after they had passed out of the family's possessions.

Byrd's *History of the Dividing Line Betwixt Virginia and North Carolina* recorded a journey he made in 1728 as one of the commissioners appointed to establish the boundary between the two Colonies. This was wild, little known frontier country, and Byrd kept a candid account in shorthand of daily events for the public record as well as for his own reflection. A catchall book, a personal journal that was also partly history, travel, and jottings about nature, it included sketches of the surveying party and of people he met, remarks on Indians, satires, tentative essays, and notes on whatever else interested him. He also wrote a shorter version, or "secret history," using material left out of the original and commenting on the habits and conduct of some of the members of his party to whom he gave cover-names such as "Firebrand," "Meanwell," and "Orion."

A fine raconteur, Byrd loved the witty anecdote that could be recalled over wine at dinner. He also had a strong inclination for making his friends ridiculous, and since he could never resist tossing a barb, his journal has a consistently acid tinge. As a Virginia aristocrat, Byrd never bothered to conceal his contempt for the lesser members of his party or for the denizens of "Lubberland" he met on the frontier, who lived so much on pork, he wrote, "that it don't only incline them to the Yaws . . . but makes them extremely hoggish in their Temper, and many of them seem to Grunt rather than speak in ordinary conversation." He took some pains to write an easy, urbane prose in the manner of the English essayists, and (except for Franklin) wrote as good prose as anyone in America before Irving. His brief account of the Carolinian frontiersman is a good sample of his skill at characterization and of his aristocratic hauteur:

Surely there is no place in the World where the Inhabitants live with less Labour than in N Carolina. It approaches nearer to the Description of Lubberland than any other, by the great felicity of the Climate, the easiness of raising Provisions, and the Slothfulness of the People.

Indian Corn is of so great increase, that a little Pains will Subsist a very large Family with Bread, and then they may have meat without any pains at all, by the Help of the Low Grounds, and the great Variety of Mast that grows on the Highland. The Men, for their Parts, just like the Indians, impose all the Work upon the poor Women. They make their Wives rise out of their Beds early in the Morning, at the same time that they lye and Snore, till the Sun has run one third of his course, and disperst all the unwholesome Damps. Then, after Stretching and Yawning for half an Hour, they light their Pipes, and, under the Protection of a cloud of Smoak, venture out into the open Air; tho', if it happens to be never so little cold, they quickly return Shivering into the Chimney corner. When the weather is mild, they stand leaning with both their arms upon the corn-field fence, and gravely consider whether they had best go and take a Small Heat at the Hough; but generally find reasons to put it off till another time.

Thus they loiter away their Lives, like Solomon's Sluggard, with their Arms across, and at the Winding up of the Year Scarcely have Bread to Eat.

To speak the Truth, tis a thorough Aversion to Labor that makes

People file off to N Carolina, where Plenty and a Warm Sun confirm them in their Disposition to Laziness for their whole Lives.

His account of the crossing of the Great Dismal Swamp shows his narrative style at its best:

15. The Surveyors pursued their work with all Diligence, but Still found the Soil of the Dismal so Spongy that the Water ouzed up into every foot-step they took. To their Sorrow, too, they found the Reeds and Bryars more firmly interwoven than they did the day before. But the greatest Grievance was from large Cypresses, which the Wind had blown down and heap'd upon one another. On the Limbs of most of them grew Sharp Snags, Pointing every way like so many Pikes, that requir'd much Pains and Caution to avoid.

These Trees being Evergreens, and Shooting their Large Tops Very high, are easily overset by every Gust of Wind, because there is no firm Earth to Steddy their Roots. Thus many of them were laid prostrate to the great Encumbrance of the way. Such Variety of Difficulties made the Business go on heavily, insomuch that, from Morning till Night, the Line could advance no further than 1 Mile and 31 Poles. Never was Rum, that cordial of Life, found more necessary than it was in this Dirty Place. It did not only recruit the People's Spirits, now almost Jaded with Fatigue, but serv'd to correct the Badness of the Water, and at the same time to resist the Malignity of the Air. Whenever the Men wanted to drink, which was very often, they had nothing more to do but to make a Hole, and the Water bubbled up in a Moment. But it was far from being either clear or well tasted, and had besides a Physical Effect, from the Tincture it receiv'd from the Roots of the Shrubbs and Trees that grew in the Neighbourhood. . . .

16. The Line was this day carried one Mile and a half and sixteen Poles. The Soil continued soft and Miry, but fuller of Trees, especially White cedars. Many of these too were thrown down and piled in Heaps, high enough for a good Muscovite Fortification. The worst of it was, the Poor Fellows began now to be troubled with Fluxes, occasioned by bad Water and moist Lodging: but chewing of Rhubarb kept that Malady within Bounds. . . .

17. . . . Since the Surveyors had entered the Dismal, they had laid Eyes on no living Creature: neither Bird nor Beast, Insect nor Reptile came in View. Doubtless, the Eternal Shade that broods

over this mighty Bog, and hinders the sunbeams from blessing the Ground, makes it an uncomfortable Habitation for any thing that has life. Not so much as a Zealand Frog could endure so Aguish a Situation.

It had one Beauty, however, that delighted the Eye, though at the Expense of all the other Senses: the Moisture of the Soil preserves a continual Verdure, and makes every Plant an Evergreen, but at the same time the foul Damps ascend without ceasing, corrupt the Air, and render it unfit for Respiration. Not even a Turkey-Buzzard will venture to fly over it, no more than the Italian Vultures will over the filthy Lake Avernus, or the Birds in the Holy-Land, over the Salt Sea, where Sodom and Gomorrah formerly stood.

The Decline of Verse

The poetry written in America during the late seventeenth and early eighteenth centuries had little to recommend it; the colonial muse, as Moses Coit Tyler later remarked, "sounded no note that was not conventional and imitative." There was no scarcity of poets, but nearly all of them wrote in the manner of Pope, Dryden, Watts, Thomson, Waller, or any other much esteemed Englishman. A popular favorite was Sir Richard Blackmore, court physician to Queen Anne, whose long, mediocre, moralized poems, such as "The Creation, A Philosophical Poem Demonstrating the Existence and Providence of God" (1712), Americans greatly admired—Cotton Mather quoted Blackmore more frequently than he did Milton. The verse they wrote was fluent, graceful, bland, and utterly lacking in vitality; it was written to please, teach, and coincide with prevailing poetic postures. For example, Roger Wolcott of Connecticut, writing in 1725, disposed of the same Calvinist principle of saving grace in two couplets and a routine metaphor that Wigglesworth wrestled with for a full canto:

Vertue still makes the Vertuous to shine,
Like those that liv'd in the first week of time;
Vertue hath force the vile to cleanse again,
So being like clear shining after rain.

Thomas Makin and John Beveridge of Pennsylvania wrote Horatian verse, much of it in Latin; Francis Knapp copied Pope, and so did Benjamin Colman, Mather Byles (who corresponded with Pope personally), John Adams (a Rhode Island minister), John Seccomb, and nearly everyone except Jane Turell, a Boston child-prodigy who composed much-admired hymns at eleven and also imitated Edmund Waller. William Livingston, a young New York lawyer who also wrote Addisonian essays, provided an example of the current style in his *Philosophical Solitude: Or, the Choice of a Rural Life* in 1747. Apparently unaware that he could find plenty of rural life in a half-hour's walk from New York, he spent his poem describing a rather sensuous maiden called "Solitude" who abjured the bustle of cities and closed with a typical apostrophe to rural quiet:

With her I'd spend the pleasurable day,
While fleeting minutes gayly danced away . . . ,
Oft in her panting bosom would I lay,
And in dissolving raptures melt away,
Then lulled by nightingales to balmy rest,
My blooming fair should slumber at my breast.

In the 700 lines of his poem, it is difficult to discover one that exhibits any semblance of originality.

Philadelphia was a nest of minor poets, glib, facile, bright young men—Jacob Taylor, Henry Brooke, Joseph Shippen, Aquila Rose, James Ralph, George Webb—who wrote what Franklin called "knicknackeries." The *Juvenile Poems* of Thomas Godfrey, a Philadelphia youth who died young, appeared in 1765; his verse was undistinguished, but published with it was his blank verse drama "The Prince of Parthia," written in 1759, which was to be called later the first "American" play.

In the South, poets wrote much the same way. There were many of them, for young Southerners were also attracted to fashionable versifying. In South Carolina there were men such as Charles Woodmason, Dr. Thomas Dale, James Kirkpatrick, and

Rowland Rugeley, several of whom published in the London papers and enjoyed minor reputations in England. In Virginia, Henry Potter, John Markland, John Mercer, and Robert Bolling wrote competent verse by contemporary standards; Bolling contributed to the London *Imperial Magazine* as well as to the *Virginia Gazette*. That poetry flourished in Augustan Virginia is attested to by the fact that the *Gazette*'s index for the years 1736–1780 shows two and one-half pages of entries under "Poems."

The best of the Southern poets in the early eighteenth century was Robert Lewis. Educated at Eton and possibly also at Oxford, Lewis came to Maryland in 1725 to teach school. In 1728, he published a translation from the Latin of an English poet's attack on the Welsh that seems to have attracted the attention of the Colony's government. Although Lewis' preface to the poem lamented in conventional fashion the artistic barrenness of the new country, where

Rough woods embrown the Hills and Plains,
Mean are the Buildings, artless are the Swains,

Lewis found sufficient inspiration in the American landscape to write one of the era's most popular poems, "Description of Spring, A Journey from Patapsco to Annapolis, April 4, 1730," which was reprinted at least four times in the London papers with appreciative critical comments. With echoes of Milton's "L'Allegro" and Thomson's "Seasons," the poem has a directness, freshness of observation, and descriptive appeal unusual among the mannered, conventional, nature poems produced at the time. To Lewis belonged the distinction of introducing the Southern mockingbird with grace and taste to American verse:

But what is He, who perch'd above the rest,
Pours out such Musick from his Breast!
His Breast, whose Plumes a cheerful White display.
His quiv'ring Wings are dress'd in sober Grey.
Sure all the Muses, this their Bird inspire!

And he, alone, is equal to the choir
Of warbling songsters who around him play,
While Echo-like, He answers every Lay. . . .
Oh sweet Musician, thou dost far excel
The soothing song of pleasing Philomel!
Sweet is her Song, but in few Notes confin'd;
But thine, thou Mimic of the feath'ry kind,
Runs thro' all Notes!—Thou only know'st them All,
At once the Copy—and th' Original.

His "Food for Criticks," published in the *Maryland Gazette* in
1731, was quite probably the best nature poem written in colonial America. A man who obviously loved to hunt, fish, and
roam the woods, he observed American nature directly and cata-
loged it appreciatively, as demonstrated in his picture of a Maryland river:

Oh happy stream, hadst thou in Grecia flow'd,
The bounteous blessing of some watry god
Thoud'st been, or had some Ovid sung thy rise
Distilled perhaps from slighted virgins eyes.
Well is thy worth in indian story known,
Thy living lymph and fertile borders shown.
Thy shining roach and yellow bristly breme,
Thy pick'rel rav'nous monarch of the stream;
The pearch whose back a ring of colours shows;
The horned pout who courts the slimy ooze;
The eel serpentine, some of dubious race;
The tortoise with his golden spotted case;
Thy hairy muskrat, whose perfume defies
The balmy odors of arabian spice;
Thy various flocks who shores alternate shun,
Drove by the fowler and the fatal gun.

His responsiveness to the strangeness, wonder, and beauty of
American nature, despite his conventionality of context and language, foreshadowed what Philip Freneau and William Cullen

Bryant would do later and little better. Earlier than they, and with as sensitive a vision, Lewis saw the American wilderness as Eden, where one might

Taste nature's bounty and admire her bloom;
In pensive thought revolve long vanish'd toil,
Or in soft song the pleasing hours beguile;
What Eden was, by every prospect told,
Strive to regain the temper of that age of gold;
No artful harms for simple brutes contrive,
But scorn to take a being they cannot give;
To leafy woods resort for health and ease,
Not to disturb their melody and peace.

Although better known than Lewis, William Dawson of Virginia was not half so good a poet. Dawson, professor and later president at William and Mary College, published *Poems on Several Occasions, by A Gentleman of Virginia* in 1736, leaving its authorship in aristocratic anonymity. Having read the Cavalier poets, he imitated Herrick rather than Pope:

Come, my Sylvia, come away;
Youth and Beauty will not stay;
*   Let's enjoy the present now.*
Heark, tempestuous Winter's Roar,
*   How it blusters at the Door,*
Charg'd with Frosts, and Storms, and Snow.

The most interesting poem published during these years was authored by Ebenezer Cooke (or Cook), a shadowy figure in Maryland history but obviously a prickly, independent character. *The Sot-Weed Factor: Or, a Voyage to Maryland. A Satyr . . . in Burlesque Verse* (1708) recounts the adventures of a young man who served as tobacco-factor in Maryland and describes "the laws, government, courts, and constitutions of the country, and also the buildings, feasts, frolics, entertainments, and drunken humours of the inhabitants of that part of America."

Cooke's poem belongs in the strong, satiric tradition of the South, quite different from any that flourished in New England; this tradition drew ultimately from the powerful political and religious arguments of seventeenth-century Maryland and Virginia. *The Sot-Weed Factor's* precursors were the broadside and pamphlet satirists of the early colonial battles among clergy, governors, landowners, and minor aristocracy; its most direct ancestor is George Alsop's *Character of the Province of Maryland* (London, 1666), an attack on British misconceptions of Maryland society. Alsop, who served some time in Maryland as an indentured servant, was a clever man, and his book (as Moses Coit Tyler called it later) was the only product of its time that could compare with Nathaniel Ward's *Simple Cobler* for dash and energy. Dedicated to Lord Calvert, the book aimed

To maintain the truth
'Gainst all the rabble-rout that yelping stand,
To cast aspersions on thy Maryland.

A strong book for strong tastes, Alsop's part-verse, part-prose defense was jocular, often coarse, sometimes close to obscenity. "If I have composed anything," he wrote truculently, "that's wild and confused, it's because I am myself," and he thumbed his nose at those critics who

Arms all akimbo, and with belly strut,
As if they had Parnassus in their gut

stood ready to murder his "poor infant" of a book.

Ebenezer Cooke was a poet in the same tough, powerfully satiric tradition. A mixture of wit, vulgarity, and wild imagination, his poem, though heavily indebted to Samuel Butler's *Hudibras,* rings with a fierce individuality of its own. "Condemn'd by Fate to Wayward Curse, of Friends unkind, and empty purse," the youth is cheated by "a Pious, Conscientious Rogue" of a Quaker, gulled by "an ambidextrous quack" of a lawyer-physician, victimized by the "Punch and Rum Judges" of the

courts, threatened by "a Ravenous Gang" of thieves in Baltimore, solicited by a "blushing chambermaid" in "loose and slut-
tish Dress," and finally ships off angry and penniless to England,
leaving behind a violent curse on the Colony and all its people:

May Cannibals transported o'er the Sea
Prey on the Slaves, as they have done on Me;
May never Merchant's trading Sailes explore
This Cruel, this Inhospitable Shoar;
But left abandon'd by the World to Starve,
May they turn Savage, or as Indians wild,
From Trade, Converse, and Happiness exil'd;
Recreant to Heaven, may they adore the Sun,
And into Pagan superstitions run—
For Vengeance Ripe—
May Wrath Divine then lay those Regions wast,
Where no Man's Faithful, nor a Woman's Chast.

Cooke apparently returned to Maryland, however, publishing
a few poems signed "E. Cook, Laureat," though there is little
evidence that he was either poet laureate of Maryland or that it
had one. He appeared again with a much-softened version called
Sotweed Redivivus (1730), so mild that it is doubtful that he
wrote all of it.

LITERATURE
AND
CULTURE
IN A
REVOLUTIONARY
SOCIETY
1730–1790

 *THREE*

ENLIGHTENMENT AND
REVOLUTION

The American-ness of the American Revolution

The United States, unlike other modern Western nations, began its history without having to overthrow a nobility, a state church, an entrenched master class, or any other aspects of the feudal structure with which Europeans had to contend. It was formed during an extraordinary time of revolution —of a political revolution that destroyed old orders of society and politics; of a scientific revolution that had already changed man's conception of himself and the universe; at the onset of a technological revolution that soon would give man new controls over his environment.

The Revolution that shaped this nation was distinctively American and therefore, is not easily compared to any other. Its aim was not to destroy an established order, but to found a new one without interference from the old. There were no mobs, no *sans culottes,* no Terror. It did not free landless peasants or enslaved workers, nor was it led by a proletariat. Nearly all Americans involved in it, whether Rebel or Tory, shared a common English heritage of Lockean, Whig liberalism; even American radicals, as it turned out, were hardly more than cautious liberals by later European standards. They already had land, property, comparative well-being, and (for the times) relatively large amounts of political liberty and economic democracy—though naturally they felt that they had not nearly enough.

Difference and Destiny

At the close of their revolution, these Americans faced the future with a strong sense of fresh beginnings, of hope and *newness*. With virtually no history of their own, they felt little responsibility to the past; with no record of failure to disillusion them, they were sanguine about the future. They were impatient of traditional, "established" institutions, for they had just disestablished some. As Crèvecoeur summed it up in 1782, "The American is a new man, who acts upon new principles." Thomas Pownall, who served as royal governor of both Massachusetts and South Carolina, recognized this quality when he said that America was founded "totally and entirely on a New System of Things and Men."

Part of the American's emerging sense of self-consciousness was his gradual realization, even before the Revolution, that he and his nation-to-be were different from all the other established nations. The Constitutional Convention marked the final rejection by Americans of Britain and Europe, but the delegates at Philadelphia were very lately ex-British subjects as well as very new American citizens. They knew that the British political tradition had many virtues; the stability, expertise, and economy of the British system presented an alluring model. How new should the new nation be? As the delegates debated their proposed pattern of government, Charles C. Pinckney of South Carolina rose to make a penetrating comment, which went directly to the center of the answer.

Americans, said Pinckney, are neither British, European, Roman, nor Greek. "We have universally considered ourselves as the inhabitants of an old instead of a new country," he continued. "The people of this country are not only very different from the inhabitants of any state we are acquainted with in the modern world, but I assert that their situation is distinct from that of either Greece or Rome, or of any state we are acquainted with among the ancients. . . ." Therefore, he concluded, the Convention must think and plan in terms of "a new country" where "there will be few poor and few dependent," a country where "there is more equality of rank and fortune than in any other country in the world." Few of the men at Philadelphia, and probably not Pinckney himself, fully comprehended the implications of his speech. But gradually they did perceive, as the Convention proceeded, that the United States was *sui generis,* new in the world, something without precedent. This feeling was to become stronger as time passed.

Americans were conscious not only of being new, but of being different. They knew that they were not simply Europe projected on another continent, but a different civilization with a separate future. British and European commentators and travelers never let them forget it; for the most part, they usually treated the new nation with curiosity or contempt, forcing Americans constantly to study, analyze, and explain themselves. As Franklin once remarked bitterly, an American in England "was understood to be a kind of Yahoo," his feelings hardly worth noticing. New Americans, in defending their right to exist, had to answer the question "What is an American?" many times.

None of them would deny that his country was new, or that it was different. The fact that it was new, as James Kirke Paulding explained in *Letters from the South* (1817), merely meant that it would take a little time to grow up, to "progress from infancy to maturity, from maturity to age." At the same time, Americans gradually began to realize that to be different from Britain and Europe was not necessarily wrong or shameful. Indeed, it might be of distinct advantage to the United States, as Jefferson said, to have "the American hemisphere to itself" and to proceed on its way as far from the old nations as possible. It might well be, they concluded, that the United States, because it *was* new and different, was superior to Europe, and that God had willed it so.

Americans believed they saw convincing proof of this in the past, which seemed to reveal a sequence of events pointing to the creation of the United States as a Providentially chosen nation. Dr. Richard Price of London, Franklin's friend, went so far as to suggest that in the "progressive course of human improvement" the American Revolution ranked second only to "the introduction of Christianity among mankind." As the Puritans were convinced that God had ordained a Christian common-wealth in the new hemisphere, so the revolutionaries began to believe that He had also designed a free and secular one.

The fact that the United States was new and providential, of course, was not all that contributed to the American sense of destiny. While most political philosophers agreed that men were much the same everywhere and that a beneficent Deity had be-stowed His blessings on all men, it seemed that Americans pos-sessed advantages not given to others. Evidence seemed to show, a contributor to a Connecticut magazine wrote in 1786, that God had "reserved this country to be the last and greatest theater in the improvement of mankind." For the first time in history, men in America had the chance to put into practice principles of government and society impossible to test else-where. What happened to America, then, was of utmost signifi-cance. If the "bold and sublime" American experiment worked, Thomas Paine said in *The American Crisis,* his generation had it "in our power to make a world happy—to teach mankind the art of being so—to exhibit, on the theater of the universe, a charac-ter hitherto unknown—and to have, as it were, a new creation entrusted to our hands. . . ."

The United States was superior to England and Europe, there-fore, because it was *not* like them; because it had left behind the prejudices, superstitions, and ignorances of the Old World; be-cause it had been chosen to be the precursor of a new kind of New World. Nothing new and good could be built on Europe's "moldering pillars of antiquity," said Noah Webster, and Joel Barlow agreed that the Old World, where for centuries "human reason and the rights of human nature have been the sport of change and the prey of ambition," offered little hope of progress.

The Uses of Patriotism

Americans had long believed that their land was a refuge, as William Penn once expressed it, from "the anxious and troublesome solicitations, hurries, and perplexities of woeful Europe." The success of the Revolution seemed to demonstrate that the United States should continue to serve as a haven for the world's oppressed. Shortly after the war, *The Pennsylvania Gazette* described the new states as a shelter where "the indigent and oppressed, whom the lawless hand of European despotism would crush to earth, can find succour and protection, and join common fellowship. . . ."

Simply to act as a haven, however, was not enough. The United States had a larger mission: to prove the ability of men to govern themselves and to lead other nations of the world toward the same kind of society. America, by the force of its example, Joel Barlow believed, should "excite emulation through the kingdoms of the earth, and meliorate the condition of the human race." The responsibility of America was to exemplify and extend the concepts of liberty, equality, and justice to the world at large—this was "the great design of Providence," James Wilson said at the Constitutional Convention, "in regard to this globe."

In order to accomplish this mission, it was imperative that Americans cultivate their "Americanness" and develop their own life and culture. Nationality must be nurtured, Europe avoided, and patriotism encouraged. "Every engine should be employed to render the people of the country national," wrote Noah Webster, "to call their attachment home to their own country; and to inspire them with the pride of national character."

Europeans often found this American nationalism bumptious and flamboyant (a British traveler in 1810 thought that "the national vanity of the United States surpasses that of any other country, not excepting France"), but it had a serious cultural purpose. If the United States was to succeed as an experiment in self-government, the men who governed themselves must have deep faith in their system; the patriotic impulse was therefore essential to the creation of the national character.

The Arrival of the Enlightenment

The intellectual and cultural structure of ideas within which Americans achieved their independence was provided by two great movements—the Age of Reason and the Age of Romanticism. The United States emerged at a time when the Western world was in transition from Renaissance to Enlightenment. Each of these periods involved quite different views of man, the world, and the Deity beyond them. Voltaire was living when the Continental Congress signed the Declaration of Independence; John Locke wrote a charter for the Carolinas; Rousseau, Franklin, and Montesquieu were friends; Sir Isaac Newton and Cotton Mather were contemporaries.

Puritanism, though a powerful component of earlier American intellectual life, was parochial and confined primarily to New England. The Enlightenment provided the first nationalized ideological pattern for American thought. By the middle of the eighteenth century, Puritanism was waning in importance, while the ideas of the Enlightenment flooded American shores. As the Reverend Charles Backus told his Connecticut congregation in 1788, "The present age is an enlightened one. Theories capable of being corrected and improved by experiment, have been greatly elucidated. Principles venerable for their antiquity have been freely examined, and the absurdities exposed . . ." In this spirit of confidence and optimism, Americans set out to build their society and culture.

The Age of Reason rested upon three major principles: the perfectibility of man; the inevitability of progress; and the efficacy of reason. It emphasized the scientific method over the theological, reason over faith, skepticism over tradition and authoritarianism. The thinkers of the Enlightenment believed that by submitting himself, his society, his past, and the universe to rational analysis, man could discover the laws by which he might someday fully understand all human and natural activity. Having found these principles, men could so direct their energies and construct their institutions that their progress would be swift and sure. This was the era of Voltaire, who brought everything to the bar of reason; of Newton, who drew a new design for the universe; of Locke, who created a new image of man and society.

There was an American Enlightenment, but it was late, eclectic, and singularly American. First, there was a cultural lag in the transmission of patterns in thinking from one side of the Atlantic to the other. Ideas conceived in Europe often had their effect a half-century or more later in America under quite different circumstances and to meet different needs. The Founding Fathers worked with ideas already old by European standards—on another continent, for different purposes, with changed meanings, and mixed with borrowings and adaptations. Goethe, Wordsworth, Coleridge, Schiller, and Kant were writing at nearly the same time that Americans still cited Newton, Grotius, Pufendorf, and Locke.

Second, Americans selected from British and European thought those ideas they needed or those in which they had special interest. They adopted Locke's justification of a century-old English revolution to vindicate their own; they used French "radicalism," aimed at Bourbon kings, to overthrow a tyranny that did not really exist. They ranged through the Enlightenment, blending old ideas with new and using them for their own purposes.

The Enlightenment in England was a relatively conservative compromise of new and old ideas with British conditions. The British produced some authentic rebels—William Godwin, Horne Tooke, Thomas Paine, Joseph Priestley (of whom the last two came to America), and others—but their Enlightenment was better represented by such moderate radicals as Charles James Fox and Edmund Burke. The French *philosophes* carried their rationalism to quite un-British extremes, and therefore Americans found the French version of the Enlightenment much more useful. Edmund Burke, counted a liberal in England, eventually found it necessary to protest both French and American extremism in the name of Enlightenment moderation. Paine answered Burke, while Jefferson and other American intellectuals read the French and British philosophers, praised them, and appropriated from them what they needed.

Romanticism and American Culture

The rise of Romanticism disturbed the orderly patterns of The Age of Reason. Beginning about 1750, European and British philosophers and critics took renewed interest in ideas relatively neglected since the earlier eighteenth century. These were reconsidered, extended, and diffused into a loose system rather unsatisfactorily called "Romantic," which spread through Britain, Europe, and America. Men on both sides of the Atlantic, after examining some of the attitudes of the Enlightenment, altered their conceptions of the world, human nature, and society. Many of these ideas were not new, nor were they ever arranged into a unified system. Nevertheless, the climate of opinion that characterized intellectual activity during the closing decades of the eighteenth century and the opening decades of the nineteenth was consistent enough to call those years the Age of Romanticism.

The Romantic view of society rested on three general concepts. First, was the idea of organism—that things were wholes, or units, with their own internal laws of governance and development. This held true of men and societies, of the individual and the state. Second was the idea of dynamism—of motion and growth. Beliefs and institutions were assumed to be pliable and therefore capable of manipulation and adaptation. The age, as A. O. Lovejoy has remarked, had a "dislike of finality." Third was the idea of diversity—that differences of opinions, cultures, tastes, societies, and characters have value, as opposed to the norms of uniformity established by the Enlightenment. To the Age of Reason, rationalism meant conformity; diversity meant irrationality and therefore error. To the Romantic, consensus seemed much less important than individual judgment, and diversity seemed "natural" and "right."

The Enlightenment viewed man as a mixture of passion and reason. Its philosophers were convinced that unless mind controlled heart, neither men nor societies could move together in harmony. They placed importance on the emotional aspects of man's nature, stressing the validity of the emotions and intuitions. Eventually they concluded that these inward elements blended into a quality of mind higher than the reason—the Fancy, or the Imagination, they sometimes called it, "reason in its higher form." In this vein Wordsworth defined the Romantic Imagination as "absolute power . . . clearest insight, amplitude of mind, and Reason in its most exalted mood." Because each individual possessed this power, Romanticism placed great value on personal, private judgment, as opposed to authority, tradition, and privilege.

Some aspects of Romanticism fitted the facts and necessities of American life; some did not. Romanticism in America (reinforced by the frontier tradition) developed as a more constructive and individualistic movement than in Britain or Europe, where it frequently took the form of attacks on established institutions, standards, and morals. Individualism produced rebels (which Americans could understand), but the American Romantic rebel had much less than his British and European counterpart to rebel against and a more open society in which to function. There was no need for him to attack entrenched injustices, old inhibitions, or ancient social stratifications, for they did not exist in the same manner as they did abroad. Americans could never accept what they considered Byron's irresponsibility, Goethe's personal amorality, or the moody sentimentalism of the young Frenchmen and Germans.

The Era of Confidence

At the close of the eighteenth century, Americans regarded their brief past with satisfaction and looked to the future with self-assurance. Crusty John Adams, who did not always agree with the easy optimism of the times, looked back in old age at what his generation had done and found it good. "Nevertheless," he wrote Jefferson, "according to the lights that remain to us, we may say that the eighteenth century, notwithstanding all its errors and vices, has been, of all that are past, the most honorable to human nature."

The beginnings of American culture came in a time of confidence. Americans had committed themselves to an experiment in government based on familiar Enlightenment principles— progress, natural rights, the dignity and rationality of man, the benevolence of God—and they believed that they could make this experiment work. They considered that they owed very little to custom, precedent, tradition, or authority. They believed they were special and different, a *new* people possessed, as David Humphreys of Connecticut said, of "superior advantages for happiness over the rest of mankind."

Their task, as they conceived it, was to found an *American* civilization whose goal, Jefferson said, was nothing less than "the happiness of associated man." Nathaniel Ames expressed the essence of this spirit when he wrote in his journal on December 31, 1800: "Here ends the eighteenth century. The nineteenth begins with a fine clear morning wind at S.W.; and the political horizon affords as fine a prospect with the irresistible propagation of the Rights of Man, the eradication of hierarchy, oppression, superstition, and tyranny over the world. . . ."

Society at Mid-Century

To the European traveler, American colonial society at mid-century seemed not unlike England's. American cities resembled English provincial towns, colonial upper classes imitated the gentry, colonial leadership looked to the home country for guidance. The colonist depended on the British army for protection, on British subsidies for his economy, on British manufacturing for the apparatus of living, and on British laws for his governance. William Eddis, writing as late as 1774, observed "little difference . . . in the manners of the wealthy colonist and the wealthy Briton."

Eddis' comment was both true and misleading. The average man did not send his sons to England for an education, bought his furniture from a local artisan, built his own house, and followed neither London's fashions nor its morals. He considered himself English, yet with a difference; in the back of his mind he was somehow separate. Memories of England, brought by the

seventeenth-century colonists, had long since faded. Class structure was more flexible than England's, distinctions blurred, opportunities for leadership open to more people. The frontier, the
Awakening, migration, time, and distance had done their work.

By mid-century there was also an American "backcountry"—a
distinctively native region unlike anything England or Europe
had ever known—which developed for a hundred years beyond
the line where settlement stopped and wilderness began. During
the eighteenth century, this empty country filled in. Waves of
migration moved into western Pennsylvania, upper New York
State, the Shenandoah Valley, the pine lands of Carolina, even
into Georgia and Kentucky. Trails penetrated the forests, and
hamlets cropped up, but the land remained a country of small
farms freshly wrested from the woods and linked rather tenu-
ously with the coast and the cities.

There were foreigners here, people with accents—Scots, Germans, Welsh—tough, hard-working emigrants from England
and Europe who moved in with and beyond Byrd's "lubbers."
Since institutions like courts, schools, and churches did not catch
up to the backcountry quickly, lawsuits, marriages, baptisms,
theology, booklearning, and such things tended to be self-made
and informal. The society that grew up in the backcountry was
individualistic, aggressive, equalitarian, violent—certainly new,
and most certainly American.

Mid-century society exhibited a number of visible differences
between city and country, upper and lower social classes, wealthy
and poor, and illustrated cleavages of interest and character
among the several Colonies. Andrew Burnaby, who traveled
through America from 1759 to 1760, thought that "fire and
water are not more heterogenous" than North and South, but
Burnaby could not see, of course, the unifying forces at work
beneath the surface of American life. The colonists were mostly
native-born, no longer English in origin, and possessed of a common pride in their accomplishment at conquering the wilderness, the French, and the Indians to create what was obviously a
successful society. They had, as well, common cause in their dis-
satisfaction with England. At the Stamp Act Congress of 1765,

the first explicit signal of opposition to the mother country, Christopher Gadsden of South Carolina expressed the American feeling quite succinctly: "There ought to be no New England man, no New Yorker, etc., known on the Continent, but all of us Americans."

Publishing and Journalism

By mid-century, improvements in colonial communications had increased so swiftly that the American writer had access to a much broader public than before. Facilities for printing and publishing spread through the Colonies. Roads and mails improved magazines, newspapers circulated more freely, people had more to read and read more. Boston and Charleston were linked by road in 1732, the year intercolonial mail service began, to be greatly improved by Franklin when he became deputy-postmaster for the Colonies in 1753. Packtrains made regular trips to the backcountry in the 1720s, while the "Great Wagon Road" from Philadelphia to Boone's Gap opened a new route to the West and South. Both stagecoach and packetboat lines were in operation by the 1750s, allowing traveling booksellers to wander far beyond the range of city bookstores.

The demands of the reading public for books, which were too expensive for the average citizen to own, brought libraries. The Anglican Society for Propagating the Gospel began to establish its own church libraries in 1701 (twenty-nine in Maryland alone), and other church groups followed. Franklin's Library Company of Philadelphia, organized in 1731, had many imitators (seventeen before 1763), and so did others such as Newport's Redwood Library (1747), Charleston's Library Society (1745), and New York's Society Library (1754). There were few well-known authors whose works were not available in any of the Colonies by the beginnings of the war.

Until the early eighteenth century, sizeable publishing jobs were handled in England, since the colonial printer's work usually consisted of legal papers, pamphlets, sermons, notices, broadsides, and especially almanacs. There were seventy almanac series running by 1750, as almanacs commanded the largest audience of any kind of publication until the rise of the newspaper and periodical later in the century. However, as population grew, so did printing; Boston was a major publishing center by 1720, Philadelphia equaled and surpassed it by mid-century, and New York was not far behind.

Printing came late to the Southern Colonies, where craftsmen appeared and disappeared until William Parks came to Annapolis from England in 1726. Parks published the work of poets Richard Lewis and Ebenezer Cook and in the early 1730s moved his press to Williamsburg, where he printed William Dawson's poetry and Stith's *History of Virginia*. Until his death in 1750, he remained the most important colonial printer south of Philadelphia, and his importance to literary-minded Southerners was recognized by them. One grateful poet named Dumbleton celebrated Parks' establishment of a paper mill by writing:

The sage Philosophers have said,
Of nothing, can be nothing made;
Yet such thy will, O Parks, brings forth
From what we reckon nothing worth. . . .
The Bards, be sure, their Aids will lend;
The Printer is the Poet's Friend;
Both cram the News, and stuff the Mills,
For Bards have rags, and little else.

Newspapers eventually became the most numerous publications, and every printer hoped to found a successful one. The Boston *Publick Occurrences*, started in 1690, lasted only four days, but the Boston *News-Letter*, begun in 1704, became the first newspaper deserving of the name. The Boston *Gazette* and the Philadelphia *American Weekly Mercury* followed in 1719, James Franklin's *New England Courant* in 1721, Benjamin Franklin's *Pennsylvania Gazette* in 1731. New York had its first paper in 1725; Parks' *Maryland Gazette* was the first in the South; the *South Carolina Gazette* was second in 1732, and Parks' *Virginia Gazette* followed in 1736. After 1730, newspapers appeared in all the Colonies; these were usually one-sheet weeklies later expanded in size and occasionally published twice or more a week.

Newspapers carried news, of course, but they were also important means for the transmission of ideas and culture, since they printed verse, history, essays, and information culled from publications all over Europe. They were expected to provide a wide range of instruction and entertainment, fulfilling the function later assigned to magazines. Colonial laws governing what might be printed varied widely, but in general editors had considerable freedom if they avoided the hotter political issues. By 1765, the year of the Stamp Act, there were forty-three newspapers in the Colonies—twenty in New England, thirteen in the Middle Colonies, and ten in the South.

The influence of newspapers on colonial American writing was incalculable. Their existence supplied authors with market and audience, while the appearance after mid-century of periodical magazines encouraged writing even more. Eighteenth-century magazines were a sort of *omnium gatherum* of essays, poetry, digests of news, reports, and whatever else the editor found interesting. William Smith's *American Magazine, or Monthly Chronicle for the Colonies,* founded in 1757, for example, in one issue included Smith's own essay series, Thomas Godfrey's poems, essays on music, Parliamentary news, and songs by Francis Hopkinson. Between 1741 and 1789 thirty-seven magazines appeared, many lasting a year or less, but before the turn of the century such expert editors as Matthew Carey, Josiah Meigs, Isaiah Thomas, and Noah Webster made magazine publishing pay.

The Poetry of Imitation

Formal literary writing in the Colonies over the latter half of the eighteenth century was still dominated by English literary tradition and English literary masters. The forms, aims, and standards of American writing, both before and after independence, reflected rather accurately (with a lag of a decade or so) what Englishmen read and wrote. Colonial writers reflected in their work what Quarles, Cowley, Herbert, and Vaughan wrote in the early seventeenth century, and Dryden and Samuel Butler wrote later. When Addison, Steele, and Swift appeared, Americans wrote like them too. Alexander Pope ruled American poetry absolutely, for he represented all the qualities —wit, grace, rationality, decorum—that the eighteenth-century colonist deemed desirable. His *Essay on Man* went through 105 American editions before 1840, while the Reverend John Adams paid him the ultimate New England compliment by putting the Psalms into Popean couplets. There were faint stirrings of originality here and there, but eighteenth-century colonial writing was hardly American in any real sense.

The poet of the period who showed most promise, Francis Hopkinson (that "curious, ingenious man," John Adams called him), did not take his craft seriously. Born in Philadelphia in 1738, educated in law and science, Hopkinson became a successful lawyer, judge, and political figure. He served in the Continental Congress and was one of the signers of the Declaration of Independence. A charming and complex man of diverse and undeniable talents, a lover of social graces and the refinements of good living, Hopkinson never brought his obviously great poetic gifts into focus. He wrote excellent satires and light verse; amused himself with painting, sculpture, architecture, and science; composed songs and played several instruments very well; and produced three volumes of collected works that ranged lightly and perceptively over the culture of his times as few others did. Yet he left little of permanence, and his talent remained unrealized.

All American poets were busy imitating somebody. Besides Pope, they copied Thomson's *Seasons* (Thomson's poetry had ten American editions between 1790 and 1820), Gray's graveyard elegies, Pomfret's *Choice,* the primitivism of MacPherson's *Ossian,* and English topographical poetry such as Pope's *Windsor Forest* or Dyer's *Grongar Hill.* Collections such as Elihu

Hubbard Smith's *American Poems* (1793) and *The Columbian Muse* (1794) reverberated with echoes of fashions in English verse.

There was no lack of American poets, but it was difficult to find any who did not sound like someone else. Ann Bleecker, a New York lady whose daughter published her verse in 1793, wrote "graveyard" poems with some skill. James M'Clurg, a Virginia physician, wrote stylish *vers de societé*, after the manner of Cowley. His most famous poem was *The Belles of Williamsburg* —a light, pleasant apostrophe to his Virginia friends:

Wilt thou, advent'rous pen, describe
The gay, delightful, silken tribe,
　That maddens all our city?
Nor dread, lest while you foolish claim,
A near approach to beauty's flame,
　Icarus' fate may hit ye. . . .

Describing some of Williamsburg's prettiest, he invokes the muse in praise of Myrtilla, Laura, Cordelia, and others until, "fatigued by beauty's blaze," he promises to love them all. M'Clurg's poem received wide circulation later when John Esten Cooke included parts of it in his book *The Virginia Comedians* (1854), but it stood as a bright spot in the midst of the deadly serious musings of most of his contemporaries. Elijah Fitch, a Massachusetts clergyman, attempetd a long instructional religious epic (echoing Milton and Pope) called *The Beauties of Religion* (1789) and designed "to paint religion in her native beauties . . . to give just views on religion, and to persuade love and practise to it." The first three books identified the various desires of the human soul for religion and explained the sufficiency of the Gospel in supplying them. The fourth book contained the story of an infidel who "after a debauch, awakes with a resolution to pursue nothing but the pleasures of the world" and in so doing eventually "expires in misery." The final book contains the story of a True Christian whose faith, by contrast, brings him "the joyful truths sent down from Heav'n" with "joy that doth his heart dilate."

Nathaniel Evans, a young Philadelphian who died at thirty, wrote a number of conventional love poems to a lady who married another man, odes, elegies, and pastorals in the style of Blair, Cowley, and Gray, and a long poem on peace. Few of his poems, which were collected after his death by friends, displayed much originality of thought, although Evans had a certain skill at versification. His stanzas on mutability, a favorite poetic topic of the period, addressed to his friend Will, showed that he could handle overused materials with taste and sensitivity:

Pears, apples, cheese, dear Will, and wine,
If thou wilt grace my house, are thine
(For these are in my pow'r).
When the last ray of yon bright sun
Shall round its whirling axle run
And hasten the sixth hour. . . .
Live! Live, my Will, for now's the day;
Time, like a current, glides away,
On the evanescent wind;
Unstaid by stout Herculean force,
Nought can protract its rapid course,
And fleeting moments bind.
Shadows we are, or empty dust,
And vapor-like dissolve we must,
Nor are we more secure;
Nought can escape the dreary pit
But virtue and immortal wit,
Which endless shall endure.

Thomas Godfrey, who had more talent than most, spent it on pastorals and elegies written in the style of Gray, Collins, and Milton's *Il Penseroso*. Phyllis Wheatley, Negro servant girl to wealthy John Wheatley of Boston, was taught by the family to read and write after her purchase at a slave auction in 1761. She proved extraordinarily quick at learning and attracted the attention of a number of gentlemen at Harvard. Her *Poems on Various Subjects* (1773, 1779), mostly Popean imitations, made her a nine days' wonder; some doubted her authorship, but John Hancock, Mather Byles, and Samuel Mather all attested to her authenticity. Her poems ranged from translations of Ovid and serious religious poetry (she joined the congregation of Boston's Old South Church) to her most famous single poem, her widely quoted ode to Washington, which she sent to him in 1775 as he assumed command of the Continental Armies; it closed with the lines:

Proceed, great chief, with virtue on thy side,
Thy ev'ry action let the goddess guide;
A crown, a mansion, and a throne that shine,
With gold unfading, Washington! be thine.

Ballads and Broadsides

The most vigorous American verse was written by the ballad and broadside makers, hawked in the streets, or sung in taverns. Songs and ballads appeared by the ream throughout the eighteenth century, continuing the long English ballad tradition that dealt with catastrophes, massacres, battles, crimes, and other events of popular interest. (Young Franklin, for example, dashed off "The Lighthouse Tragedy" and "Teach the Pirate" to capitalize on current events.) Collections such as Tilden's *Miscellaneous Poems* (1716) or Benjamin Church's *Patriot Muse* (1764) reprinted the better examples of such popular verse, many of them, of course, dealing with the wars against the French and Indians.

There were also many ballads on Braddock and Wolfe; John Maylem and George Cockings, among others, wrote ballads about Louisburg; there were dozens on the Battle of Quebec. They ranged in sophistication from Nathaniel Niles' "The American Hero," done in difficult Sapphic meter, to the rustic doggerel of Peter St. John's "American Taxation":

While I relate my story,
  Americans give ear;
Of Britain's fading glory
  You presently shall hear;
I'll give a true relation,
  Attend to what I say,
Concerning the taxation
  Of North America.

As temperatures rose in the conflict with Britain, every Parliamentary act, Crown order, or Board of Trade directive generated retaliatory ballads. The Tea Act, for example, elicited "The Blasted Herb," "The Fated Plant," "A Lady's Adieu to Her Tea-Table," "A New Song to an Old Tune," and "Virginia Banishing Tea, By a Lady," which began:

Begone, pernicious baleful Tea,
With all Pandora's ills possessed,
Hyson, no more beguiled by thee,
My noble sons shall be oppressed.
To Britain fly, where gold enslaves
And venal men their birthright sell;
Tell North and his brib'd clan of knaves,
Their bloody acts were made in hell!

After Lexington and Concord, "The King's Own Rangers," "A New Story for the Grenadiers," "The Enemy's First Coming to Boston," "A Song for the Redcoats," "The Patriot's Prayer," and hundreds of other songs followed the progress of American arms. "The Present War" was typical:

Britons grown big with pride
  And wanton ease,
And tyranny beside
  They sought to please
Their craving appetite;
They strove with all their might,

They vow'd to make us fight,
  To make us bow.
The plan they laid was deep,
  Even like hell;
With sympathy I weep
  While here I tell
Of that base murderous brood,
Void of the fear of God,
Who came to spill our blood
  In our own land.

Particular battles and heroes brought others—Joseph Warren's death, André's capture, Arnold's treason, Burgoyne's defeat, Howe's retreat, victories at Trenton or King's Mountain:

T'was on a pleasant mountain
  The Tory heathens lay;
With a doughty major at their head,
  One Ferguson they say.
Cornwallis had detached him,
  A thieving for to go,
And catch the Carolina men
  Or bring the rebels low. . . .

or the haunting "Hale in the Bush," which appeared after Nathan Hale's execution:

The breezes went steadily through the tall pines,
  A saying oh, hush! a saying oh hush!
As stilly stole by a bold legion of horse,
  For Hale in the bush, for Hale in the bush.
"Keep still" said the thrush as she nestled her young,
  In a nest by the road, in a nest by the road,
"For the tyrants are near and with them appear,
  What bodes us no good, what bodes us no good."

The Loyalists naturally had ballad-makers too. Jonathan Odell, a defiant Anglican minister, and Joseph Stansbury, a witty Philadelphia businessman, though in a hopeless minority, kept up a poetic fusillade equal to the best the patriots produced. Odell's charge to Washington in 1780 was as angry as anything the rebels wrote:

Was it ambition, vanity, or spite,
That prompted thee with Congress to unite?
Go, wretched author of thy country's grief,
Patron of villainy, of villains chief;
Seek with thy cursed crew th' eternal gloom,
Ere Truth's avenging sword begin thy doom.

Stansbury, appealing to the proud British naval tradition, exhorted England's sailors to put down treason with firmness and valor:

Then, Britons, strike home—make sure of your blow:
    The chase is in view; never mind a lee-shore.
With vengeance o'ertake the confederate foe:
    'Tis now we may rival our heroes of yore!
        Brave Anson and Drake,
        Hawke, Russell, and Blake,
With ardor like yours we defy France and Spain!
        Combining with treason,
        They're deaf to all reason:
Once more let them feel we are Lords of the Main.
        Lords of the Main—aye, Lords of the Main—
The first-born of Neptune are Lords of the Main!

Satire: The Cutting Edge

Poetry written during the latter portion of the eighteenth century was most likely to be satiric. Newspapers furnished a convenient medium for satiric comment on current issues and personalities, and satire also furnished a useful outlet for the passions brought to the surface of public life by argument and war. The British satiric tradition, firmly established by such masters of the form as Dryden, Butler, and Pope, gave the Americans excellent models; nor were English and Loyalists their only targets. New lines of cleavage in colonial life and the emergence of differences of class, manners, fashions, and tastes supplied materials for social satire, while the growth of cities provided the urbane, worldly audience satirists needed. A sophisticated literary form, verse satire required equally sophisticated writers and readers, both of whom were beginning to appear in American society.

Satiric verse, therefore, tended to attract the most vigorous and skillful writers. Robert Spiller estimates that there still exist about 300 satires from the latter decades of the eighteenth century—probably not more than a fraction of those actually written. Some showed more talent than others. Francis Hopkinson, who wrote Addisonian essays and designed the American flag, lent his considerable talents to the Revolutionary cause in *A Pretty Story* (1774), a prose satire after Swift, and *The Battle of the Kegs* (1778), a mock epic based on an attempt to blow up some British ships by floating powder kegs down the river, thus leading the British to fire in panic at everything they saw. A good-natured, swinging ballad meant to be sung, it was Hopkinson at his wittiest:

'Twas early day, as poets say,
    Just when the sun was rising,
A soldier stood on a log of wood,
    And saw a thing surprising.

As in amaze he stood to gaze,
    The truth can't be denied, sir,
He spied a score of kegs or more
    Come floating down the tide, sir.

A sailor too in jerkin blue,
    This strange appearance viewing,
First damn'd his eyes, in great surprise,
    Then said, "Some mischief's brewing."

The cannons roar from shore to shore,
  The small arms make a rattle;
Since wars began I'm sure no man
  E'er saw so strange a battle.

Such feats did they perform that day
  Against these wicked kegs, sir,
That years to come, if they get home,
  They'll make their boasts and brags, sir.

Later, in 1787, he published *The New Roof,* a rather pretentious allegory comparing the Philadelphia convention to a band of carpenters and mechanics building a new house:

Come muster, my lads, your mechanical tools,
Your saws and your axes, your hammers and rules;
Bring your mallets and planes, your level and line,
And plenty of pins of American pine:
For our roof we will raise, and our song still shall be,
Our government firm, and our citizens free.

Come, up with the plates, lay them firm on the wall,
Like the people at large, they're the groundwork of all;
Examine them well, and see that they're sound,
Let no rotten part in our building be found:
For our roof we will raise, and our song still shall be
A government firm, and our citizens free.

Philip Freneau, a Jersey sea captain and a classmate of Madison's at the College of New Jersey, threw himself into the Revolutionary argument, served a sentence on a British prison ship, enlisted in the Continental Army, sailed in the coastal trade, and in his later years served in political journalism on Jefferson's side. Freneau wrote against the British army, its generals, George III, Parliament, rival poets, and political opponents with a brilliance and savagery unmatched during the era. He could skewer a man with a phrase—as he did Lord Montague ("A

little fat man, with pretty white hair") or George III ("A royal
King Log, with a toothful of brains")—and his stanzas on Corn-
wallis drip with contempt and anger:

Foe to the human race, Cornwallis yields!—
None e'er before essay'd such desperate crimes,
Alone he stood, arch-butcher of the times,
Rov'd uncontroul'd this wasted country o'er,
Strew'd plains with dead, and bath'd his jaws with gore?
　　'TWAS thus the wolf, who sought by night his prey,
And plunder'd all he met with on his way,
Stole what he could, and murder'd as he pass'd,
Chanc'd on a trap, and lost his head at last.
　　WHAT pen can write, what human tongue can tell
The endless murders of this man of hell!
Nature in him disgrac'd the form divine;
Nature mistook, she meant him for a—swine . . .
　　CONVINC'D we are, no foreign spot of earth
But Britain only, gave this reptile birth.
That white-cliff'd isle, the vengeful dragon's den,
Has sent us monsters where we look'd for men.
When memory paints their horrid deeds anew,
And brings these murdering miscreants to your view,
Then ask the leaders of these bloody bands,
Can they expect compassion at our hands?—

The flood of satiric poetry during and after the Revolution
virtually inundated everything else in literature. Satire not only
lent itself admirably to wartime uses but also to the political
struggles that began within the country from almost the time of
Yorktown. Lampoons, mock-heroics, Hudibrastics, burlesques,
tirades, "Rolliads" and "Anarchiads" (modeled on contemporary
British political satire) crowded the newspapers and magazines
for the next twenty years. For example, *The Echo,* a journal that
ran for fourteen years, published little else. Brockholst Livingston's anti-Jefferson *Democracy* (1790) was followed by Lemuel
Hopkins' *Democratiad* (1795); Alsop, Dwight, and Hopkins

collaborated on *The Political Greenhouse* (1799); Thomas Green Fessenden's *Jeffersoniad; or Democracy Unveil'd* (1805), was a vicious attack on Jefferson. (Young William Cullen Bryant's *Embargo,* written in 1809, was a childish imitation of these.) The anti-Federalists replied with St. George Tucker's *Probationary Odes* (1796), which lampooned Hamilton and Adams, and John Williams' *Hamiltoniad* (1804). Pope, Churchill, and Butler gave the Americans models to copy; the combative atmosphere of the times furnished the impetus; and political life provided plenty of materials.

The "Connecticut Wits": Trumbull, Dwight, Barlow

The group called the "Connecticut Wits" produced a loosely knit body of satire over a twenty-year span that maintained a respectably high level of achievement. Yale graduates, most of them professional or businessmen to whom poetry was a polite avocation, they were all conservative in politics, theology, and literary tastes (except Joel Barlow, who changed his views and affiliations) and wrote poetry heavily indebted to Pope, Butler, and Churchill.

The chief "Wits" were David Humphreys, Dr. Lemuel Hopkins, Richard Alsop, Theodore Dwight, his cousin Timothy Dwight, Joel Barlow, and John Trumbull. Barlow, Hopkins, Humphreys, and Trumbull collaborated on *The Anarchiad* (1786–1787), a long poem on contemporary politics; Theodore Dwight and Alsop, with others' help, wrote much of *The Echo* (1791–1805) and probably most of *The Political Greenhouse* (1799). Humphreys wrote against dull-witted critics and political radicals, while Hopkins, a physician, attacked medical quacks. Whatever real poetic talents they possessed (Trumbull and Barlow perhaps had the most), none of them produced more than a few lines of memorable verse or broke away for a moment from the boundaries of British convention.

John Trumbull entered Yale at thirteen as a precocious lad with a sharp wit and a sense of humor. After graduation he stayed at Yale as a tutor, wrote essays under the name of "The Correspondent," and published an impish, clever satire, *The Progress of Dulness* (1771–1773). Through his three major characters—Dick Hairbrain, a foppish coxcomb; Harriet Simper, a silly coquette; and Tom Brainless, a rustic dullard—he disposed of fashionable society, the Church, and his alma mater by having Brainless take his degree at Yale in divinity, marry Harriet after Hairbrain had discarded her, and accept a country pulpit where he did neither good nor harm to anybody. Though the form of his satire was common and its subject matter had been familiar to English verse for at least forty years, Trumbull pumped a good deal of zest and vitality into it. His description of the lazy, worthless college boy of the seventies rang true for generations of them to come:

> So said, so done, at college now
> He enters—well, no matter how;
> New scenes awhile his fancy please,
> But all must yield to love of ease.
> In the same round condemn'd each day,
> To study, read, recite and pray;
> To make his hours of business double—
> He can't endure th' increasing trouble;
> And finds at length, as times grow pressing,
> All plagues are easier than his lesson.
> With sleepy eyes and count'nance heavy,
> With much excuse of non paravi
> Much absence, tardes and egresses,
> The college-evil on him seizes.
> Then ev'ry book, which ought to please,
> Stirs up the seeds of dire disease;
> Greek spoils his eyes, the print's so fine,
> Grown dim with study, or with wine;
> Of Tully's Latin much afraid,
> Each page, he calls the doctor's aid;
> While geometry, with lines so crooked,
> Sprains all his wits to overlook it.

His sickness puts on every name,
Its cause and uses still the same;
'Tis tooth-ache, cholic, gout or stone,
With phases various as the moon;
But though through all the body spread,
Still makes its cap'tal seat, the head.
In all diseases, 'tis expected,
The weakest parts be most infected.

Trumbull then joined John Adams' law office to study law and entered into the revolutionary controversy in 1775 with a poem against the British blockade. He then began a mock-epic burlesque of loyalists and mob-minded patriots, *M'Fingal,* publishing the first part in 1776 and completing it in 1782. He wrote the poem, he said, to give "in a poetical manner, a general account of the American contest . . . which no history could probably record, and with as much impartiality as possible, satirize the follies and extravagances of my countrymen as well as of their enemies."

M'Fingal went through thirty pirated editions and was circulated widely, Trumbull's biographer wrote, by "the newsmongers, hawkers, pedlars, and petty chapmen of the day." He imitated Swift and Butler but added to them a rough humor that was quite American. A good craftsman, Trumbull used his favorite measure, octosyllabic couplet, with great skill, as is illustrated in his account of the great mock-epic encounter between Squire M'Fingal's Tories and the Sons of Liberty:

This said, our 'Squire, yet undismay'd,
Call'd forth the Constable to aid,
And bade him read, in nearer station,
The Riot-act and Proclamation.
He swift, advancing to the ring,
Began, "Our Sovereign Lord, the King"—
When thousand clam'rous tongues he hears,
And clubs and stones assail his ears.
To fly was vain; to fight was idle;

By foes encompass'd in the middle,
His hope in stratagems he found,
And fell right craftily to ground;
Then crept to seek an hiding place,
'Twas all he could, beneath a brace;
Where soon the conq'ring crew espied him,
And where he lurk'd, they caught and tied him.
   At once with resolution fatal,
Both Whigs and Tories rush'd to battle.
Instead of weapons, either band
Seized on such arms as came to hand.
And as famed Ovid paints th' adventures
Of wrangling Lapithae and Centaurs,
Who at their feast, by Bacchus led,
Threw bottles at each other's head;
And these arms failing in their scuffles,
Attack'd with andirons, tongs and shovels;
So clubs and billets, staves and stones
Met fierce, encountering every sconce,
And cover'd o'er with knobs and pains
Each void receptacle for brains;
Their clamors rend the skies around,
The hills rebellow to the sound;
And many a groan increas'd the din
From batter'd nose and broken shin.
M'Fingal, rising at the word,
Drew forth his own militia-sword;
Thrice cried "King George," as erst in distress,
Knights of romance invoked a mistress;
And brandishing the blade in air,
Struck terror through th' opposing war.

Trumbull believed that his future lay in law, however, and not in
poetry. He opened his own firm in New Haven, served as Judge
of the Supreme Court of Errors, and wrote no more poems.

   Timothy Dwight, Jonathan Edwards' grandson, who was best
known as president of Yale (1795–1817), did not have Trum-

bull's talent, but he had greater tenacity and purpose. Dwight served as an army chaplain in the Revolution and, like Trumbull, taught at Yale as a tutor. His Biblical allegory, *The Conquest of Canaan* (1785), consisted of eleven books of heroic couplet (one of the longest poems in American history) dealing with Joshua's Canaanite wars. Heavily indebted to Milton and to Pope's translation of Homer, and with overtones of Goldsmith, the poem is also a somewhat vague double allegory referring to the Puritans' conquest of New England and Washington's defeat of the British army. The English poet William Cowper liked it and wrote an admiring review for the London journals.

The Triumph of Infidelity (1788), another long production of Dwight's, defended Calvinism against infidelity, deism, Catholicism, rationalism, Hume, Voltaire, and various liberal American divines. An amateurish and heavily derivative poem, it is less notable for its art than for the zeal of its indignation. His indictment of the "smooth divine" who was more concerned with good living and the approval of his congregation than with their salvation had the sting of good satire:

Each week he paid his visitation dues;
Coaxed, jested, laughed; rehearsed the private news;
Smoked with each goody, thought her cheese excelled;
Her pipe he lighted, and her baby held.
Or placed in some great town, with lacquered shoes,
Trim wig, and trimmer gown, and glistening hose,
He bowed, talked politics, learned manners mild,
Most meekly questioned, and most smoothly smiled;
At rich men's jests laughed loud, their stories praised;
Their wives' new patterns gazed, and gazed, and gazed. . . .

Dwight's most pleasant poem was not satire at all; *Greenfield Hill* (1794), a pastoral in the English tradition of topographical poetry, grew out of his love for his own New England home at Greenfield, Connecticut. Dwight originally planned to write each of its seven parts in the manner of a prominent English poet; he found this too difficult, though the reader could easily recognize traces of Pope, Dyer, Thomson, Milton, Pomfret, and a half-dozen others. Its purpose was to survey life in New England, count its blessings, and admire its scenery. A relaxed and personalized poem with quite readable descriptive portions, it also had long passages of almost impervious dullness. But when Dwight became emotionally involved with his subject, as in his stanzas contrasting a New England village with one of Old England, he wrote effectively:

> *Sweet-smiling village! loveliest of the hills!*
> *How green thy groves! How pure thy glassy rills!*
> *With what new joy, I walk thy verdant streets!*
> *How often pause, to breathe thy gale of sweets;*
> *To mark thy well-built walls! thy budding fields!*
> *And every charm, that rural nature yields;*
> *And every joy, to Competence allied,*
> *And every good, that Virtue gains from Pride!*
>
> *No griping landlord here alarms the door,*
> *To halve, for rent, the poor man's little store.*
> *No haughty owner drives the humble swain*
> *To some far refuge from his dread domain;*
> *Nor in one manor drowns a thousand lots;*
> *The wealth, which shivering thousands want beside;*
> *Nor in one palace sinks a hundred cots;*
> *Nor in one manor drowns a thousand lots;*
> *Nor, on one table, spread for death and pain,*
> *Devours what would a village well sustain.*

A third member of the "Wits," Joel Barlow, diverted much of his unsteady talent into politics, editing, pamphleteering, and diplomacy. He too graduated from Yale, served as a tutor there, and later served as an army chaplain. After the war, he settled in Hartford as a lawyer to combine with several of the other Wits on some political satires. By 1783 he had completed an American epic, *The Vision of Columbus* (published in 1787), which he intended "to inculcate the love of rational liberty . . . and show that on the basis of the republican principle all good morals, as well as good government and hopes of permanent peace, must be founded." A highly inflated poem of almost 5,000 lines, patterned closely on *Paradise Lost,* it was spectacularly unsuccessful, however sincere his effort.

Barlow's interests soon diverged from those of his fellows; he went to France in 1788 as a land agent and remained in Europe for eighteen years. Here the Connecticut Yankee turned cosmopolitan, his New England Calvinism became deism, his political conservatism changed into French radicalism. When the French Revolution erupted, he took up its cause against Burke and its British critics in a long poem, *The Conspiracy of Kings* (1792), modeled on Juvenal and Pope, and in a number of prose pamphlets, the most effective being his answer to Burke, *Advice to the Privileged Orders* (1792).

After his return to the United States, Barlow took up residence in Washington. Still determined to provide the United States with its own great epic, he reworked *The Vision of Columbus* as *The Columbiad* (1807), making it half again as long and no better than before. He did make it the most expensive book yet published in America, with eleven engravings done by the best contemporary artists chosen and supervised by Barlow's friend Robert Fulton, who contributed one of his own. Madison sent him to France as American ambassador, and he died in 1811 while trying to reach Napoleon on his retreat from Moscow.

Barlow's *Hasty Pudding* (1793), a mock epic written to his favorite New England dish during a siege of homesickness in France, was an agreeably homespun poem that still appears in anthologies. His praise of the thoroughly American corn-meal concoction beloved by New Englanders was attractive and effective indigenous verse:

Delicious grain, whatever form it take,
To roast or boil, to smother or to bake,
In every dish 'tis welcome still to me,
But most, my Hasty Pudding, most in thee.
Let the green succotash with thee contend;

Let beans and corn their sweetest juices blend,
Let butter drench them in its yellow tide,
And a long slice of bacon grace their side;
Not all the plate, how famed soe'er it be,
Can please my palate like a bowl of thee.
Some talk of hoe-cake, fair Virginia's pride!
Rich johnny-cake this mouth has often tried;
Both please me well, their virtues much the same,
Alike their fabric, as allied their fame,
Except in dear New England, where the last
Receives a dash of pumpkin in the paste,
To give it sweetness and improve the taste.
But place them all before me, smoking hot,
The big, round dumpling, rolling from the pot;
The pudding of the bag, whose quivering breast,
With suet lined, leads on the Yankee feast;
The charlotte brown, within whose crusty sides
A belly soft the pulpy apple hides;
The yellow bread whose face like amber glows
And all of Indian that the bakepan knows,—
You tempt me not; my favorite greets my eyes,
To that loved bowl my spoon by instinct flies.

His best poem, however, was his *Conspiracy of Kings,* an attack on the enemies of the French Republic written out of his concern for the fate of those republican principles that he saw emerging from both French and American revolutions. His topic and form forced him to concentrate his gifts (which were too limited and pedestrian, certainly, for the epic) into Popean couplets, yet his deep involvement with his subject gave the poem an urgency and energy that his verse otherwise lacked. His opening address to the tyrants of Europe showed Barlow at his best:

Ye speak of kings combin'd, some league that draws
Europe's whole force, to save your sinking cause;
Of fancy'd hosts by myriads that advance,
To crush the untry'd power of new-born France.

Misguided men! these idle tales despise;
Let one bright ray of reason strike your eyes;
Show me your kings, the sceptred horde parade—
See their pomp vanish! see your visions fade!
Indignant man resumes the shaft he gave,
Disarms the tyrant, and unbinds the slave,
Displays the unclad skeletons of kings,
Sceptres of power, and serpents without stings.

Lawyer, diplomat, politician, pamphleteer, and revolutionary, Joel Barlow had neither time nor opportunity to develop his talents fully, yet of all the Wits he might have been the most successful.

 *FOUR*

EXPANDING LITERARY HORIZONS

The Revolution and Literature

The impact of the revolutionary controversy and the war on American writing was so great as to be difficult to assess. Had the war not diverted the normal course of events, it is reasonable to assume that during the seventies and eighties there would have been a sizeable amount of belletristic writing couched in conventional literary forms in the Colonies, for in 1776 a new generation of writers—among them Freneau, Hopkinson, Dwight, Barlow, and Trumbull, all talented men—were already at work. But there was not much room or much energy left over for literature through the revolutionary years. It became a weapon against the British, an instrument for drawing the Colonies together, a medium for exchanging and disseminating ideas.

"An age employ'd in edging steel, Can no poetic raptures feel," wrote the poet Philip Freneau, for writers were busy exploring the new ideas transforming society; they were often more concerned with the necessity of expressing these ideas than with the literary art with which they were expressed. War not only "drove out the tranquil forms of literature," as Moses Coit Tyler later said, but gave greater impetus to the combative forms —to satires, burlesques, parodies, political essays, polemics, anecdotes, ballads, and broadsides. There were many things to say, arguments to be made, positions to maintain, people and principles to attack and defend. To be effective, revolutionary writing had to appeal to a larger body of people than an educated elite and had to be written to American and not to London standards or styles.

137

The Decline of Calvinist Orthodoxy

At the time of the Revolution, there were approximately 3,000 churches in the United States; the majority of these were Calvinist, belonging to Presbyterians and Congregationalists whose differences lay more in matters of church government than in creed. The Anglican Church was seriously divided by the war, supplying on the one hand the largest number of signers of the Declaration of Independence and on the other the largest body of Loyalist sentiment. The Methodists, whose emissaries had arrived only in 1769, were increasing rapidly; so too were the Baptists, though both sects were still relatively small and dispersed. Lutheran and Reformed Church membership lay chiefly in German- and Dutch-settled areas. The small Catholic population was concentrated in Maryland; in 1782 there were still fewer than twenty-five priests in America.

The decline of old-line Calvinist churches, predicted by Cotton Mather earlier in the century and hastened by the Great Awakening, seemed to have arrived. Ministers of the Revolutionary and postwar years generally believed America, as the Presbyterian Assembly noted, to be "in a low and declining state," marked by "a general dereliction of religious principles and practice among our citizens," while orthodox churchmen everywhere prayed for strength to combat "indifference and irreligion."

What the Enlightenment had done to theology, of course, was to suggest that religious ideas ought to be tested by reason, and that each man's reason was capable of testing them. At first, orthodox church doctrine seemed to stand up perfectly well under rational scrutiny. Cotton Mather found it easy to accept the Enlightenment without abandoning any of his Calvinist principles. As corrrespondent of the Royal Society and an enthusiastic scientific amateur, he believed that scientific rationalism reinforced his faith and wrote *The Christian Philosopher* in 1721 to show how it did. The majority of the American clergy, like Mather, believed that Newton, Locke, and company could be absorbed into their faith without creating any serious prob-

lems and probably strengthening it. Mather read Locke and
Newton with pleasure (he called Newton "our perfect dicta-
tor"), and most educated clergymen knew something of the
Enlightenment scientists and philosophers.

Deism and "Infidelity"

But there were those to whom the orthodox
Calvinist diagram of the world did not seem to match the one
drawn by Science and Reason. As the eighteenth century proceeded, what Mather's generation found to be a satisfactory adjustment of faith and science no longer sufficed. By the time of
the Revolution, the older Protestant churches and the newer
evangelical sects faced a serious threat from a religio-philoso-
phical movement imported from Europe under the name of
"deism." Derived from the Enlightenment's trust in scientific rationalism, in tune with the secular and rationalistic temper of
the times, deism exerted a powerful attraction to the intellectual
leaders of the revolutionary generation. Cutting through the in-
tricacies of theology, the deist rested his "rational" religion on
four major premises: first, that nature, viewed by reason, was the
only valid source of God's revelation; second, that nature so
viewed was "a harmonious, magnificent order" (Paine's phrase),
which is natural law; third, that man and his institutions might
partake of that order; and fourth, that the duty of man was to
bring himself and his society into harmony with that natural,
divine law.

God, the deist thought, was eminently rational and benevolent; man was rational, altruistic, and naturally free. To find religious truth, one judged his faith by the standards of reason as a
scientist found truth in nature; he rejected myth, mystery, and
irrationality, meeting God through nature and finding in nature
the laws He placed there for man's guidance. The deist hoped to
find a theology that met the test of credibility; against the
"affections" of the Awakening and the doctrinalism of Puritanism, he set the primacy of rationality.

There were, of course, varying shades of deism, which left

ample space for individuality. Some, like Thomas Paine, rejected
both institutionalized religion and scriptural authority; others,
like Franklin or Jefferson, remained within their churches, followed what they wished of church discipline, and used the evidences they found in nature to reinforce their Christian principles. But in general, deists agreed that true religion was personal
rather than institutional, more concerned with reason than with
faith, more rooted in Science than in scripture.

Despite differences and rivalries, the orthodox Protestant sects
recognized the threat of rationalistic religion. Ministers of all
faiths preached against deist "infidelity" and warned of the
devil's part in promoting it. The Reverend Timothy Dwight
preached 200 sermons against the deistic heresy to his Yale students and wrote a savagely satiric poem, *The Triumph of Infidelity* (1788), to expose its evils. Dozens of books and pamphlets
kept up the attack, but in time the furor lessened.

Actually, deism's period of popularity was brief and confined
to a relatively small group of intellectuals. It demanded too much
sophistication and subtlety to make it a likely creed for the
masses; it had no established body of doctrine, no church organization, no missions, no preachers. It was a bookish religion,
drawn from libraries and laboratories, whose rational approach
to God had neither the attraction of the Calvinists' rugged cer-
tainties nor the evangelicals' emotionalism. "No heart was ever
won by reason's power alone," wrote Timothy Dwight, showing
that he knew the psychology of religious belief better than the
deists. "Happily," noted the Reverend David Lindsley in 1805,
"the reign of atheism has passed away and the fopperies of infidelity are no longer in fashion."

Nevertheless, traces of deism's influence remained in American religious attitudes—its appeal to the reasonable and cred-
ible, its reliance on the practical test, its concern for order and
predictability that marked it as part of the Enlightenment. Most
of all, deism was fundamentally optimistic and progressive. Instead of relying on God's providential interventions, deism suggested that men could change things for the better. Deism gave

men a measure of control over their affairs; it postulated that man was morally and intellectually teachable. Its influence in the shaping of the American mind was eventually not theological, but rather a matter of temperament and spirit.

The Unitarian View

The unitarian movement in American theology, which paralleled the rise of deism in the later eighteenth century, had much more direct effects. The "heresy" of denying the Trinity to accept only one God appeared in England and Europe in the sixteenth and seventeenth centuries and grew within English Calvinism with the extension of religious toleration in the eighteenth. American unitarianism resembled the English brand in some ways but was not strongly influenced by it, being more an indigenous growth arising out of the general trend away from traditional Calvinism in the middle years of the century. It would be misleading to consider unitarianism in terms of its opposition to the theological doctrines it discarded; it was less a system than a position.

Essentially, unitarianism was a quiet, gradual revolt against the Calvinists' distrust of human nature, their emphasis on man's darker side, and the whole mechanical apparatus of election and salvation. Unitarian-minded ministers stressed the positive aspects of Christianity and its ethical and social elements; they emphasized man's ability to improve himself, his rational faculties, his moral and spiritual potentialities. Their version of Christianity, rather than Calvinism's, fitted much better the perfectionism and optimism of the Age of Reason and Revolution; it was, William Ellery Channing said, an "enlightened Christianity."

There were unitarian congregations before there were organized Unitarian churches, as the movement spread through both Presbyterian and Congregational groups. Anglican King's Chapel in Boston formally adopted unitarian principles in 1787, but the earliest church to bear the name was Philadelphia's First

Church in 1796. Before the close of the century, most of New England's liberal ministers had adopted unitarian views, while Harvard, in particular, soon became their stronghold.

Attacked constantly by the orthodox as a negative system of loosened standards, a way of "not believing" that encouraged insincerity and infidelity, the movement finally found a spokesman in William Ellery Channing of Boston, whose famous sermon on "Unitarian Christianity" in 1819 articulated the position with conviction and finality. "Calvinism, we are persuaded," said Channing, "is giving place to better things. It has passed its meridian and is sinking fast to rise no more." A "Conference of Liberal Ministers," called in 1820, furnished a meeting ground for those dissatisfied with orthodoxy and six years later became the American Unitarian Association of 125 churches, among them twenty of the oldest congregations in New England.

By reason of its wide acceptance in the proper places and its avoidance of open hostility to older Calvinistic sympathies, Unitarianism, as deism could not, gave respectability and status to religious liberalism. Whereas one might attack Paine as an atheistical wrecker of the Christian faith, one could hardly call such men as Channing, Jared Sparks, or James Freeman emissaries of infidelity. As Channing predicted, the movement helped to hasten the demise of the older Calvinism by offering a view of man and deity much more in tune with the optative mood of the times.

A hopeful faith, Unitarianism, like deism, gave men assurance that they could make themselves and their world better, and by emphasizing the ethical and social responsibilities of Christians, it encouraged them to do so. By replacing a deterministic philosophy with an optimistic one, it helped to liberate intellectual and artistic energies in such a way as to encourage self-trust and self-expression as Calvinism had not, and deism could not. From the Unitarians' cheerful confidence to the ebullient self-reliance of transcendentalism and Jacksonism was not a long step.

Journals, Travels, and Sermons

The most popular forms of prose during the Revolutionary years were the essay and pamphlet, whose functions were public and secular. When American attention focused on the argument with Britain and the war, such once-favorite forms as the journal, travel narrative, and sermon declined in popularity. Prominent ministers and public figures continued to keep journals, for the most part published posthumously and sometimes bound in with volumes of sermons or addresses. The Reverend Nathaniel Emmons' memoirs, for example, were included in six volumes of his sermons; President Ezra Stiles of Yale left fifteen volumes of unpublished journals; Alexander Graydon's *Memoirs of a Life Lived Chiefly in Pennsylvania,* based on his life in the seventies and eighties, did not appear until 1811.

Most of the journals that appeared, however, were wartime products whose interest lay less in the writer's inner life than in his military adventures. Major Robert Rogers' soldierly account of his expeditions against the French at Detroit, published in 1765, was one of the best of these. There were many more, among them James Thacher's description of his service with the Massachusetts militia in the Revolution; Return Meigs' diary kept on Arnold's expedition against Quebec; William Feltman's journal of the Yorktown campaign; Samuel Curwen's account of what it was like to be a Loyalist in wartime. George Rogers Clark's splendid journal of his western campaigns of 1778–1779, however, remained unpublished until 1869.

Travel books were no longer so much in vogue. Improved transportation made it possible for people to travel more widely than before, so that Madame Knight's journey or Alexander Hamilton's trip seemed no longer so adventurous. By the later eighteenth century, the traveler who wrote a book was more likely to be a scientist, trained or amateur, whose purpose was to observe and record scientific data. Lewis Evans, who published his *Geographical . . . and Historical Essays* (1755, 1756), was a professional cartographer whose concise, controlled prose even Dr. Samuel Johnson called "elegant." John Bartram's *Observa-*

tions on the Inhabitants, Climate, Soil, Rivers, Productions, Animals . . . , etc. (1751) was an account by a amiable Quaker scientist of a botanical field trip from Pennsylvania to Canada.

William Stork's *Description of East Florida* (1766) was a beautifully written scientific book. James Adair, who spent forty years as a trader with the frontier tribes, published in 1775 what was essentially a pioneer anthropological study—unfortunately, it was marred by his conviction that Indians were the lost tribes of Israel. The only popular journal of the older type was Jonathan Carver's *Travels Through the Interior Parts of North America.* Carver, a young and adventurous soldier who started out in 1776 to cross the whole North American continent, reached the Minnesota country in 1777 and returned to the East in 1788. His book, published in London in 1798, sold widely in England and Europe.

The most influential travel book in eighteenth-century America was William Bartram's *Travels Through North and South Carolina, Georgia, East and West Florida* . . . , published in 1791. Bartram, trained as a botanist like his father John, was also a painter and romantic philosopher. He wrote a fluent, simple, sentimental prose that appealed to British and European readers, who seized on it eagerly as a source of instruction about American nature. Since he was himself strongly influenced by the "noble savage" tradition and by the British poets, his anecdotes of the frontier and the wilderness sometimes gave his readers a curious picture of America. For example, Bartram had one of his settlers remark as he lay beneath a tree contemplating the landscape and smoking a pipe, "Welcome, stranger. I am indulging in the rational dictates of nature, taking a little rest, having just come in from the chace and fishing."

Wordsworth, Coleridge, Campbell, Chateaubriand, and others drew much of their information about American life and scenery from Bartram, and his book was still being read in late Victorian England. Scientist though he was (and his book contains much sound scientific observation), he also had a strain of the poet in him, as he believed that nature contained spiritual principles of great value to mankind. His remarks on the Ephemera—insects

whose brief life span of a few hours also intrigued Franklin—
provide a good sample of his style:

Solemnly and slowly move onward, to the river's shore, the
rustling crowds of the Ephemera. How awful the procession! innumerable millions of winged beings, voluntarily verging on to
destruction, to the brink of the grave, where they behold bands of
their enemies with wide open jaws, ready to receive them. But as if
insensible of their danger, gay and tranquil each meets his beloved
mate in the still air, inimitably bedecked in their new nuptial
robes. . . .
The importance of the existence of these beautiful and delicately
formed little creatures, whose frame and organization are equally
wonderful, more delicate, and perhaps as complicated as those of
the most perfect human being, is well worth a few moments' contemplation; I mean particularly when they appear in the fly state.
And if we consider the very short period of that stage of existence,
which we may reasonably suppose to be the only space of their life
that admits of pleasure and enjoyment, what a lesson doth it not
afford us of the vanity of our own pursuits!

Volumes of sermons continued to appear throughout the latter years of the century, but they seemed to lack the vigor and
intensity of their predecessors. Nathaniel Emmons, for example,
published 200 sermons during his lifetime and a hundred separate religious essays. His collected sermons in six volumes (ten
more volumes have never been published), though their scholarship was impressive and their theology sound, did not have the
conviction of the earlier Calvinists. The most widely published
and read sermons were those that dealt not with theology, but
with issues of empire, war, and politics; after 1765, hundreds of
these appeared in pamphlet form, usually within a few months
after they had been preached.
The part played by the clergy in encouraging resistance to
England and in gathering support for the Revolution was an
extremely important one. That "black Regiment, the dissenting
clergy," a Loyalist observed in 1780, had much to do with incit-
ing colonial feeling against England; Alice Baldwin, in her study
of New England sermons during the revolutionary years, con-

cluded that "there is not a right asserted in the Declaration of Independence which had not been discussed by the New England clergy before 1763." Since Americans had listened to militia-day and election-day sermons for a hundred years, they were accustomed to hearing military and political issues discussed from the pulpit, and, as Loyalist preacher Jonathan Boucher said, "much execution was done by sermons" against England and Tories.

Revolutionary sermons ranged from scholarly and legal to emotional and incendiary, depending on the position of preacher and congregation vis-à-vis England. The Reverend Samuel Langdon of Harvard, for example, told his congregation that war with England would be a war against a wicked people who deserved it:

> In a general view of the present moral state of Great Britain it may be said: There is no truth, nor mercy, nor knowledge of God in the land. By swearing, and lying, and killing, and stealing, and committing adultery, their wickedness breaks out. . . . As they have increased, so have they sinned, therefore God is changing their glory into shame.

Jonathan Mayhew chose the hundredth anniversary of the decapitation of Charles I to remind the English of what happened when monarchs demanded "unlimited submission" of their loyal subjects. The people, he repeated, possessed the right to rebel against any government whose actions contravened the laws of nature and reason—in fact, in Mayhew's opinion failure to resist tyranny was itself "highly criminal."

After the outbreak of war, ministers served as chaplains, preached to the troops, and sermonized on the conflict at every possible occasion. George Duffield, William Smith, and Jacob Duchè of Philadelphia, Jacob Green of New Jersey, Oliver Hunt of South Carolina, Samuel Cooper of Boston's Brattle Street Church—these and others preached and published sermons with such titles as "The Duties of the Christian Soldier," "Discourses On the Rights of Kings," "The American Line," and "The Present Conflict Reviewed." Hugh Henry Brackenridge, serving as chaplain to the Pennsylvania Line, preached and published *Six Political Discourses Founded in the Scripture,* placing the Bible directly behind the American cause.

Most Loyalist preachers, who ran some danger of persecution, either left the country or remained quiet. Anglican Jonathan Boucher preached through Virginia and Maryland in 1775 with a brace of pistols lying at hand in the pulpit, but he finally had to leave for England, where long after the war he published his Loyalist sermons as *A View of the Causes and Consequences of the American Revolution* (1797). Except in areas occupied by the enemy, pulpit orators thundered weekly against Howe, Gage, the Hessians, George III, Parliament, and Tories. The Reverend Nathaniel Whitaker, of Salem, Massachusetts, chose for his sermon on the perfidy of Loyalists the text, "Cursed be he that holdeth back his hand from blood," and drew for his hearers a frightful picture of a future America under British and Tory rule:

Behold these delightful and stately mansions for which we labored, possessed by the minions of power. See yon spacious fields, subdued to fruitfulness by the sweat and toil of our fathers and ourselves, yielding their increase to clothe, pamper, and enrich the tyrant's favorites who are base enough to assist him in his cursed plot to enslave us. Does this rouse our resentment? Stop a moment, and I'll show you a spectacle more shocking than this. What meagre visages do I see in yonder fields, toiling and covered with sweat to cultivate the soil? Who are those in rags, bearing burdens and drawing water for these haughty lords, and then cringing to them for a morsel of bread? They are—O gracious God, support my spirits—they are my sons and my daughters . . . again loaded with irons and dragging after them, wherever they go, the heavy, galling, ignominious chains of slavery!

Pamphlets and Politics

The political essay, whether published in a newspaper or pamphlet, was the most characteristic type of American prose written during the latter half of the eighteenth century.

For at least a hundred years the dominant form of public discourse in England and the Colonies, the American revolutionary generation found it perfectly suited to its needs—brief, readable, inexpensive to produce, and easy to sell. The colonial reader was accustomed to theological disputation and exposition in pamphlet form, so when the British replaced the heretics after 1760, King George or Lord North substituted for Satan's emissaries, and Parliament or the Board of Trade replaced the erring theologians of the Awakening, the colonial public knew exactly what to expect. The revolutionary generation also had the great English pamphleteering tradition to draw on—Milton, Dryden, Swift—and newer models like Defoe, Johnson, "Junius," Burke, and others. Sometimes read aloud at public gatherings, and sometimes (depending on the temper of the audience) burned at public meetings, these pamphlet-essays sold in tremendous amounts—Thomas Paine's famous *Common Sense,* for example, sold over 100,000 in three months, which meant that a fairly large percentage of the entire colonial population must have read it.

The number of political essays written during the period 1760–1800 reached high into the thousands; some 2,000 pamphlets still remain—no doubt a fraction of those lost. Together they constitute the most brilliant body of political prose written in America, far surpassing the level of those later elicited by the argument over slavery and union. Public life and public issues attracted the best minds of the day, men whose wits had been honed on the classics, debates, politics, oratory, and journalism. The form demanded real skill, for the colonial audience was a critical one, easily able to tell the amateur from the expert. Good political writing required perfect control of plain, convincing, persuasive English; clear organization and impeccable logic; brevity and directness; and a very thorough understanding of audience psychology. It was a demanding and challenging kind of writing, worthy of the best efforts of good minds.

How pamphlet wars developed is illustrated by an exchange that extended from 1764 to 1765 among four participants. James Otis of Boston had already demonstrated his skill with his

Vindications of the House of Representatives (1762), an attack on the Writs of Assistance, which, John Adams said, made every man who read it "ready to take arms." In July, 1764, Otis published *Rights of the British Colonies Asserted and Vindicated,* which outlined a plan for the permanent position of the Colonies within the empire. In September, Oxenbridge Thacher, another Boston lawyer, continued Otis' argument with *The Sentiment of British America;* he was supported by Rhode Island's Stephen Hopkins, whose *Rights of the Colonies Examined* appeared in December, 1764. Two months later, an anonymous *Letter from a Gentleman at Halifax to his Friend in Rhode Island* answered all three. Hopkins then replied in a series of essays directed to "A Friend in Rhode Island" in *The Rhode Island Gazette,* while Otis returned in March with *Vindication of the British Colonies Against the Aspersions of the Gentleman from Halifax.* The "Gentleman" returned with *A Defence . . . from Halifax* in April, which brought a reply from Otis—*Brief Remarks on the Defence . . .*—in June. (The "gentleman," exposed as Martin Howard, a Newport Loyalist, was beaten, hanged in effigy, and driven out by the Sons of Liberty in August.) All of these pamphlets were done with skill, care, and precision by four literate, well-educated men with a thorough command of the language and a wide knowledge of law, history, and the classics.

The Stamp Act of March, 1765, opened the gates for the first wave of the pamphlet flood. Otis, John Dickinson of Pennsylvania, John Adams, Daniel Dulany of Maryland, and dozens of others rushed into print. The Stamp Act Congress, which met in October, produced seventeen pamphlets alone, while sermons against the Act poured out of the presses. After 1765 the stream of political writing swelled each year. Every Revolutionary leader of consequence, often under a pseudonym, wrote essays for the papers, letters to the public, or pamphlets. Richard Bland and Arthur Lee of Virginia; James Wilson of Pennsylvania; Alexander Hamilton of New York, still a college student; Josiah Quincy, Jr., of Boston, who died young in 1775; the redoubtable Otis; John Adams, whose *Novanglus* papers of 1774 were among the most effective opening shots of the pamphlet war in New England—these and many others contributed to the patriot cause.

Samuel Adams, powerfully persuasive but no stylist, wrote letters to the newspapers under such names as "Vindex" or "A Son of Liberty" so effectively that the British named him "chief incendiary" and excepted him from the list of colonial leaders to be offered amnesty. Franklin's two essays on British policy, *Rules by Which a Great Empire May be Reduced to a Small One* (1773) and *An Edict by The King of Prussia* (1773), were among the most effective satiric pieces written by anyone in the decade.

John Dickinson published his first pamphlet, "The Late Regulations Respecting The Colonies," on the occasion of the Stamp Act and his last, "On The Present Situation in Public Affairs," thirty-two years later, thereby earning his sobriquet as "Penman of the Revolution." An accomplished stylist, he prompted Franklin to say of his essays, "You feel, as you read, that you are paying attention to the language of an honest gentleman." His reasonableness and clarity are aptly illustrated in the advice given to his countrymen in *Letters from a Farmer in Pennsylvania* (1767–1768) to maintain "a firm but peaceable resistance" to Britain:

Every government, at some time or other, falls into wrong measures; these may proceed from mistake or passion. But every such measure does not dissolve the obligation between the governors and the governed; the mistake may be corrected; the passion may pass over.

It is the duty of the governed to endeavor to rectify the mistake and appease the passion. They have not at first any other right than to represent their grievances and to pray for redress, unless an emergency is so pressing as not to allow time for receiving an answer to their applications, which rarely happens. If their applications are disregarded, then that kind of opposition becomes justifiable, which can be made without breaking the laws, or disturbing the public peace. This consists in the prevention of the oppressors reaping advantage from their oppressions, and not in their punishment. For experience may teach what reason did not; and harsh methods cannot be proper, till milder ones have failed.

If at length it becomes undoubted that inveterate resolution is formed to annihilate the liberties of the governed, the English history affords frequent examples of resistance by force. What particular circumstances will in any future case justify such resistance can never be ascertained till they happen. Perhaps it may be allowable to say, generally, that it never can be justifiable until the people are *fully convinced* that any further submission will be destructive to their happiness.

Nor were the Tories silent. Daniel Leonard's *Massachusettensis* (1775) was so persuasive that John Adams thought him the most dangerous Loyalist propagandist in New England. Samuel Seabury's "Westchester Farmer" letters of 1774–1775 (to which Hamilton replied) and Joseph Galloway's twenty-two pamphlets, many written from England, were excellent briefs for the Loyalist position.

Tom Paine: The Bold Propagandist

The prince of revolutionary pamphleteers was Thomas Paine, one of the most skillful political propagandists of any age. Paine was born in England, and after failing as a corsetmaker, schoolteacher, sailor, and excise officer, in 1774, at the age of thirty-seven, came to America bearing some circumspect letters of recommendation from Franklin. He had already developed a clear and forceful pamphlet style and an excellent grasp of the techniques of persuasion. The ordinary man, he said, "feels first and reasons afterward . . . ; say a bold thing, and they will begin to think."

The controversy between Crown and Colonies exactly fitted Paine's interests and talents, and in January, 1776, he published *Common Sense,* which had much to do with crystallizing public support for independence. *Common Sense* went through fifteen editions before the end of the year; Washington credited its "sound doctrine and unanswerable reasoning" with convincing more colonists of the necessity of separation than any other single document.

Paine served with the Continental Army on General Greene's staff and at intervals brought out thirteen pamphlets called "The Crisis" in which he traced the course of the war and exhorted the populace to greater effort. The recurrent themes of the "Crisis" series—the implacable tyranny of England, the necessity of independence, the common interest of the Colonies in obtaining it—were precisely those principles of the revolutionary cause that needed most support, and Paine's shrewd, effective arguments provided it through the critical years of the war.

Paine's pamphlets were constructed out of clear, compact, bold prose that no ordinarily intelligent reader could fail to understand. He had a gift for speaking directly to the public, neatly balancing his appeal between a man's self-interest and his ideals, and putting it all into eminently reasonable terms. He offered his readers, he said, "simply facts, plain arguments, and common sense," though he loaded his facts expertly and oversimplified complex arguments. He possessed a gift for the memorable phrase—"Government, like dress, is the badge of lost innocence"; "'Tis the business of little minds to shrink"; "Wisdom is not the purchase of a day"—that stuck in the mind. His prose was deceptively simple, for within it he sometimes built rather complicated rhetorical patterns with carefully balanced sentences, subtle repetitions, and ingenious twists of phrasing; this is illustrated, in his remarks on why government is needed, albeit the best may be none:

Society in every state is a blessing, but Government, even in its best state, is but a necessary evil; in its worst state an intolerable one; for when we suffer, or we are exposed to the same miseries *by a Government,* which we might expect in a country without government, our calamity is heightened by reflecting that we furnish the means by which we suffer.

On the other end of the scale, the arresting simplicity of the opening trumpet call of his famous *American Crisis* (written, so the story has it, on a drumhead by campfire light during Washington's retreat across New Jersey in 1776) is Paine at his brilliant best:

These are the times that try men's souls. The summer soldier and the sunshine patriot will, in this crisis, shrink from the service of their country; but he that stands it *now,* deserves the love and thanks of man and woman. Tyranny, like hell, is not easily conquered; yet we have this consolation with us, that the harder the conflict, the more glorious the triumph. What we obtain too cheap, we esteem too lightly: it is dearness only that gives every thing its value. Heaven knows how to put a proper price upon its goods; and it would be strange indeed if so celestial an article as FREEDOM should not be highly rated. Britain, with an army to enforce her tyranny, has declared that she has a right (*not only to* TAX) but "to BIND *us in* CASES WHATSOEVER," and if being *bound in that manner,* is not slavery, then there is not such a thing as slavery upon earth. Even the expression is impious; for so unlimited a power can belong only to God.

After the war, acclaimed by Congress and the people for his services to the nation, Paine turned his attention to Europe, where other revolutions seemed in the making. He witnessed the early events of the French Revolution and did his best to assist the beginning of something similar in England. He was a member of the French Revolutionary Convention, participated in its deliberations, and finally in 1793 was imprisoned and narrowly escaped the guillotine because he opposed the execution of the King. His American citizenship and the intervention of James Monroe, the American ambassador, saved him; meanwhile, he had published *The Rights of Man* (1791, 1792), had been charged with libel and treason in England, and had been hanged in effigy by a London mob.

After his release from prison, Paine remained in Paris, in poor health and on the edge of poverty. He continued to write, publishing his strongly deistic and anticlerical *Age of Reason* (1794–1796), his political tract *Dissertation on First-Principles of Government* (1795), and his ideas on tax and land reform,

Agrarian Justice (1797). However, *The Age of Reason* and his bitter attack on the President in his *Letter to Washington* (1796) aroused powerful antagonisms in the United States, and when Paine returned to America in 1802, he found himself discredited and vilified as a drunkard, atheist, and dangerous radical. He lived in obscurity at New Rochelle, New York, stripped of his right to vote and subject to constant abuse until he died in 1809. Even after death he remained controversial—the Quakers refused to admit his body to their burial ground, and his bones were finally sent to England, sold at auction as a curiosity, and lost.

A tactless and intemperate man of strong feelings, Paine aroused equally strong feelings in others. He was neither a learned man nor an original thinker, and many of his ideas were borrowed from his contemporaries. But he was one of the most gifted political writers who ever lived, and no one did more by his pen for revolutionary America. He was absolutely unafraid to stand up for his principles, and no man fought harder—in three countries—for the freedom in which he believed. The appearance of men such as Otis, Dickinson, Adams, Paine, and others meant that the political essay in America had come of age. During the Revolution, these writers outgrew their models; they thought and wrote as Americans, in an American style, and in American prose.

Aristocrat in the Forest: Crèvecoeur

Michel-Guillaume Jean de Crèvecoeur was neither a political writer nor an American, but he wrote a book that, for its perceptive comments on the American scene, belongs firmly in American literature. Born into a noble French family in Normandy and educated in England, he arrived in Canada about 1754 with Montcalm's army, as a lieutenant who specialized in map making and surveying. About 1759 he came to the American Colonies, and in 1765 he took out British citizenship in New York under the name of John Hector St. John.

What he discovered of this new society filled him with excitement; he traveled widely through the Colonies, fascinated by their diversity and vitality. Later he married an American girl, bought a farm sixty miles from New York City in Orange County, and settled down to an idyllic life as a gentleman farmer. However, during the Revolution he was suspected of Tory sympathies; he refused to join the rebels and was subjected to such harassment that he returned to France. His *Letters from an American Farmer,* dedicated to the French philosopher Raynal and written in English, was published in London in 1782.

The "letters" were epistolary essays written "for the information of a friend in England." Twelve in all, they presented an enthusiastic view of American society as well as discussions of American institutions, information about farming, flora and fauna, and imaginary conversations between an idealized American farmer and his wife. The *Letters* sold extremely well both in Europe and America; it was reprinted five times in England within ten years and translated into both French and German. In 1783 Crèvecoeur returned to New York as French consul to find his wife dead, his house burned, and his three children in a stranger's home. He remained in the United States for nearly ten years, then went back to France for the rest of his life.

An admirer of Rousseau and a child of French romanticism, Crèvecoeur found in America exactly what he was prepared to find—a land of happy husbandmen living in a free, simple, virtuous, egalitarian society close to a benevolent nature. "Sentiment and feelings," he once wrote, "are the only guides I know." What he attempted, in an early and tentative way, was to establish the meaning of the name "American" in terms of its relation to the Enlightenment and the future world. The most famous passage of the *Letters* defined his concept of "Americanism" best; he believed it to be essentially individualistic, subsumed into a society "animated with the spirit of industry which is unfettered and unrestrained, because each person works for himself." "What, then, is an American?" Crèvecoeur asks:

He is an American, who, leaving behind him all his ancient prejudices and manners, receives new ones from the new mode of life

he has embraced, the new government he obeys, and the new rank he
holds. He becomes an American by being received in the broad
lap of our great *Alma Mater*. Here individuals of all nations are
melted into a new race of men, whose labours and posterity will
one day cause great changes in the world. Americans are the western
pilgrims, who are carrying along with them that great mass of arts,
sciences, vigour, and industry which began long since in the east;
they will finish the great circle. The Americans were once scattered
all over Europe; here they are incorporated into one of the finest
systems of population which has ever appeared, and which will here
after become distinct by the power of the different climates they
inhabit. The American ought therefore to love this country much
better than that wherein either he or his forefathers were born.
Here the rewards of his industry follow with equal steps the progress of his labour; his labour is founded on the basis of nature,
self-interest; can it want a stronger allurement? . . . The American is a new man, who acts upon new principles; he must therefore entertain new ideas, and form new opinions.

Letter III, in which Crèvecoeur makes his famous distinction
between Americans and Europeans, was the most thoroughly
considered of all the essays and the most important piece of
writing he ever did. It had three general concerns: first, it explored the differences between American and European society;
second, it analyzed American regional groupings, recognizing
for probably the first time the unique significance of the American frontier; and third, it interpreted for the first time the process of assimilation by which the European became "this new
man," this American.

In the first instance, Crèvecoeur explains that American society is energetic, dynamic, "animated with the spirit of an industry which is unfettered and unrestrained, because each person
works for himself." It is also "a modern society," built of new
materials on a new continent. Not for the New World is the
spectacle of "great lords who possess everything, and a herd of
people who have nothing"; instead the Americans are a people
"of middle means . . . of decent competence," united "under
the silken bands of a mild government . . . possessors of the

soil they cultivate, members of the government they obey, and the framers of their own laws." Theirs is, in fine, a society in which "man is as free as he ought to be . . . the most perfect society in the world."

While it "does not afford that variety of tinges and gradations which may be observed in Europe," American society, Crèvecoeur explains, has differences of its own kind. There are distinguishable types of Americans because different environments produce different men. "Men are like plants," he continues, which differ among themselves "from the peculiar soil and exposition in which they grow." An American environment, therefore, produces Americans, their distinctive nature deriving from "the air we breathe, the climate we inhabit, the government we obey, the system of religion we possess, and the nature of our employment." Seacoast society, he explains, has bred "a bold and enterprising class" of sailors, merchants, and city dwellers—aggressive, cosmopolitan, resourceful, even obstinate. The next line of settlement has produced farmers, "independent freeholders" such as the "farmer" himself. Beyond them, at the "extended line of frontiers," are the lawless, violent, improvident frontiersmen, those "off-casts" of society—a "mongrel breed, half-civilized, half-savage," Crèvecoeur calls them—who in making the first penetration of the wilderness are themselves touched by its wildness. Yet it is these "ferocious, gloomy, licentious" people, ironically, who provide the necessary first step toward the evolution of a stable, agrarian society. They open the path for

the arrival of a second and better class, the true American freeholders . . . more industrious people who will finish their improvements, convert the loghouse into a convenient habitation, and . . . change in a few years that hitherto barbarous country into a fine fertile, well-regulated district.

But whatever may be the regional differences among Americans, they disappear as all are "melted into a new race of men." In a long and carefully organized passage in Letter III, Crèvecoeur details the psychological changes that turn Europeans into Americans. The immigrant comes, with Europe's past clinging to him, to a huge, lovely country, which is empty, open, and quite unlike Europe, "where every place is overstocked." "He no sooner breathes our air," writes James, the author's Scots narrator, the "farmer" of the title, "than he forms schemes and embarks on designs he never would have thought of in his own country." His first step toward Americanization is his rejection of Europe's "ancient prejudices and manners"; his next comes with his realization of the opportunities the country offers to him. "Has he a particular talent, or industry?" asks Crèvecoeur. "He exerts it in order to procure a livelihood, and it succeeds." He finds independence, higher wages, plentiful food, and most important of all, he "alters his scale . . . he now feels himself a man, because he is treated as such." He begins to think in different terms—American terms—since he has become "a new man, who acts upon new principles; he must therefore entertain new ideas and form new opinions."

So out of this "promiscuous breed," this "mixture of English, Scotch, Irish, French, Dutch, Germans, and Swedes . . . that race called Americans has arisen." The change from European to American, as Crèvecoeur describes it, rested on that second chance, the opportunity to begin again, that lay at the center of the American myth. It is significant that the word *new* appears seventeen times in Letter III, and often in company with such words as *metamorphosis, regeneration,* and *resurrection.* These Americans, men born again in the New World Eden, Crèvecoeur believes to be the hope of the world—"western pilgrims, who are carrying along with them that great mass of arts, sciences, vigour, and industry which began long since in the east; they will finish the circle . . . and one day cause great changes in the world."

The theme of America as land of opportunity and hope winds through Letter III and imposes unity on it. Crèvecoeur constantly emphasizes the openness of American society, its mobility, and fluidity. There is in America quite literally "room for everybody"—thousands of acres of untaxed, uncultivated land, a prospect that must have exerted a tremendous appeal to land-hungry Europeans. In this "great American asylum," the "poor of Europe" may find peace and prosperity; the good things of life, lacking for the mass of Europeans, are here for the working and asking. Here "servant may rise to master . . . the slave of some despotic prince become a free man," writes James; he who has hitherto been a cipher now finds "for the first time in his life, he counts for something."

Crèvecoeur's prose style, strongly infused with the fashionable rhetorical patterns and sentimentality of his Parisian kinsmen, was neither American nor English. He liked little elegancies of prose and was prone to Gallic artificialities and exuberances— yet his style fitted his temperament and his message. He was an ebullient and thoroughly likeable man of sensibility and feeling; the *Letters* reflect him and his fresh enthusiasm for his adopted land perfectly. In the closing letters of the collection, he tempered his enthusiasm for the American future considerably, no doubt reflecting on his own wartime troubles, but his portrait of America as it appears in the first five letters is a sympathetic and perceptive articulation of the myths of America as Paradise and Hope, as they appeared in the first generation's version of the American Dream.

The Literary Essay

The development of the literary essay in America depended, as it had in England, on the growth of the newspaper and the magazine. American essayists naturally copied the great British practitioners of the form—Addison, Steele, Swift, Goldsmith, Johnson, Butler—throughout the eighteenth century. The essay caught on quickly in the Colonies; Harvard students, only twelve years after the appearance of *The Tatler* in London, put together a series called *The Telltale* in obvious imitation. *The New England Weekly Journal* had a "Will Pedant" writing in *Spectator* style in the 1720s; Franklin wrote as "Silence Dogood" in his brother's *Courant* in 1722; *The Virginia Gazette* had a "Monitor" in 1736.

By mid-century, few papers lacked a "Lounger," a "Hermit,"

or a "Scriblerus" pretending to be Addison or Swift. One of the better early essayists was William Livingston of New York, a lawyer and mediocre poet who edited and wrote essays for his own papers, *The Independent Reflector* (1752–1753) and *The Occasional Reverberator* (1753), and who continued to write under different names for another twenty years. Like other Americans working in the essay form, Livingston learned to write an easy, graceful, polished prose derived from British models, which became the standard American prose style by mid-century.

The familiar essay remained a popular form throughout the eighteenth century and into the nineteenth. Almost every American writer of literary pretensions tried his hand at it, for it lent itself admirably to the various needs of the era. The struggle among political factions, literary criticism, social satire, the manners of a self-consciously sophisticated society, and the fads and follies of a gawky young nation fitted all the requirements of the essay form. Like their English models, American essayists posed under names such as "Oliver Oldschool" (Joseph Dennie); "Tomocheeki" (Philip Freneau); "The Gleaner" (Judith Warren); or "The Prompter" (Noah Webster). Joseph Dennie's "Lay Preacher" series, most of them published in his *Portfolio* magazine after 1800, represented the best examples, perhaps, of the late British-derived manner. The opening paragraphs of his essay "On the Pleasures of Study" are a good example of how he hoped, he said, "to unite the familiarity of Franklin with the simplicity of Sterne." However, Dennie wrote a prose of slightly overblown elegance that resembled neither very closely:

Whenever I reflect upon my habitual attachment to books, I feel a new glow of gratitude towards that Power, who gave me a mind thus disposed, and to those liberal friends, who have allowed the utmost latitude of indulgence to my propensity. Had I been born on a barbarous shore, denied the glorious privileges of education, and interdicted an approach to the rich provinces of literature, I should have been the most miserable of mankind. With a temperament of sensibility, with the nerves of a valetudinarian, with an ardent thirst for knowledge, and very scanty means for its acquisition, with a mind often clouded with care, and depressed by dejection, I should have resembled the shrinking vegetable of irritableness, and like the mimosa of the gardens, have been doomed to be at once stupid and sensitive. The courses of nature and fortune having taken a different direction, parental benignity having furnished me with the keys, and discipline and habit having conducted me through the portico of education, I have ever found, whether walking in the vestibule of science, or meditating in the groves of philosophy, or hearkening to historians and poets, or rambling with Rabelais, such excellent companions, that life has been beguiled of more than half its irksomeness. In sickness, in sorrow, in the most doleful days of dejection, or in the most gloomy seasons in the calendar, study is the sweetest solace and the surest refuge, particularly when my reading is directed to that immortal book, whence the theme of this essay is taken. In an hour of adversity, when I have caught up this precious volume, I have found, instantly, the balm of Gilead and the medicine for the mind. The darkness of despair has been succeeded by the brightest rays of cheerfulness, and in place of grim phantoms, I have found comfort, peace, and serenity.

Narratives of War and Prison

Authors aimed both the political essay and the periodical essay at an educated, book-reading public. At the popular level of entertainment, the man in the street had something more exciting and attractive to catch his interest—narratives of war and prison life written by the dozens during and after the Revolutionary War. Library of Congress entries number over 200 surviving examples, some published fifty years after Yorktown. These narratives replaced or augmented the Indian captivity tales and (except for the elimination of the old-fashioned religious exhortations) followed much the same pattern, supplying adventure, heroism, villainy, horror, and hairbreadth escapes in highly satisfactory proportions.

The hero's opponents now were not redskins but redcoats; the victim's trial of captivity was not in an Indian village but in British prisons at Dartmoor or Halifax, or in prison ships like *Jersey* or *Hunter*. Yet like the Indian stories, the prisoner tales illustrated how the individual, buttressed by his bravery and dedication to a cause, stood up against suffering and won out over temptation—as in Ethan Allen's story of the sick young militia-man who chose to die in prison rather than take the Crown oath and go free. Whereas the Indian captivity tale instilled a moral lesson in the reader, the prison narrative imparted a patriotic one.

The wartime narratives had sufficient details to satisfy the most lurid imagination. Jonathan Davis saw a Yankee prisoner beaten to death while "running the gauntlet" in Plymouth prison; John Shaw saw berserk British guards put a whole com-pany of prisoners to the sword; David Perry saw a sailor, under sentence of 800 lashes, die at 600, the last 200 laid on the bloody bones of his back. Thomas Dring, whose escape from the infa-mous *Jersey* is still a classic of its kind, told how the prisoners inoculated themselves against smallpox with a common pin and pus from the sores of a dying victim and, strangely enough, sur-vived. From the Tory side, the *Narrative of the Exertions and Sufferings of James Moody* (1783), recounting the imprison-ment and escape of a Loyalist officer from the British army, was cut to exactly the same pattern and sold equally well in Boston and London.

A few of these wartime tales were written by educated men such as Henry Laurens, who served as President of Continental Congress, was captured at sea in 1780, spent fifteen months in the Tower of London, and published his *Narrative of Capture and . . . Confinement* after being exchanged for General Corn-wallis. Most of these tales, however, were plain and unvarnished, sometimes ill-written, and done by ordinary men with force, real-ism, and vigor. In them sounded authentic American voices speaking an American rather than an English tongue. Ethan Allen, of Ticonderoga fame, spent three years as a prisoner and in *A Narrative of Ethan Allen's Captivity* (1779) told about his experiences in soldierly prose. He reported thus on prisoners held captive by the British in New York:

The private soldiers who were brought to New York were crowded into churches and environed with slavish Hessian guards, a people of a strange language who were sent to America for no other design but cruelty and desolation, and at others by merciless Britons, whose mode of communicating ideas being intelligible in this country, served only to tantalize and insult the helpless and perishing; but above all was the hellish delight and triumph of the Tories over them, as they were dying by hundreds. This was too much for me to bear as a spectator, for I saw the Tories exulting over the dead bodies of their murdered countrymen. I have gone into the churches and seen sundry of the prisoners in the agony of death, in consequence of very hunger, and others speechless and very near death, biting pieces of chips; others pleading for God's sake for something to eat, and at the same time shivering with the cold. Hollow groans saluted my ears, and despair seemed to be imprinted on all of their countenances. The filth in these churches, in conse-quence of the fluxes, was almost beyond description. The floors were covered with excrements. I have carefully sought to direct my steps so as to avoid it, but could not. They would beg for God's sake for one copper, or morsel of bread. I have seen in one of these churches seven dead at the same time, lying among the excrements of their bodies.

It was a common practice with the enemy to convey the dead from these filthy places in carts, to be slightly buried, and I have seen whole gangs of Tories making derision, and exulting over the dead, saying, 'There goes another load of damned rebels."

Combined with the still-popular Indian stories and with the traditional "providence" tales of earlier America, these wartime narratives provided a rich repository of materials for the Ameri-can novel-to-be and readied the public for its appearance.

Franklin: The Enlightenment Incarnate

Benjamin Franklin represented more fully than any other man of his time the temper and personality of the American eighteenth century: its sound judgment and common sense; its political principles and humanitarian activities; its in-terest in science and the natural world; its belief in the potential-ities of the individual; its rationalistic religion. His life spanned eighty-four years of that century—born and bred in the provincial Boston of Mather and Sewall, living through the Revolution into the Republic of Washington and Jefferson, alert to and involved in every aspect of the era's rich and complex life.

Son of a tallow chandler and soap boiler, young Franklin was apprenticed to his brother's print shop, but at seventeen he ran away to New York and then Philadelphia to make his fortune. He soon made it, becoming a wealthy man and Philadelphia's first citizen, and then retired from business in 1748, hoping to spend a quiet, contemplative life in his library and laboratory. However, he was appointed deputy postmaster for the Colonies, a post he held for nearly twenty years, and after 1757 served as colonial agent for Pennsylvania in London. From 1770 to 1775 he represented not only Pennsylvania but Georgia, New Jersey, and Massachusetts in their dealings with King and Parliament. In 1775, giving up hope of finding any way to resolve the imminent clash between Colonies and empire, he returned to America.

Franklin wrote little about his political beliefs, preferring to deal in practicalities. Because of his sympathy for the causes of farmer and artisan, the political leaders of Pennsylvania at first classified him as "a sort of tribune of the people" and did not fully trust him. Penn once wrote that he was "a dangerous man . . . of uneasy spirit," but it would be hard to make Franklin into a political radical. He knew too much about the average man to be overly optimistic about him, just as he had seen too much of the ruling class to trust its wisdom. The ideal government, he once said, was that which suffered neither from "too much power in our governors nor too little *obedience* in the governed."

Franklin threw in his lot with the cause of independence because he could see neither hope nor usefulness in a middle course. He was not a political philosopher like Jefferson and could not have put his beliefs into the ringing phrases of the Declaration. He was rather a practical organizer, a political tactician; but he was no less a believer than the Virginian in liberty, reason, and justice. Franklin thought that most men were reasonable and responsible; if properly educated and controlled, they could establish and maintain a government that would allow them to live in peace and security.

He was deeply involved in the Revolution. He served on the Pennsylvania Committee of Correspondence, as delegate to the Second Continental Congress, on the Committee to draft the Declaration, and as the new nation's first representative to France (perhaps the most important and delicate task ever assigned to an American diplomat). In 1778 he successfully secured the French alliance, the greatest single factor in the ultimate victory of the American cause, and in 1783 he served with Adams and Jay on the committee which signed the peace treaty at Ghent. He then returned to the United States to begin two terms as governor of Pennsylvania, and finally, at eighty-one, he sat in the Philadelphia convention with men half his age to write the Constitution.

Franklin's greatest pleasure, he said, came from his scientific pursuits, "the philosophical studies and amusements" to which he hoped to devote his life after his retirement from business. He had a consuming curiosity about the world and a great desire "to extend the power of man over nature" so that it would be controllable and useful. Though science was crowded out of his life by his public career, which gave him only a few years of leisure for study and experiment in middle life, he was no amateur scientist, but one of the dozen or so first-rank scholars of his century; he was responsible for some of the most notable basic research done in his time. He began his first experiments as a youth in 1729 and in 1742 initiated the series of experiments in electricity on which his fame rested. He was a member of the Royal Society of London, holder of the Copley Medal for original research and of seven honorary degrees, master of five languages, member of the French, Dutch, Swedish, Italian, and Spanish Academies, and author of more than a hundred papers on electricity, medicine, chemistry, botany, meteorology, hydraulics, engineering, ethnology, and agronomy. He published his first scientific paper at twenty-three (on heat conductivity) and his last, on oceanography, at seventy-nine.

Franklin contributed most to the infant science of electricity.

He rejected the accepted "two fluid" theory of electricity, recognizing the existence and function of "positive" and "negative" charges (terms which he coined); he performed basic research on the principle of the battery and proved the identity of electricity in natural and manufactured form by his well-known lightning experiment. But most of all, Franklin helped to explain and tame the new, strange force so recently discovered and so soon to change the world. Franklin never believed nature to be mysterious or uncontrollable, and he took the fear out of the popular attitude toward it. His amazingly inventive mind was as fascinated by little things as by the broadest theories of knowledge. The same man who worked with electricity was equally absorbed with inventing a device to remove objects from high shelves, a clock with three wheels and two pinions, bifocal spectacles, a smokeless fireplace, and a harmonica made of thirty-seven glass spheres.

Like Jefferson, Franklin preferred to keep his religious principles to himself. He had little interest in theological disputation or speculation, evolved his own set of Christian principles, and tried to live by them. Raised as a Boston Presbyterian, he broke with its theology but retained much of the Puritan's moralism and concern with self-discipline. Like his Calvinist forebears, he believed that morality was required for an orderly life and an orderly society; he recognized his own frailties, as he did those of others, and worked hard to overcome them.

Certain aspects of Calvinism repelled him—its emphasis on the failings of human nature, its dependence on faith, its denial of much of human self-reliance—for he was a commonsense believer in reason and in the individual's ability to control and improve himself. He was, in effect, a deist who found proof of God in His world and works; the most acceptable way to worship this deity, he wrote, was to serve his fellowmen and to translate Christian principles into practical life. "I would rather have it said," he wrote, "He lived *Usefully,* than he died *Rich.*" He contributed to a Protestant church and a Jewish synagogue, helped his friend John Carroll become the first Catholic archbishop in the United States, attacked no sect, and worshiped God in his own way.

If Madam Knight, as legend has it, was Franklin's first teacher in dame-school, he had a good beginning, but he educated himself far beyond the rudiments of literacy. He read widely in the course of his trade as a printer and editor, but he did much more. He recalled reading Bunyan in his youth, Defoe, Shaftesbury, Swift, Plutarch (probably in Dryden's translation), and especially Addison and Steele. Throughout his life he read continuously—the *Autobiography* mentions over seventy major authors he seemed to have known thoroughly, ranging from the Greeks to contemporary philosophers—and the man who organized the Junto Club and the Library Company of Philadelphia probably read most of the books they owned.

Franklin as Literary Man

Franklin never considered himself a literary man, yet it is clear that during his entire life he depended on the skill of his pen. As editor, publisher, agent, statesman, scientist, diplomat, and public figure, he wrote pamphlets, historical narratives, essays, parables, allegories, reports, aphorisms, epigrams, satires, dialogues, and even ballads and verse, either for amusement or for quite specific and practical ends. His writings, like the Puritans', were for the most part "useful," but the range of his writing is exceptionally wide. As Herman Melville said, Franklin was "everything but a poet."

Like other young men he tried his hand first at the essay, publishing fourteen papers for his brother's paper in 1722 under the name of "Silence Dogood" and six more as "The Busy-Body" in Philadelphia from 1728 to 1729. From the age of sixteen he wrote steadily in a variety of forms, but he never gave up the essay. His last manuscripts contained a playful piece on the problems of a left-handed man in a right-handed world and a splendid essay "On the Art of Procuring Pleasant Dreams." During his middle years he wrote on serious topics—economic and political issues, education, science, and the like—and in the Revolutionary controversy he wrote some expert and savage Swiftian satires, such as *Rules by Which a Great Empire May Be Reduced to a Small One* (1773) and *The Sale of the Hessians* (1777). Late in life he enjoyed writing (and printing on his own press) "bagatelles," graceful and urbane little missives, such as *The Whistle* or *The Ephemera,* which were in perfect neoclassical taste.

Franklin wrote vivid, economical, uncluttered prose in the tradition of the "plain style" he learned from Addison, Steele, Swift, and Defoe. Like many other young men of his time, he assiduously modeled his prose on *The Spectator,* heeding Defoe's warnings against "a superfluous crowding in of insignificant words." His style, however, was not simply a copy of his models, for Franklin was concerned with developing his writing so that he might be "a tolerable English writer" in his own way. The norm of English style, he believed, should be that of intelligent, informed conversation; words should be used "as near as possible to those spoken," and most of all, as he wrote philosopher David Hume, the author should emphasize clarity, for "one cannot be too clear."

Then too, Franklin was a professional journalist who considered writing to be his trade, was proud of it, and never stopped learning the art. He explained in the *Pennsylvania Gazette* that a good editor, like any other writer, should have "great Easiness and Command of Writing and Relating Things clearly and intelligibly, and in few Words," without "affected Words and highflown Phrases." He also admired the kind of scientific writing advocated by the Royal Society's Thomas Sprat, who urged writers "to reject amplifications, digressions, and swellings" in favor of "clear senses and a native easiness." The best writing, Franklin believed,

should proceed regularly from things known to things unknown, distinctly and clearly without confusion. The words used should be the most expressive that the language affords, provided they are the most generally understood. Nothing should be expressed in two

words that can be as well expressed in one; that is, no synonyms
should be used, or very rarely, but the whole should be so placed
as to be agreeable to the ear in reading; summarily it should be
smooth, clear, and short, for the contrary qualities are displeasing.
. . . In this sense, that is best wrote which is best adapted for obtaining the end of the writer.

The result is a prose style with grace, force, flexibility, and order;
an instrument ideally suited to the expression of Franklin's ideas
and a reflection of the personality behind the pen. No other
stylist of Franklin's era could have matched the easy, artful
charm of the opening paragraphs of the *Autobiography*:

Dear Son, I have ever had a Pleasure in obtaining any little Anecdotes of my Ancestors. You may remember the Enquiries I made
among the Remains of my Relations when you were with me in
England; and the journey I undertook for that purpose. Now imag-
ining it may be equally agreable to you to know the Circumstances
of *my* Life, many of which you are yet unacquainted with; and ex-
pecting a Weeks uninterrupted Leisure in my present Country Retirement, I sit down to write them for you. To which I have besides
some other Inducements. Having emerg'd from the Poverty and
Obscurity in which I was born and bred, to a State of Affluence and
some Degree of Reputation in the World, and having gone so far
thro' Life with a considerable Share of Felicity, the conducing Means
I made use of, which, with the Blessing of God, so well succeeded,
my Posterity may like to know, as they may find some of them suitable to their own Situations, and therefore fit to be imitated. That
Felicity, when I reflected on it, has induc'd me sometimes to say,
that were it offer'd to my Choice, I should have no Objection to a
Repetition of the same Life from its Beginning, only asking the
Advantages Authors have in a second Edition to correct some Faults
of the first. So would I if I might, besides corr[ecting] the Faults,
change some sinister Accidents and Events of it for others more
favourable, but tho' this were deny'd, I should still accept the Offer.
However, since such a Repetition is not to be expected, the next
Thing most like living one's Life over again, seems to be a *Recollection* of that Life; and to make that Recollection as durable as possible, the putting it down in Writing. Hereby, too, I shall indulge
the Inclination so natural in old Men, to be talking of themselves

and their own past Actions, and I shall indulge it, without being troublesome to others who thro' respect to Age might think themselves oblig'd to give me a Hearing, since this may be read or not as any one pleases. And lastly (I may as well confess it, since my Denial of it will be believ'd by no Body) perhaps I shall a good deal gratify my own *Vanity*. Indeed I scarce ever heard or saw the introductory Words, *Without vanity I may say,* &c but some vain thing immediately follow'd. Most People dislike Vanity in others whatever share they have of it themselves, but I give it fair Quarter wherever I meet with it, being persuaded that it is often productive of Good to the Possessor and to others that are within his Sphere of Action: And therefore in many Cases it would not be quite absurd if a Man were to thank God for his Vanity among the other Comforts of Life.—

The Autobiography as Art

Franklin's *Autobiography* alone entitles him to a place within the American literary tradition, for it is done with deliberate literary art and is a classic of its genre. Written in four sections at different times (1771, 1784, 1788, and 1789), the early portion was apparently not intended for publication, whereas the latter parts, written in old age and illness, have quite a different tone. In middle life, in good health and pleased at the chance to relive his youth, Franklin wrote with satisfaction about his upward climb in society; when he resumed his manuscript thirteen years later as one of the nation's most honored men, he made it a more formal account of his participation in history-making events, as he was conscious that he was writing for posterity. Well acquainted with the strong native tradition of memoirs and journals, Franklin consciously wrote his *Autobiography* within this tradition.

The *Autobiography* is not fiction, but Franklin wrote it as an artist would, creating plot, character, and setting, with a firm grasp of narrative technique and a good sense of character description. He chose important moments from the life of his chief character, the boy called Franklin—his entry into Philadelphia, his unfortunate trip to England, the temptation of the landlady's daughter—and handled them artfully as dramatic incidents. His account of Braddock's defeat, for example, becomes a moral exemplum illustrative of the pitfalls of pride by ending with the ironic twist of the hapless General's dying words, "We shall better know how to deal with them next time." The thumbnail sketches of such people as the eccentric Keimer, the slippery Keith, his romantic poet-friend Ralph, or the pious Catholic lady, are constructed with considerable skill. In a broad sense, the *Autobiography* is a kind of true novel of how a young man, by reason of his charm, wit, and ability, met the challenge of the city and achieved wealth, power, moral stability, and self-assurance in a tough, competitive society.

Beneath the surface account of Franklin's life, two themes pervade the *Autobiography*. He saw his past as material for a moral tale that might teach the reader how to identify critical decisions and avoid mistakes in his own life. In this sense, the first half of the narrative, especially, belongs in the same tradition with Bunyan, the Puritan memoir, and the moralistic literature of the seventeenth century. As partial justification for his account of himself, and to forestall charges of self-pride, Franklin reminded his son and his readers that his life might serve to exhibit certain lessons, "fit to be imitated" by any who "find themselves in similar circumstances." How Franklin learned to recognize temptation, to assess and control himself, to find the proper meanings in experience, and finally to emerge as master of himself—this is one of the major purposes of the book.

The book's second theme lies in its exploration of the relationship of the individual to society. Franklin, a youthful rebel, learned how to adjust himself to society's rules so that he was neither at war with the world nor subservient to it. His story is a study in accommodation, of reasonable compromise between one man and other men so that both may live in harmony. Franklin made it clear at the outset that he was a vain, selfish, and occasionally foolish youngster who had to learn how to balance his self-interest with the interests of others—a major human problem in all ages, and one of the reasons for the durability of Franklin's treatment of it. He eventually discovered, paradoxically, that selflessness rather than selfishness advanced the fortunes of both individual and society. What he found in reviewing his life was the validity of the doctrine of Christian brotherhood; by reasoning it out and testing it, he found that if one fulfills his obligations to society, society will honor its obligations to him. Unlike Thoreau, who fought society to preserve his individuality, Franklin outwitted it.

Despite its literary value, the *Autobiography* does not present a satisfactory version of Franklin. It is incomplete, since it carries him only to the age of fifty-one when he stood on the threshold of greatness, and it tends to oversimplify him by failing to do justice to his amazing versatility. It shows little of his life as a scientist, no more than hints at his family and social life, says almost nothing of his political career, and nothing at all of his middle and later years. The most serious deficiency of the *Autobiography* is the image that it is likely to project of Franklin as "Poor Richard." It is a success story of no small proportions, but by oversimplifying Franklin into a shrewd tradesman of homely aphorisms, the narrative has sometimes left its readers with a false likeness of him. Franklin did believe that portions of his book might serve to exemplify "the effects of prudent and imprudent conduct in the commandment of a life of business," but he did not mean that posterity should judge him only in terms of his rags-to-riches success story or by *The Way to Wealth*.

Unfortunately, thousands of readers have fixed Franklin in the popular mind as the first apostle of frugality, good management, and regular hours. There is some truth to the picture, but the fact is that "the little cares and fatigues" of business did not really interest him, and that he retired at forty-two when he decided he had money enough to do what he wanted, though he could easily have been the richest man in the Colonies. He did not wish it said of him, as Poor Richard said of another, "He does not possess wealth, wealth possesses him."

Franklin was one of those rare men who attain distinction by incorporating in themselves the spirit of their time and place. He felt no discord with his era, no lack of harmony with his society. His temperament suited the times, and the times encouraged the fullest development of his powers. He spoke the language of the Enlightenment (though with a native American accent) as clearly as Addison, Pope, or Defoe and like them was its true son. The qualities of mind displayed in his life and writings are distinctively those of the Age of Reason—tolerance, serenity, assurance, good will, intelligent skepticism, common sense, wit, belief in man's rationality, hope for his betterment, faith in his progress. Franklin symbolized and confirmed the ideals of his age by being an eminently successful human being within its spiritual and intellectual framework. For those who wish to know what life was like in eighteenth-century America, Franklin's *Autobiography* contains its essence, recorded in the clear and steady prose of one of its greatest men.

THE
CREATION
OF AN
AMERICAN
LITERATURE
1790–1830

 *FIVE*

AN EMERGENT NATIONAL CULTURE

From Revolution to Peace

The years between Washington's election as President in 1789 and the Peace of Ghent in 1814 brought great alterations in American life. The change from knee-breeches and powdered wigs to pantaloons and short hair, from the graceful formality of the minuet to the continental gaiety of the waltz, from the flowing folds of London-style dresses to "bare arms and bosoms" in the French manner, exemplified a different style of life. The United States was a booming, wealthy nation, which grew from less than 4 million in 1790 to more than 7 million in 1810. New York's population, second to Virginia's, was soon to exceed it; Pennsylvania, North Carolina, Massachusetts, and South Carolina followed in that order, with Kentucky—raw frontier in 1790—in seventh place.

New York was by this time the largest city at about 100,000, Philadelphia (53,000) next, Baltimore third, Boston fourth. Yet the country was still overwhelmingly rural; in 1810, only 5 percent of the population lived in towns of more than 8,000. Vermont, Kentucky, Tennessee, Ohio, and Louisiana entered the Union in these years, and settlers pushed into what were to be Alabama, Mississippi, and Michigan. With the Louisiana Purchase in 1803, the United States dominated the continent, which it had once shared with France, Britain, and Spain; its frontier reached the Mississippi.

Until the war between France and England temporarily ruined American ocean commerce, the United States prospered mightily. Though still an agricultural nation, its manufacturing boomed and after the War of 1812 increased even faster. The capitalization of cotton factories alone increased from a half million in 1800 to 40 million in 1815—a rate of increase matched by other industries. American industry could compete successfully in foreign markets, it found, while the settlement of the West opened up new domestic markets each year. By Monroe's time, the country possessed a wealthy, expanding economy, which the cultural scene was quick to reflect.

The most disturbing problem derived from America's relationships with Britain and Europe. Independence, unfortunately, did not bring freedom from "entangling alliances" as Washington and Jefferson had hoped. Alliance with France, a decisive factor in the Revolution's success, was severely strained by the French Revolution and its aftermath; sympathy for the French Republic, strong at first, faded when its political direction seemed to change. The fall of the French Republic, the rise to power of Napoleon, and the struggle between the English-European coalition and Napoleon's France finally drew the United States into conflict. After the War of 1812, which equally well might have been with France, America looked westward for the next half-century. The war settled little diplomatically, militarily, or politically, yet it marked the end of the American colonial complex.

It was hardly a "second war of independence," as it is sometimes named, but in a subtle sense there is some reason for so calling it. Out of the old clash between a growing sense of nationality and the old persistent feeling of dependence on Europe came a newer spirit of self-reliance. Troops from East and West, city and frontier, fought together and won victories—bumbling and bickering and defeats were easy to forget. The lingering sense of inferiority disappeared in the waving folds of Francis Scott Key's "Star Spangled Banner," and Americans could tell themselves that they had met and defeated (or at least had not been defeated by) the world's greatest military and naval power. The war knit the nation together. "It has renewed," said Albert Gallatin, who served in Jefferson's cabinet, "and reinstated the national feeling and character which the Revolution had given, and which were daily lessening. The people now have more general objects of attachment. . . . They are more Americans, they feel and act more as a nation."

The Search for a National Culture

As the United States took on political shape and stability, Americans sought to evolve a culture of their own. Having gained political independence, they searched for a unique and personal way of expressing (in literature, drama, and the arts) the fundamentals of their Americanism. There were "two things wanted," Royall Tyler wrote in the preface to *The Algerine Captive* (1797)—"that we write our own books of amusement, and that they exhibit our own manners." The United States was the cultural heir of Britain and Europe; bearing in on the new republic was the great legacy of Western, Christian, classical tradition that it shared with the Old World. The American problem was how to choose from this powerful heritage those things that might delineate and exemplify the American way of life. No American in his right mind wished to cut himself off from his cultural inheritance; but how might he make it his own, rather than something borrowed or transferred?

Immediately after the Revolution, critics, editors, and authors agreed on the need for a native, original, indigenous art. "We are called to sing a New Song," said Nathaniel Appleton, "A Song that neither We nor our Fathers were ever able to sing before." "America must be as independent in *literature*," wrote that indefatigable nationalist Noah Webster, "as she is in *politics.*" Since any valid cultural achievement must grow out of "difference of country, of habits, and of institutions," Edward Channing wrote in his essay *On Models in Literature* (1816), a *distinctively* American literature must cultivate the unique American condition and express its distinctive qualities. A nation of free men, everyone assumed, would naturally produce great art; it was highly probable, predicted David Ramsay in 1794, ". . . that the free government of America will produce poets, orators, critics, and historians equal to the most celebrated of the ancient commonwealths of Greece and Italy." John Trumbull put the same thought into couplets:

This land her Swift and Addison shall view,
The former honors equalled by the new;
Here shall some Shakespeare charm the rising age,
And hold in magic chain the listening stage. . . .

Dozens of similar exhortations and predictions rang through the journals after 1783.

Problems and Obstacles

It was not so easy to produce great art on demand. No Swifts, Addisons, or Shakespeares suddenly appeared to answer Trumbull's prophecy. Some critics pointed out that the tendency to hail any ambitious bard (and there were dozens) as a new Milton or Homer was likely to do no more than encourage bad poetry. Joseph Dennie, the acerbic editor of *The Portfolio,* warned zealous young writers that to be national, however laudable, was not necessarily to be good; Noah Webster himself agreed that enthusiastic patriotism was not a substitute for authentic talent.

The production of the native American literature demanded and heralded by the critics labored under certain handicaps. For one thing, a great deal of the creative energy of the period was diverted into business and politics. There was, no doubt, as large a percentage of men of talent in the United States as in any other nation, but with a state to construct and a continent to exploit, here was far too much to do to expend effort in making poems. The emergence of party warfare, culminating in the Federalist-Antifederalist battles of the 1780s and early 1800s; the problems of foreign policy raised by post-Revolutionary relations with Britain, by the French Revolution, and the War of 1812; the struggle over the Articles and the Constitution—these and other issues of the turbulent decades that lay between Yorktown and the era of "good feelings" demanded the full attention of the nation's best minds.

Then, too, one of the reasons Americans had wanted independence was to be able to manufacture, trade, and therefore make profit in foreign and domestic markets without interference, and the new nation was filled with young businessmen ardently doing exactly that. Politics and commerce, Samuel Miller explained in his *Retrospect of the Eighteenth Century* (1802), often stifled culture, diverting it into nonartistic channels. It was very difficult in his times, remarked John Quincy Adams, "to be a man of business and a man of rime"; bank shares and epics, Joel Barlow said, did not mix.

Furthermore, there were those who doubted that a society built on the principle of equality could ever support a significant culture. Was not democracy more likely to produce a kind of diffused mediocrity? "The spirit of democracy," editorialized the *Boston Anthology* in 1807, "blasts everything beautiful in nature and corrodes everything in art." A more serious problem, as Washington Irving pointed out a few years later, was that the United States lacked "the charms of storied and poetical association . . . the accumulated treasures of age." America had no usable past to stir the artist's fancy, "no annals for the historian . . . ," James Fenimore Cooper wrote later in *Notions of the Americans* (1828), "no manners for the dramatist, no obscure fictions for the writer of romance . . . nor any of the rich artificial auxiliaries of poetry."

Other quite practical problems confronted the aspiring novelist, poet, or critic. The United States had no tradition of literary patronage among the wealthy, and there were very few artists and writers who had the personal resources needed for a full-time career. America lacked an audience of both the size and perception necessary for the professional literary man, who must, as Freneau told his fellow poets, "graft his authorship upon some other calling." For this reason, young men of artistic talent often drifted off into other pursuits and gave up writing—as John Trumbull, whose gifts were undeniable, turned to law instead of poetry in his early thirties. In the United States, books were produced chiefly, John Pickering wrote in 1816, "by men, who were obliged to depend upon other employments for their support, and who could devote to literary pursuits those few moments only, which their thirst for learning, stimulated them to snatch from their daily avocations." For this reason, young Henry Wadsworth Longfellow's father warned him against being a poet, for, as he told his son, "there is not wealth and munificence enough in this country to afford sufficient encouragement and patronage to merely literary men."

There was also the practical matter of the lack of an adequate copyright law in the United States. As late as 1830 only one book in every three came from an American press. An American writer of the early nineteenth century found his market thin indeed, as he was in competition with cheap (or pirated) reprints of English authors. Such competition was, of course, formidable, for it included not only the great English masters of the past but new popular writers such as Burns, Scott, Jane Austen, and later the fashionable Romantic poets. An English novel, for example, cost the American purchaser only half of its London price; a typical circulating library list of 1804 showed over 2,000 English and French titles.

American readers, John Adams wrote with some justification, were "disposed to encourage a thousand foolish republications from Europe rather than one Useful work of their own growth." Anxious to locate the obstacles to native literature, *The Monthly Register and Review of the United States* published in 1807 a survey of reasons given by the critics. This included "a comparatively thin population" without "a sufficient quantity of wealth to create a demand for costly books"; "easy means and abundant sources of personal revenue" in trade and agriculture that drew men away from letters; a "scarcity of public libraries" and a "want of literary awards and honors"; defects in public education; the problems of copyright; and the government's failure to encourage and patronize writers.

Yet the outlook for the American author was not wholly bleak. He wrote for a relatively well-educated public, and in America, unlike Europe, the habit of reading books was not restricted to the upper classes; Americans, an observer remarked as early as 1772, had a taste for books "that made almost every man a reader." Boston in the 1770s had fifty bookstores, Philadelphia had thirty or more, and the spread of circulating libraries across the Colonies in the eighteenth century made books available everywhere in surprising quantity. By 1825, it was calculated, the libraries of New York, Boston, Philadelphia, and Baltimore had more than twenty times as many books to lend as the entire nation had owned in 1800.

American writers understandably lacked self-confidence, often preferring to accept the fashionable and avoid the untried. Sydney Smith, the English critic, advised them to give up their nationalistic nonsense, and "make it their chief boast . . . that they are sprung from the same race with Bacon and Shakespeare and Newton." With all their trying, Smith wrote in his famous sneer that rang through the States, "Who reads an American book?" Despite all the demands for "fresh, new literature," readers and writers alike hesitated to depart from British and European standards. It was safer to imitate Pope (on whose eminence everyone agreed) or Scott (who was generally conceded to be the greatest novelist of all time) than to strike out in new directions. James Kirke Paulding, in his poem *The Backwoodsman* (1818), whose subject matter was deliberately American, voiced the American author's plaint:

Neglected Muse of this our Western clime,
How long in servile, imitative rime,
Wilt thou thy stifled energies enchain,
And tread the worn-out path still o'er again!

The Literary Predicament

The American writer faced a real dilemma. The flow of models and ideas from England and Europe was difficult to resist. It gave him—virtually forced upon him—manner, method, meaning, and symbol with which American nature, the American past, and American society did not fit. How could one properly put the Indian into the "noble savage" tradition, or put American experience and materials into the Gothic tradition of Walpole, the journalistic narrative of Defoe, the primitivism of Ossian, the medievalism of Scott, or the manners-comedy of Jane Austen, when it was clear that they did not belong there? How could the American writer find meanings applicable to his experience from the body of conventional English and European symbols—lakes, mountains, birds, flowers, castles, villages, and so on —when it was obvious that they were simply not the same on this side of the Atlantic? No one was quite sure of how to use the old literary heritage and combine it with the new American experience. Two sets of answers emerged after 1800, both assuming that American literature should be *American,* but differing in how that quality of Americanism should be obtained.

One group advised choosing the best English models but using American characters, settings, and ideas, producing literature to English standards written by Americans. Judge Parsons of Boston told Harvard students that an American author ought to cultivate a thorough knowledge of the English masters to give his own work "an elevated tone" and to assimilate "something of their speed and impetus." Fisher Ames ridiculed the pretensions of the literary nationalists, writing that "national claims ought to be abandoned as worthless the moment they are found to need asserting."

The other group, convinced that American nature could never be forced into the classical-pastoral tradition, that American society could never be interpreted in English-aristocratic terms, and that American ideas could never be expressed by the symbols of an outworn, feudal Europe, demanded a completely American art—in style, form, manner, language.

Choices and Resources

The first step toward cultural independence, of course, was to declare America's freedom from English and European domination. But after having declared this freedom, critics wondered what should be selected from the great body of

British and Continental literature, which, after all, no American could or should complètely reject. This was a difficult problem, one which critics of the 1790s and early 1800s discussed endlessly. They more or less agreed upon two principles of selection. First, American artists must exercise great care in following foreign models, lest they destroy their own native genius. Let there be, warned Webster, "no servile imitation of the language, manners, and vices of foreigners." Second, they must reject anything in any foreign culture that was immoral, untrue, or subversive of American principles. As Barlow wrote in *The Columbiad,* Americans might profitably learn from English or European writers whose works were "true and useful," but must avoid all "false and destructive ones that have degraded the species in other countries." The writer, in the opinion of Andrews Norton, who spoke for the next generation, "must present no deceptive portrait of our moral nature; he must show what is good as good, and what is evil as evil." For this reason, many American critics were uneasy with authors like Goethe (whose work Alexander Everett found immoral) and Byron, whom W. H. Prescott regarded as "lawless . . . affected, violent, morbid," unacceptable "both on the ground of moral and literary pretensions."

Simply to abstain from imitating the Old World, of course, was not sufficient to create an indigenous, Americanized culture. To originate an "American style" in literature required the construction of a body of positive principles; the American author must have something American to write about and a defined, recognizably native manner of writing it. It was true, as Timothy Dwight admitted, that the United States lacked "ancient castles, ruined abbeys, and fine pictures," but on the other hand, the American artist possessed a wealth of resources that the British or European did not. Let him, then, realize, count, and utilize his literary blessings.

First of all, the American artist had the Indian and the frontier. Those who had first-hand experience with the red man tended to doubt his compatibility with poetry, yet the whole story of the conquest of the frontier and the Indian wars was an undeniably great literary resource. Charles Brockden Brown, in the preface to his novel *Edgar Huntly* (1799), suggested that "the incidents of Indian hostility and the perils of the Western wilderness" provided material far superior to anything British novelists possessed, while James Kirke Paulding in 1817 directed the attention of American writers to the "active, hardy, vigilant, enterprising, fearless" frontiersman as prime subject matter for novelists—as James Fenimore Cooper soon proved.

Second, the United States did have a history of its own, a brief but significant and eminently usable past. "Thy native land is big with mighty scenes," Mercy Warren told the young poets of 1782, while the *North American Review,* in 1817, assured young writers that the promise of American history was "infinite, its characters innumerable, and the scenery of its places full of beauty and grandeur." The Revolution, in particular, provided authors with subject matter of great dramatic, epic, and narrative possibilities, populated with heroes and villains. Every author of note made at least one attempt, after 1790, to use American history in a major work. Cooper's novel *The Spy* (1821) was not the first of its kind but the conclusion of thirty years of apprenticeship in the American war novel.

Third, there were many aspiring authors who agreed with the dramatist James Nelson Barker that American writers possessed ample materials for distinguished studies of manners in "the events, customs, opinions, and characters of American life." Irving and Cooper did not wholly agree—"I have never seen," Cooper said, "a nation so much alike, in my life, as the people of the United States"—but others hoped for an American Jane Austen. William Cullen Bryant, in his review of Catherine Sedgwick's novel *Redwood,* felt that American society displayed "an infinite variety of pursuits and subjects, [an] endless diversity and change of fortunes . . . ," and that all one needed to exploit it was "sagacity and skill."

The fourth category of available artistic material was, of course, American nature itself—vast, unspoiled, fascinating in its variety and grandeur. Though America might lack "storied and poetical associations," Irving admitted, it possessed a matchless "simple beauty" and "wild magnificence" that Europe never had.

American nature was rich in "magnificent spectacles," "immense vistas," and "sublime beauty," to use the critical vocabulary of the day. The Delaware, the Hudson, the Ohio, the Mississippi were as inspiring as the Tweed or the Thames, not simply because they were bigger. The robin, the whipoorwill, the mockingbird, the wild honeysuckle, and the daisy were equally worthy of poetry as any English skylark or daffodil. "Oak and elm," wrote Joseph Dennie, "are as good wood to supply poetical fire as cypress and yew."

The quest for an American art was fundamentally a search for the proper way to use the resources of the American land, the American past, and American society to produce something aesthetically correct, morally true, and at the same time expressive of American life and ideals. It would eventuate, Paulding said, in an art that arose out of the "feelings, associations, attachments, and associations of the people at large."

To create this literature, the writer must confront the United States clearly and directly; he must "examine objects with his own eyes," wrote novelist Charles Brockden Brown, "employ European models merely for the improvement of his taste," and build his art out of "all that is genuine and peculiar in the scene before him." To discover what critic John Neal called "the abundant and hidden sources of fertility in our own brave earth" was, then, the aim of this first generation of American artists.

The Second "Awakening" in Religion

By 1800, after decades of apathy and bickering, the shock of war, and the confusions of postwar social and economic readjustment, American Protestant churches were ripe for a revival of religious piety. Ministers in the postwar years generally agreed American Christianity to be in "a low and declining state." As in the period prior to the Great Awakening of the 1740s, many churchmen felt a sense of failure and irrelevance. The threat of French Revolutionary radicalism and of "rational" religion, the division of the nation into warring political factions, the temptations of material wealth and the restiveness of the younger generation seemed all to be parts of a general national moral disintegration. The Methodist Church, in 1795, for example, called for a resumption of national fast days to pray for relief of "our manifold sins and iniquities . . . our covetousness and the prevailing love of the world . . . profanation of the Sabbath . . . disobedience to parents, the various debaucheries, drunkenness, and such like." The Presbyterian Assembly of 1798 noted "with pain and fearful apprehension a general dereliction of religious principles and practice among our citizens, a visible and prevailing impiety."

Church buildings had been destroyed by war, congregations split, parishes disbanded. New Salem, Massachusetts, had no church services at all for twenty years; of New York City's nineteen churches, the Reverend John Rodgers reported, ten were unfit for use in 1784. Severance of connections between church and state, as provided in the new state constitutions, encouraged uneasiness and a proliferation of sects, while postwar financial inflation made support of his church difficult for the ordinary man.

There was also, as many ministers noted, a disturbing interest in those "infidel doctrines" that, wrote the Reverend Timothy Dwight, "are vomited upon us from France, Germany, and Great Britain." Church membership declined, particularly among younger people. At William and Mary, William Hill reported "rudeness, ribaldry, and infidelity" among the students, and a visitor to Princeton in 1799 found only a few undergraduates who "made any pretensions to piety."

The rebirth of revivalism, later called by historians the "Second Great Awakening," appeared first in New England in the 1790s; it was welcomed by the clergy as a providential weapon against postwar apathy and infidelity. Though Baptist and Methodist evangelicals were never really accepted by the orthodox churches, they gained hundreds of converts and sparked a resurgence of religious fervor throughout New England. Revivalist techniques, worked out in the earlier Awakening and since perfected in England, fired enthusiasm in the churches with what

Timothy Dwight observed suspiciously as "that strange new-birth, that Methodistic grace."

There was, however, a new element in the national picture not present in the 1740s—the West. There was fear in Eastern churches that this new country might be lost to infidelity and barbarism and a growing conviction that missionaries must go to the new settlements to battle Satan on his own ground. While the Second Great Awakening was certainly a reaction against Enlightenment rationalism and declining churchly influence, it was also a theological drive to the West, in order to secure this new and potentially powerful segment of the nation for ortho-dox Protestantism. The churches had several objectives, there-fore, during the Second Awakening—to reassert orthodox reli-gious and moral standards, to counteract apathy and rationalism, to awaken the nation to the dangers of wealth and worldliness, and most of all, to convert and control the West.

The wave of evangelism rolled swiftly westward and south-ward. Revivalists such as James McGready and Barton Stone car-ried the flame of "old time religion," with torchlit camp meet-ings, shouting, singing, hysteria, and other stigmata of sudden public conversion, through the Carolinas into Kentucky and Tennessee. From the mountainous Southwest it spread west and north into the lower fringes of Ohio, Indiana, Michigan, and Illinois, striking impartially into all churches. In 1811, Methodist Bishop Francis Asbury counted 400 revivals, mostly in the South and West. Methodists and Baptists, accustomed to emotionalism, welcomed the evangelistic torchbearers eagerly. Presbyterians sometimes hung back, and Congregationalists often opposed them, but revivalism flourished nonetheless.

A typical revival or "camp meeting" began on a Thursday or Friday and sometimes lasted until the following Tuesday, with continuous preaching, praying, and singing by the light of bon-fires at night. The largest meeting was probably that at Cain Ridge, Kentucky, in 1801, where nearly 20,000 people gathered for a week in fervent hysterical worship, urged on by Baptist, Methodist, and Presbyterian exhorters. A witness wrote of the

Cain Ridge meeting that there were at one time more than a hundred "sinners" laid out in rows, struck dumb by their sense of sinfulness, while "the solemn hymns, the impassioned exhortations, the earnest prayers, and the sobs, shrieks, or shouts bursting from persons under intense agitation" surged about them. The Second Awakening shook orthodoxy on its already unsteady foundations, broke up into an astonishing variety of new schismatic sects, and left the Baptists and Methodists the undisputed masters of the West. From it came the Christian Church, the Campbellites, the United Brethren, the Rappites, and many other sects.

The evangelical sects were loosely organized, flexible in creed, simple in theology. They stressed religious elements particularly appropriate to the frontier—emotionalism, personal conversion, directness—and emphasized the importance of the individual in religion rather than church or creed. The itinerant evangelist made theology a personal and communal matter; revivals were social as well as religious events. Bishop Francis Asbury, the superb administrator and organizer who introduced into the West the "circuit rider" system used by the Wesleys in England, found it perfectly adapted to the scattered settlements, just as Baptists found their "lay preacher" system equally well suited. Asbury, who traveled over 300,000 miles in the saddle himself, sent hundreds of circuit-riding ministers, like the redoubtable Peter Cartwright, into remote backwoods areas, creating a string of Methodist outposts. The evangelical churches more or less captured the lower Northwest and the Southwest and began to push far into the New England-settled Great Lakes area.

The Impact on American Life

The Second Awakening had two quite strong and lasting effects on American churches and their position in American society. First of all, it meant that the Methodists and Baptists became the two most powerful American sects. During the period from 1800 to 1830, Methodist membership increased sevenfold, Presbyterian quadrupled, Baptist tripled, and Congregational doubled. The Methodists gained 6,000 new members in the Western Conference in two years during the height of revivalism, and the Baptists added 10,000 to their rolls in Kentucky alone in three years. Presbyterian gains, while large, were more than offset by the divisions and schisms that beset them.

Second, the Awakening meant that the United States, despite the shocks of eighteenth-century rationalism and "infidelity," remained predominantly a religious-minded nation with an emotional, pietistic, moralistic spirit that would color its social, political, and economic thinking for generations to come. The shrewd French traveler Alexis de Tocqueville noted this primary fact of American life in 1831 after the Awakening had run its course. "There is no country in the world," he wrote, "in which the Christian religion retains a greater hold over the souls of men than in America. . . . Religion is the foremost of the institutions of the country."

In addition, the Second Awakening also exerted forceful secondary influences on nineteenth-century society and politics. There was a close connection, contemporary observers believed, between the extension of revivalism and the improvement of moral standards in frontier communities. The Reverend David Rice, for example, noted in 1803 that after evangelical meetings in Kentucky there was a great deal less drunkenness, swearing, and profligacy, with many communities "remarkably reformed." Missionary preachers, camp meetings, and the churches that followed them were (with the schools) powerful moral forces in a society where whiskey was cheap, violence common, and restrictions of sexual activity casual. The Methodist Discipline contained a code of conduct which Methodists were expected to follow to the letter, and the Quarterly Methodist Conference functioned as moral courts for ministers and members who violated it. Baptist conferences meted out stiff discipline to members for major and minor sins ranging from adultery to horse racing, while western Presbyterian presbyteries and Congregational congregations punished their recalcitrants in much the same way.

Politically, the evangelism of the Awakening reflected and

helped to shape the democratizing trends of the era. There were many factors involved in the rise of Jacksonian democracy, but as early as 1800 political observers noted that Methodists and Baptists usually leaned toward anti-Federalist politics, and that Jefferson's ministerial supporters seemed to be chiefly in evangelical pulpits. Baptists and Methodists formed the bulk of Jeffersonian strength in New England, while missionaries in the West found "strongly democratic" trends among the evangelical congregations of Kentucky and Tennessee. Significantly, revivalist preachers made the amusements and vices of the wealthy and conservative into sins—card playing, horse racing, dancing, billiards, gambling, cockfighting, theatergoing—giving morality a class bias that had obvious political connotations. Frontier preachers, writes W. W. Sweet, "brought home to the pioneers the fact that they were masters of their own destiny, an emphasis that fitted in exactly with the new democracy rising in the West, for both emphasized the actual equality among men." They emphasized ideas of individual worth, personal responsibility, and the equality of believers, opposed institutional rigidity and class distinctions, and had little regard for dogma and authority in either religion or politics. It was no accident that the areas "burned over" by the fires of the Second Great Awakening later supported Andrew Jackson.

Magazines and Editors

A factor in the development of American belleslettres was the expansion of printing and publishing in the post-1800 decades. By 1810, there were at least 200 paper mills in the nation and commercial presses in all of the larger towns and many smaller ones. American presses could print any kind of book that London could; printshops had evolved efficient methods, and the introduction of new machinery, such as the Columbian Iron Press (1807), increased production a hundredfold. Booksellers and printers turned into publishers—the houses of Wiley, Harper, and Carey all appeared before 1820—and magazines proliferated. To American authors and critics, the growth of the magazine was of special importance, for they (though their average life was less than twenty months) provided outlets never before available for essays, fiction, poetry, and literary criticism.

Seventy-one magazines were founded between 1786 and 1800, according to Frank Luther Mott, and several hundred more between 1800 and 1830. Like their British counterparts, they tended to be small, usually about sixty-four pages, with perhaps three-quarters of the material reprinted from other magazines. Some contributed little of importance to the American literary scene, but others, edited by skilled and able men, not only encouraged but actively solicited original materials from the best American writers. The Boston *Massachusetts Magazine,* for example, which ran for eight years (1789–1797), published history, Congressional summaries, obituaries, marriages, and general news, and also poetry, plays, stories, and music. Among the better journals were Josiah Meigs' *New Haven Gazette and the Connecticut Magazine;* Boston's *Monthly Anthology* (forerunner of the *North American Review*); the *Boston Weekly Magazine,* which specialized in drama and fiction; the *New York Weekly Magazine;* the Baltimore *Portico;* and New York's *Analectic Magazine,* which Irving edited for two years. Charles Brockden Brown edited two magazines in New York and two in Philadelphia; Noah Webster's *American Magazine* originated the "Review of New Publications" column and especially invited contributions "such as relate to this country . . . or remarks upon . . . the institutions and customs of the people, in the different states."

Matthew Carey, of Philadelphia, an Irish immigrant who arrived in 1784, founded *The American Museum* (1787–1792), a pot-pourri of reprints and thefts, which Carey aimed at the public taste. However, the *Museum* also printed more than 500 poems, among them Trumbull's *M'Fingal,* and such things as Boone's "Autobiography," the text of the Constitution, and William Hill Brown's novel *The Power of Sympathy.* Carey also turned bookseller and publisher, remaining active to his death in 1839. He published not only Mrs. Rowson but Webster, Freneau, Irving, and later Poe and Simms, as well as "Miss Porter, Lord Byron, Miss Edgeworth, W. Scott, Leigh Hunt, Tom Moore, Miss Burney, etc. etc. . . . ," becoming one of the most successful and important publishers in the nation.

Joseph Dennie of Philadelphia, whose "Farrago" and "Lay Preacher" series (1792, 1796) placed him among the foremost American essayists, edited *The Portfolio,* probably the best of the literary periodicals, from 1801 to his death in 1812. A conservative Federalist in political and literary matters, Dennie served his era well as a critic and an arbiter of taste. He refused to praise poor work because it was "native," and by stressing excellence over patriotism furnished a useful antidote to some of the spread-eagle demands for quick epics and "national" novels. Himself a Shakespearian scholar, Dennie reprinted a great many of the English and European classics as well as such new poets as Campbell, Moore, and Leigh Hunt; he also published Charles Brockden Brown and was the first American editor to introduce Wordsworth and Coleridge to the public. A precise and opinionated critic, Dennie demanded high standards, and for more than a decade, when American literature was tentatively developing its own critical theory, his influence was strong.

The Creation of Folk Types

At about the time of the Revolution, Americans began to center their interest on folk materials on themselves. Tales of witches and the supernatural began to lose appeal to a more sophisticated and enlightened generation. The Indian tribes, defeated in the East, no longer posed a threat to settled country; stories of captivity, torture, and war merged into novel and drama. The matter of traditional folk tales, imported and adapted to the American locale, attracted Americans less than their own characters, types, and regional cultures. The struggle to make an independent nation crystallized a sense of native identity that, as Richard Dorson has shown, encouraged the development of a new set of American folk types suited to a new and native kind of American folk literature.

The first of these was the "backwoods roarer," who began to appear in folk stories in the 1780s as a "half horse, half alligator," who might be a wagoner, boatman, scout, or hunter—tough, boasting, aggressive, crude, cruel, independent. Books by foreign travelers—Michaux in 1804, Janson in 1807, Schultz in 1808, for example—nearly always repeated stories about these "frontier gamecocks," while newspaper or almanac anecdotes about them were common by 1810. Playwrights found the type immensely popular, and with the appearance of Mike Fink (an actual person who died about 1823) in Neville's *Last of the Boatmen* (1828) and the publication of Davy Crockett's *Narrative* (1834) it was firmly established in American popular literature.

After the turn of the century, the figure of the foreigner began to appear in folk stories, reflecting the American's increased consciousness of his uniqueness and his own national characteristics. The dialects and curious ways of Dutchmen, Irishmen, Englishmen, and others made them excellent subjects for anecdotes, as Irving found when he created "Diedrich Knickerbocker." H. H. Brackenridge, in using a comic Irishman named Teague O'Regan, complete with brogue, in his novel *Modern Chivalry,* likewise followed popular folk patterns, and the fact that William Dunlap (who knew public tastes well) put a Yankee, a Negro, a Frenchman, a Dutchman, an Irishman, and an Englishman into his play *A Trip to Niagara* in 1828 shows how familiar these character stereotypes had become by that time.

More important for literary purposes was the creation of the Yankee—the slick, shrewd, commonsense, rural bumpkin who emerged as a staple figure in fiction, drama, song, and folk tale after 1800. Americans possessed, of course, a long tradition of rogue tales brought from Europe into which the Yankee fitted, but he was soon thoroughly nativized. Madam Knight saw his prototype, "a tall country fellow, with his alfogeous full of tobacco," in Connecticut on her trip to New York in 1705, and he emerged fully developed in folk literature within the next century. The folk Yankee usually appeared in two guises—the slick rogue who sold wooden nutmegs to the gullible or the rustic simpleton. The shrewd Yankee peddler was a stock figure in newspaper and almanac anecdotes (many copied out of English jest books), while the country boy come to camp in "Yankee Doodle" represented him in his other manifestation.

Whatever his costume, the Yankee remained the most important folk figure in America for the next century. (For that matter, he survives in the "Toby shows," which still tour the Midwest.) Royall Tyler's "Jonathan," played by the great comedian Wignell in 1787, was the first of a succession of stage Yankees. James Nelson Barker's *Tears and Smiles* (1807) had "Nathan Yank"; Tyler tried to repeat his success with *A Yankey in London* in 1809 and *A Yankey in England* in 1815; Samuel Woodworth's hit play of 1825, *A Forest Rose,* presented "Jonathan Ploughboy." Alphonso Wetmore's *The Pedlar* (1821) not only had a Yankee but a "backwoods roarer," a combative boatman, a funny foreigner, a comic sailor, and added another folk hero, the "Old Continental," or Revolutionary veteran. The Yankee was almost as popular in fiction. Paulding used "Brother Jonathan" as his essay commentator, while Irving immortalized him as Ichabod Crane. He appeared in fifteen books before 1830 when Seba Smith's "Major Jack Downing" set the pattern for the character who persists as "Uncle Sam."

The half-century or so after the close of the Revolution saw a growing tradition of folk humor and folk tale, more indigenously American than before, containing within it three new character types—the rough frontiersman, the Yankee, and certain nationality and racial figures from the melting pot of immigration. These, added to the great stock of folk materials inherited from the past, helped to form a great reservoir from which the humorists, regionalists, and realists of the nineteenth century could draw.

Pamphlet Warfare and The Federalist

Pamphlets continued to provide a convenient channel for the expression of ideas after the Revolution. After independence was won, there were still many things that Americans had to say, and there was no less controversy after the war than before. Discussions of theology, politics, philanthropy, taxes, reform, education, and scores of other topics elicited hundreds of these little books, some notable, many not. Anthony Benezet, a French-born Philadelphia Quaker, wrote tracts on the slave trade, temperance, the Indian, Quaker doctrine, and many other topics; Ethan Allen, the tough Vermont soldier, wrote a highly controversial deistic tract, *Reason the Only Oracle of Man* (1784), which Timothy Dwight called the "first formal publication in the United States, openly directed against the Christian religion." Dr. Benjamin Rush of Philadelphia, the ranking American medical scientist, wrote pamphlets on capital punishment, the study of classical languages, education, war, biography, and slavery. Throughout the period, the pamphlet remained a useful and widely popular vehicle for introducing issues to the public.

The argument over the Constitution brought a flood of these pamphlets, second in number only to those produced by the Revolution. The campaign for and against its adoption by the states, which lasted for twenty months through 1787–1789, involved the first full-scale examination of the basic principles of the new American government. Much was at stake, for the change of direction proposed by the Constitution—from a confederated to a nationalized state—was a fundamental one. To adopt or reject the document written at Philadelphia, as Richard Henry Lee said, was a crucial decision for "ages and millions yet unborn," and the debates over it drew the best minds in the nation into them.

The proposed Constitution emerged from the Philidelphia Convention on September 27, 1787, and was to be effective as soon as nine of the thirteen states ratified it. Those who opposed it were neither against liberty nor for anarchy; they distrusted the kind of centralized government suggested at Philadelphia and argued with some justice that the Convention had far exceeded its original charge to improve the Articles of Confederation. Those who approved the document believed with equal sincerity that the kind of government represented by the Articles had failed and could in no way be adapted to the future needs of the Republic.

Ratification proceeded fairly swiftly in the smaller states; by January 1788 five states (Delaware, New Jersey, Georgia, Connecticut, and Pennsylvania) had ratified. In Massachusetts, the sixth state, the struggle was long and hard, with ratification succeeding only after a close vote. Maryland and South Carolina followed, and the ninth state, New Hampshire, finally ratified on June 21, 1788. Legally, the Constitution was in force, although it was obvious that without the approval of the two powerful states of New York and Virginia it could never successfully operate.

In New York State, Governor George Clinton led the opposition. To counteract Clinton and his supporters, Alexander Hamilton asked John Jay of New York, and James Madison of Virginia to assist him in writing a series of essays explaining and defending the new instrument of government. (William Duer also contributed two papers, which are not usually included with the series.)

Jay, a wealthy New York lawyer who had served as Secretary of Foreign Affairs under the Articles, had written much of the New York State Constitution. Madison, known best for his part in the Philadelphia Convention, was a sound legal and political scholar. Hamilton's attendance at the Convention had been irregular and his influence not large; he was known best in New York for his political acumen and organizational skill. Despite their collaboration, the three men were not wholly agreed in their political principles. Jay was a strong conservative, Madison a Virginia liberal, and Hamilton a convinced nationalist, but they did agree on the necessity of adopting the Constitution if the nation was to survive.

The Federalist series, numbering eithty-five papers in all, appeared between October 1787 and April 1788. Hamilton probably wrote about fifty-one, Madison twenty-six, and Jay five, while three were joint efforts of Madison and Hamilton. Jay fell ill and dropped out of the series shortly after it began; Madison left New York for home in March 1788 and contributed no papers after that. The central argument of the series was that the Articles did not provide the national government with sufficient authority to maintain liberty, security, and property; and that the Constitution, which remedied those deficiencies, ought to be adopted in its place.

While *The Federalist* series was undoubtedly influential in consolidating support for the Constitutional forces, not a little of the outcome in New York was due to the skill of Hamilton and his fellow politicians. Even so, the margin of victory in New York in July 1788 was breathtakingly small (30–27), and the Convention, in approving the document, demanded, as several other states had done, that a bill of rights be attached to it.

The Federalist was, of course, a purely partisan project, which was never intended to be an objective presentation of general political principles. Written in haste for quite practical reasons, it nevertheless made its point directly, without undue appeal to prejudice or emotion, that to be free men must govern themselves, to govern themselves they must have order and stability, and that to have order and stability they must adopt a set of rules by which all abide. Some of the papers are muddy, hasty, and repetitious; others, such as Madison's X or Hamilton's XXVIII on judicial review, are political classics. Beyond the specifics of the Constitutional debate, *The Federalist* identified and discussed with clarity and skill certain fundamental political truths of paramount importance—the function of pressure groups, the economic motivations of political life, the persistence of human self-interest, the psychology of mass politics, the continuous struggle of many against few. The series not only furnished the best analysis of the new government, but marked the high point of the American pamphleteering tradition.

The brilliance of *The Federalist* and its influence on the vote of a decisive state have tended, however, to obscure the equal brilliance displayed by others in the battle of the pamphlets. Among those who wrote in support of ratification were such men as Edmund Randolph, H. H. Brackenridge, Tenche Coxe, Noah Webster, James Iredell, James Wilson, and John Dickinson (whose essays in particular deserve reading). The anti-Federalists had their own luminaries, among them Albert Gallatin, James Monroe, Luther Martin, and George Mason. Elbridge Gerry, writing as "A Columbian Patriot"; Governor George Clinton, as "Cato"; and the "Brutus Letters" (possibly by Robert Yates of New York) are effective replies to *The Federalist* and are not inferior to it. Richard Henry Lee's *Letters of a Federal Farmer* (1787–1788), which went through four editions in three months, bears comparison with the best political writing of the era. A classically trained Virginia lawyer, Lee wrote a clear, spare style with a ring of conviction, and his pamphlet series merits more recognition than it has received within the tradition of American political prose.

The Constitutional controversy marked the last appearance of the pamphlet as a significant literary form in America. Campaigns, elections, and issues of a religious or social nature continued to generate pamphlets, though never again at the level of excellence represented by the Federalist–anti-Federalist debate. The growth of newspapers and magazines after 1800 and the introduction of the cheap printed book furnished better ways of transmitting ideas and information to the public in swift and simple form. Not until the arguments over slavery and union were put forth a half-century later, did the pamphlet again appear, and then in different guise and at a quite different level of communication.

Discovering American History

The success of the Revolution and the founding of the new government invigorated American historical writing. As Benjamin Trumbull wrote after the war, it was "the desire of many pious men, that the remarkable deliverances which the United States of America had experienced might be fully exhibited to the public, in a tribute of praise for the Great Deliverer, and for the instruction of posterity." Many historians were anxious to tell the story. The Revolution seemed to Americans to be an event of the utmost significance in the history of the world;

therefore, the events that led up to it, the war itself, and its meaning for the future had to be analyzed, explored, and interpreted. Since the Colonies had joined in a common effort to create a *nation,* its history ought to be written in *national* terms. Not that the histories of the states were to be neglected—each had its own past and each deserved to be considered as a part of the whole, but as Jeremy Belknap (who wrote a history of New Hampshire) believed, studies of the states would "lay a good foundation" for the general history of America that someone would undoubtedly write in the near future.

Much of the early historical activity centered in the states. Robert Proud's *History of Pennsylvania* (written from 1776 to 1780 and published from 1797 to 1798), by a Quaker who disapproved of war, was solemn though informative. Isaac Backus, a Baptist minister, combined a history of New England and the Baptist Church in two volumes in 1777 and 1784; Ezra Stiles of Yale collected materials for a history of New England over twenty years but never wrote it, leaving his manuscripts to his son-in-law, Abiel Holmes. Benjamin Trumbull wrote *A Complete History of Connecticut* (1797, 1818) from his own collections; Hannah Adams worked for years in colonial records before publishing her *History of New England* in 1799.

Samuel Peters and Alexander Hewatt, Loyalists who fled to England, published Tory-colored histories of Connecticut (1781) and of South Carolina and Georgia (1797). (Peters', a half-mocking satire, was a possible precursor of Irving's *Knickerbocker History.*) George Minot's *History of the Province of Massachusetts Bay* (1798), also Loyalist-flavored, continued Governor Hutchinson's earlier account. More eminent than any of these was the work of Jeremy Belknap, minister of Federal Street Church in Boston, whose *History of New Hampshire* (two volumes, 1784, 1791) was the best state history of the period. Belknap also wrote a series of historical essays, *The Foresters* (1792), and helped to found the first of the state historical societies, Massachusetts', in 1790.

"Parson" Weems and the Mythmaking Process

For a half-century after the Revolution, biography took the place of the national histories needed, but not yet written. Americans, long accustomed to looking to the lives of the eminent for guidance, possessed a sound biographical tradition more than a century old. No one doubted that the political and military heroes of the new nation would occupy important places in history, or that their lives and deeds would serve as inspirational examples for generations to come. Jeremy Belknap began a series of biographical sketches in 1789 under the title "The American Plutarch," which grew into the ambitious plan of writing brief studies of all great Americans from 1492 to the present. In 1794 he published the first volume of his *American Biography*, but he died in 1798 with the second in press. Others attempted to carry on his project, including John Eliot, a Boston minister, whose two-volume biographical dictionary (1801) was carelessly done and poorly written. William Allen, president of Dartmouth, published an *American Biographical Dictionary* in 1809, but the field of biography had already been preempted by the colorful and ubiquitous "Parson" Weems.

Mason Locke Weems was born in Maryland to a poor Scottish family. Little is known of his early years (Weems himself told more than one story), but he appeared in England in 1784 to be ordained an Anglican clergyman. He returned to America the same year to occupy a parish in Maryland and in 1791 began reprinting and selling books. After moving to Virginia in 1795, he took to the road as an itinerant book salesman, serving as agent for Matthew Carey, the Philadelphia publisher. Known as "Parson" Weems, he traveled up and down the Atlantic seaboard and in the backcountry for thirty-one years, carrying a portable bookcase, a fiddle, an inkhorn hung from his lapel, and a quill pen stuck in his hat.

A man of some education and a wide reader, Weems soon began to write books of his own. The death of Washington elicited a number of biographies, but Weems' *Life and Memorable*

Actions of George Washington (1800) was a runaway favorite, which eventually reached seventy editions. For new editions Weems merely added new materials; the famous cherry-tree story appeared in the fifth edition of 1806, was picked up for *McGuffey's Third Reader,* and entered immortality as an American legend.

Weems later wrote lives of General Francis Marion and Benjamin Franklin, neither of which ever approached the popularity of his *Washington.* A shrewd judge of public taste, he also wrote courtship and marriage handbooks, narratives of crime (done, of course, to illustrate "moral laws"), behavior books for children, and moral tracts. His biographical method was simple; since each important event in his subject's life contained a lesson for the reader, he first gave the fact, then pointed out the moral. If the necessary information was scanty, or if the right facts did not present themselves properly, he simply made them up. The result was usually more Weems than history, but was never dull or uninstructive. For better or worse he had tremendous influence on the American concept of the Revolution and its heroes—he remains one of the great mythmakers of American history. Scholars still find it difficult to modify the impressions he left on the public mind.

Interpreting the Revolution

The recent war naturally received the most historical attention. Many of its participants were still alive, and it had been, after all, as Noah Webster wrote, an event of tremendous importance "in its consequences for the human race." American historians immediately accepted the so-called "Whig" interpretation of the conflict, developed during the war by such British Whigs as Edmund Burke and Charles James Fox, who used it to discredit the party in power when they could. In the Whig view, the American Colonies, forced into war by stupid and tyrannical Parliamentary leaders, fought not only for their own rights but for those of Englishmen and mankind in general. Since the Revolutionary leaders had already used this particular version of events to vindicate independence (as Jefferson had in the Declaration), postwar historians felt they needed no other justification. In addition, they tended to see the conflict in Federalist terms—as the next-to-final act of national unity, followed logically by the adoption of the Constitution. The war "disseminated principles of union . . . ," wrote David Ramsay, "and a foundation was laid for the establishment of a nation." The Whig-Federalist point of view dominated American historical writing for the next century without serious challenge.

David Ramsay published *The History of the Revolution in South Carolina* (1785) and followed it with *The History of the American Revolution* in 1790. Ramsay, however, took a good deal of material for his second book from William Gordon's *History of the Rise, Progress, and Establishment of the United States of America* (1789). Gordon, who came to the Colonies in 1770, was the first to gain access to the papers of such men as Washington and Adams. Jedidiah Morse included a history of the war in the first edition of his famous *Geography* (1789); Noah Webster put accounts of it into his textbooks; Hannah Adams gave over half of her *Summary History of New England* (1799) to the Revolution.

Mercy Otis Warren's three-volume *History of the Rise, Progress, and Termination of the American Revolution* (1805) was perhaps the best. She began with the Stamp Act, which she regarded as the first in a chain of events leading to independence, thus setting a pattern common to Revolutionary histories for the next century. Since she was the close friend of John Adams, James Otis's sister, and the wife of a Revolutionary general, her books provided an unusual personal insight into the war. The Loyalist side of the conflict was never told. George Chalmers, a Maryland lawyer, who escaped to England in 1775, tried to tell it in his *Introduction to the History of the Colonies,* published in London in 1782, but his book did not appear in an American edition until sixty-three years later.

The Search for Historical Theory

Few writers attempted a complete history of the United States, none successfully. No one was quite sure how to begin such an important undertaking. Benjamin Trumbull planned a three-volume work to be called *A General History of the United States from the Discovery in 1492,* but he completed only the first. David Ramsay's *History of the United States from Its First Settlement,* published posthumously in 1816, remained unfinished as did his compendium of twelve volumes, *Universal History Americanized* (1819), "an historical view of the world from the earliest records to the nineteenth century, with particular deference to the state of society, literature, religion, and form of government" of the United States. Abiel Holmes, Oliver Wendell Holmes' father, brought out an outline of American history from Columbus' discovery to 1800, called *American Annals,* in 1805. Both Morse and Webster put brief historical sketches into their books, but curiously enough the only major historical study of American history as a unit done before 1820 was that of Christopher Ebeling; this was published in German in seven Teutonically thorough volumes in Germany between 1793 and 1816. Ebeling's work was excellent from a European point of view, but it was hardly American; his most valuable contribution was his collection of maps and documents, purchased by Harvard in 1818.

Possibly the most important reason for the tardiness of a *national* American history was the fact that neither of the two traditionally accepted theories of historical writing seemed to fit American needs. The seventeenth-century view of history as a chain of events, though old-fashioned, still had its adherents. The eighteenth century liked the chain analogy—George Thomson in 1791 spoke of history as "a chain consisting of many links, and to strike off one would be to discompose the whole." Others preferred the recent cyclical theory, which conceived of history as a series of cyclical movements and was based on the assumption that societies and nations rose and fell in endless sequences according to their observance or disregard of natural law—as in

Gibbon's *Decline and Fall of the Roman Empire,* the first volume of which appeared in 1776. John Adams, for example, remarked that "there is never a rising meridian without a setting sun," and Noah Webster noted that all nations "progress from their origins to maturity and decay."

Both "chain" and "cycle" theories, however, contained implications Americans found hard to accept. Neither theory placed much value on individual action; both were essentially pessimistic and deterministic. If all history was linked together by a chain of preordination, no individual could change it; if all nations rose only to fall, there seemed to be no reason to hope for a better future. Neither view fitted the American temper or expressed the American's feeling for his past and future; he had, so he believed, already changed the course of history to found a new kind of nation. It was hard for him to believe, as the Reverend Thomas Barnard said in 1795, that all the future held for him "was decline and mortification, according to the course of human affairs." There must be some way to break the chain or stop the cycle, to exempt the United States from the inexorable fate of other nations in the past.

The answer came in a new view of history, best summarized in Condorcet's *Equisse d'un Tableau Historique des Progrès,* which appeared in France in 1795. Condorcet saw history as a series of stages, each an improvement over the last, moving ever upward by the law of progress. The theory of historical progress (not new, but redefined and reinvigorated by the Enlightenment philosophers) took man off the cyclical treadmill of history and freed him from the chain of historical causation. It gave man hope for a future better than any he had ever dreamed of, for the historian could show, Condorcet believed,

by reasoning and facts, that there is no limit set to the perfecting of the powers of man; that human perfectibility is in reality indefinite; that the progress of this perfectibility, henceforth independent of any power that might wish to stop it, has no other limit than the duration of the globe on which nature has placed us.

This was precisely the view of the historical process that Americans needed before they could write their own history, for it showed that the present age was a prelude to better ones, and that the creation of the United States was the culmination of a long succession of events leading up to that better world. America was not, therefore, the apogee of a movement bound to decline; it was instead a new stage in an ever-upward succession of stages. The concept of history as the record of human progress and of American history as the most recent and convincing chapter of that record provided the basic theory for American historical writing for the next generation. Beginning with Condorcet, the ground was laid for a conception of history as inevitable progress—particularly in the United States—that rested on causes decreed by the Deity and qualities inherent in mankind. Thus George Bancroft, dean of the Romantic school of historians, beginning his monumental *History of the United States* in 1834, could see the whole course of history coming into focus at Lexington as the embattled farmers faced the redcoats, for this, he wrote, "was the slowly ripened fruit of Providence and time . . . and the light that led them was combined of rays of the whole history of the race."

 *SIX*

LITERATURE IN THE
NEW REPUBLIC

The Contours of a National Literature

The literature produced in America between 1790 and 1830 is not easily classifiable, for there is a transitional quality about the period that makes it difficult to characterize. Its writing has a formative feel that precludes setting boundaries. Irving and Bryant, for example, wrote out of almost the same milieu as Dennie, Freneau, and Brown, yet much separates them. Dennie's *Lay Preacher* essays precede Irving's *Sketch Book* by only three years, though the two represent different literary worlds; Barlow's *Columbiad* and Irving's *Knickerbocker History* were but two years apart; Freneau was still writing verse when Poe published *Tamerlane*.

The artistic accomplishments of the period obviously represent something more than a pause between the Revolution and the great nineteenth-century flowering of literature. They were years of intense, energetic (if not always distinguished) activity, out of which came the American belletristic tradition. The greater part of this activity centered in the Northern and Middle Colonies and in the urban centers of such cities as Boston, New York, and Philadelphia.

The South, too, had its share of well-read, intelligent, creative men; it was by no means a literary wasteland. But though there was much Southern writing, there was little publication—writing was considered an avocation, something not done for display or pay, and authors often published under pseudonyms and refused payment. The South had few suitable publishers, few magazines, and a relatively small critical audience. Then, too, a great deal of Southern intellectual energy poured into science, medicine, law, and politics. Certainly John Taylor of Carolina and John C. Calhoun ranked among the best political minds of the century; William Wirt, a capable essayist in the older tradition, made his name as a lawyer; George Tucker, whose essays were better than Wirt's, was both legal scholar and economic theorist.

Hugh Swinton Legaré of South Carolina, who served as Secretary of State in Tyler's cabinet, might have become one of the nation's best critics had he chosen a literary career. As it was, his work for *The Southern Review* (1828–1832) helped to make it the South's most distinguished journal before the appearance of *The Southern Literary Messenger*. There were Southern poets, and good ones, mostly unpublished, for although the South had few presses that printed poetry, it had a strong private literary tradition. Poetry of all kinds—lampoons, burlesques, political satire, light and serious verse—passed from hand to hand, circulating far more widely than later literary historians have suspected. (For example, Byrd's *History* was being read not long after its completion in manuscript form in Maryland, Virginia, and even in England.) The various *Gazettes* and other newspapers published a surprising amount of verse. Coffeehouse clubs, like Annapolis' famous Tuesday Club, furnished both inspiration and audience for Southern poets, and there were many such clubs from Baltimore to Charleston. Samuel Davies, who succeeded Jonathan Edwards as president of Princeton in 1759, was not only a powerful preacher (Patrick Henry thought him the greatest orator he ever heard) but a good poet; his *Miscellaneous Poems, Chiefly on Divine Subjects* (1751–1752) was sound, skilled, religious verse. Alexander Hamilton and James Sterling of Maryland, whose poetry was published in the newspapers but never collected, were even better. Dozens of other poets, skilled and journeymen, wrote for the periodicals.

The challenge of literature, then, attracted a number of men, North and South, who wrote a great deal (and often well) during the mid-eighteenth century. What they wrote displayed certain distinguishing characteristics.

First, the literature of the period was strongly imitative of neoclassical and contemporary English literature. The tendency of American writers was to imitate and adapt rather than experiment. Joseph Dennie's magazine, *The Portfolio,* served as a clear example. Dennie solicited, he said, articles "after the model of *The Gentleman's Magazine,*" ballads "in the style of 'John Gilpin' . . . and in the manner of Dr. Percy's," odes "in the manner of *The Rolliad,*" essays "in the manner of Addison, Johnson, or Goldsmith," "Hudibrastic poetry," and "songs adapted to the taste of the Anaversonic group." Anything unusual or unconventional was distinctly not wanted, and deviations from English fashion were unwelcome.

Since English literature itself at the time was moving from neoclassicism toward Romanticism, American literature reflected the same transition. It was not uncommon for an American poet to model his work on both Pope and Gray or for an essayist to copy both Swift and Goldsmith. Joseph Hutton, a talented and productive young Philadelphia poet, in his volume *Leisure Hours* (1801) managed to imitate Pope, Dryden, Goldsmith, Gray, Denham, Young, Cunningman, and Montgomery; his five most successful plays, for that matter, were modeled on Sheridan, Addison, and Italian opera.

Second, American literature of the time was not regional, but national. Throughout the Colonies, writers had much the same tastes, aims, and standards, and they wrote as Americans, not as New Yorkers or Virginians. They strove to use native materials and to reflect American manners and attitudes—a trend reinforced by the Romantic movement's stress on individuality and originality. The demands of literary nationalism served to counteract to some extent the belief that only England and Europe furnished acceptable subjects and standards. But though determined to be "American," writers had no clear idea of how to be so or of how to define an American style. During these years, the American writer was torn between his spirit of nationalism and his sense of literary values.

Third, American writers tended to be conventional rather than exploratory. Like English and European literature of the time, American literature was tyrannized by genres; American writers believed that what they had to say, even using native themes and materials, could best be said in the forms and language approved by accepted critical standards. Joel Barlow put his "American epic" into Popean couplet; Timothy Dwight, writing about his Connecticut home, felt he must do so in terms of Denham and Thomson. Americans, who wanted to express their cultural independence, almost unanimously chose to treat an American theme or introduce American materials in an established British genre.

Solyman Brown, in the preface to his *Miscellaneous Poems* (1818), explained rather proudly that in twenty-nine poems on American topics he had "introduced between forty and fifty kinds of measure . . . to exemplify the most approved diversities of English metre." More striking was the example of Daniel Bryan's *The Mountain Muse: Comprising the Adventures of Daniel Boone . . .* (1813). Determined to write a national epic of the West, Bryan produced a narrative poem of seven books dealing with authentically native themes of the forest, the Indian-white conflict, and frontier settlement; but written in a wild mixture of the styles of Spenser, Milton, Ossian, and Goldsmith, among others.

In effect, Americans hoped to create a native, independent literature within the framework of an established British-Continental tradition. What Americans wanted, no matter how they protested against "foreign domination," was their own Augustan age, built out of American materials and attitudes, and comfortably couched in safe, tested literary forms.

However, the literature of the period also showed the growing popularity of those forms in which the writer's ideas were shaped within a loose artistic pattern (such as the novel, poem, essay, and drama) and the decline of such once-favored forms as the sermon, journal, travel narrative, and autobiography. This, in part, reflected the increased level of sophistication of American society and a greater effort by American writers to enter into the mainstream of contemporary literature.

Fourth, a great deal of American writing was still utilitarian and moralistic. Many Americans continued to believe that novels should instruct, plays draw moral lessons, satires discover and correct error, essays debate and convince, poetry please and teach. "The writer must be chaste as well as witty," wrote Judge Joseph Story, "moral as well as brilliant." James Hillhouse, a poet himself, thought that poetry ought to "delight, purify, and exalt our moral natures, and . . . fortify us against the evil passions."

Nevertheless, in the last two decades of the eighteenth century and the first two of the nineteenth, something like a profession of letters began to emerge; with it came the realization that literature was art rather than utility. By 1810, a poet could, if he wished, write poetry more or less for its own sake, or an essayist could write for amusement as well as instruction. Charles Brockden Brown, for example, acknowledged the moral usefulness of his tales in rather perfunctory prefaces and then quickly got into the stories. Royall Tyler felt it necessary to point out the patriotic purpose of *The Contrast* before he presented the delightfully comic Jonathan, but James Nelson Barker's *Indian Princess,* only twenty years later, had no other aim than to present an exciting, tear-jerking melodrama. Freneau's sensitive examination of the honeysuckle suggested something about the evanescence of life—but it was also a private exploration of the relationship between poet and flower. While the older concept of literature as instrumentality still persisted, writers had begun to think of themselves as artists and not moralists, and so the public began to accept them.

The Prevalence of Essays

The essay in America flourished with the mushrooming growth of newspapers and periodicals. By 1800, there were a hundred newspapers in the United States and perhaps double that number by 1810; most of these and the dozens of magazines that appeared after 1800 had their "Loungers" or "Hermits" pretending to be latter-day Addisons or Swifts. As outlets for publication increased, and as a more sophisticated, urbane, wealthy society developed, the essay likewise grew in popularity; it was modeled on the great British practitioners of the form, Addison, Steele, Swift, and Goldsmith.

After 1780, the political struggles of Federalist and Republican, the manners of a self-consciously cultured society, and the fads and follies of a gawky young republic exactly fitted the requirements of the eighteenth-century essay, and few newspapers or magazines lacked a series. For example, the New York *Wasp* had "Robert Rusticoat," the Philadelphia *Tickler* "Toby Scratch," the Boston *Rover* "Roderick Rover," and the Baltimore *Scourge* "Titus Tickler." Nathan Fiske, speaking in 1801, remarked that any periodical without an essay series was doomed, and dozens of anonymous contributors, ranging from inept to highly skilled, with names such as "The Censor," "Gentleman at Large," "Lady's Friend," and "The Idler," filled the magazines and newspapers with comments on fashions, courtship, education, manners, social life, gossip, and other traditionally favored essay topics.

Through the latter years of the eighteenth century and during the first three decades of the nineteenth, the essay was perhaps the most clearly defined and popular American literary form. It provided an outlet for educated men to air their views without improper personal exposure; men who would never write for publication otherwise considered such "scribbling" an acceptable and even fashionable way of presenting one's self to the public. "Why," said John Neal in 1810, "I could give you the names of at least fifty—not to say five hundred gentlemen who . . . published essays mysteriously." There were also well-known names under pseudonyms, such as Philip Freneau ("Tomo Cheeki" and "Robert Slender"), Noah Webster ("The Prompter"), Samuel Knapp ("Ali Bey"), William Wirt ("The Old Bachelor"), Judith Murray ("The Gleaner"), and others.

Noah Webster's *Essays and Fugitiv Writings* (1790) dealt with more serious matters of politics, law, and education, while Royall Tyler's "Author's Evenings" (1801) contained some excellent literary criticism. Joseph Dennie, an avowed disciple of Addison, was one of the best and most prolific essayists of the period. His *Farrago Essays* (1792) and *The Eagle* (1793–1794) were modeled, he said, "after the designs of Addison and the harmless and playful levity of Oliver Goldsmith." *The Lay Preacher* (1796) was pronounced by one critic to be "the best popular work on the American continent." After the turn of the century, as editor of *The Portfolio,* Dennie reprinted much of the work of the great British essayists and continued his own in the "Oliver Oldschool" series.

The real master of the essay, however, and the man who deserves the title of "first American essayist," was undoubtedly Washington Irving. Irving's work owed much, obviously, to *The Spectator* in temper and style, but Irving's choice of subject matter, the development of his own style, point of view, and approach, placed him far above the level of mere imitator. His earliest work, *The Letters of Jonathan Oldstyle, Gent.* (1802), clearly derived from Addison's Sir Roger, and *Salmagundi,* issued in 1807–1808 with his brother William and J. K. Paulding, still owed a large debt to the coffeehouse tradition.

With the appearance of *The Sketch Book* in 1819–1820, however, Irving's reputation as an essayist was established both at home and abroad. *Bracebridge Hall,* the essay-like *Alhambra,* and his later volumes simply made it more secure. Recognized as a master stylist in the eighteenth-century manner, yet with a finish and charm distinctively his own, Irving domesticated the Addisonian tradition and brought it to its culmination in America.

The Outlook for Poetry: The Trap of Imitation

Poetry found hard going in the postwar period. The desire for creative literary art was strong, no doubt, but scattered and misdirected. There were a number of young men who believed that there had been too much politics and not enough poetry; among them was John Trumbull, who in his Master's oration at Yale chose not to deal with the customary topics of theology or politics but titled his "An Essay on the Use and Adavantage of the Fine Arts." Others such as Joel Barlow, Francis Hopkinson, and Philip Freneau agreed with Trumbull that the time was right for the creation of an American poetry equal to any the world had to offer.

But all of them found that the way of the poet was difficult in a nation that in two generations had suffered two wars with England, a near-war with France, and bitter political rivalries that split society apart. Trumbull abandoned literature and turned to law, Barlow to political activity, Dwight to theology and education. Freneau neglected his great lyric gifts for satire and journalism. "Barbers cannot exist as such among a people who have neither hair or beards," he once wrote despairingly. "How then can a poet hope for success in a city where there are not three persons possessed of elegant ideas?"

It was also true, of course, that in an era dominated by Coleridge, Wordsworth, Scott, Byron, and Burns, it was understandably difficult for lesser bards, American or English, to attract public notice. Though the poets blamed politics, war, moneymaking, social unrest, and other causes for public indifference to their art, they were not wholly accurate. There was a well-informed and sophisticated reading public that read Pope, Gray, Byron, and Scott with great enthusiasm, and which knew too much, in a sense, about English poetry to accept something different. The public had not yet had its fill of imitations. Poets themselves were too easily attracted by the excitement of current events, too quickly lured by satire, philosophical discussions, and by exhortations to write "national verse." The level of poetry produced in the period from 1790 to 1820, except for Freneau, was not high. There was no dearth of poets—their names were embalmed in the "cyclopaedias" of American writing so favored by the early nineteenth century—but few of them were remembered beyond their own generation.

The fact was that American poets were caught in the trap of imitation. Worship of British poetry hemmed in American versifiers and vitiated the freshness and energy that some of them undoubtedly had. What was popular in England was eagerly copied in the United States; it was easier, and much safer, for young American poets to follow accepted British masters and current English tastes than to attempt an original style. If an American wished to write poetry, he could choose the mock-heroic style already exhausted by Pope and his followers or the blank verse style of Thomson and Young. A little later he could write, if he wished, like Leigh Hunt, Southey, Moore, Montgomery, or Gray, or he could copy English "instructional poets" like Samuel Rogers, Thomas Campbell, or Felicia Hemans.

Then, after 1810, almost everybody imitated Scott or Byron. Scott's books, *The American Monthly Magazine* commented in 1817, "are in everybody's hand and his praises in everybody's mouth," which was hardly an exaggeration. The more daring younger poets imitated Byron; Merrill Heiser has concluded, after studying the period 1812–1835, that it was virtually impossible to find an American poet who was *not* influenced by Byron, including such unlikely disciples as John Quincy Adams (who imitated *Don Juan*) and Quaker John Greenleaf Whittier, who once wore a flowing tie and a soulful expression.

Examples of this derivative verse could be found in any newspaper or magazine. William Martin Johnson, a South Carolina physician, spent his artistic life writing "seasonal" poetry in the manner of James Thomson and "meditative" poetry after Gray and Collins. Carlos Wilcox of Connecticut, oddly enough, wrote in Shakespearian blank verse and Spenserian stanza. William Munford of Virginia translated Horace and Homer, wrote Popean satire, and imitated Macpherson's *Ossian*. Alexander Wilson, better known for his ornithological studies, wrote Dryden-style "odes"; Robert Johnson wrote Scottish dialect poems after Robert Burns. St. John Honeywood, a protégé of President Stiles of Yale, in 1801 published his collected poems without a single original line or thought in any of them. Samuel Woodworth, the popular playwright, wrote a great deal of rather inept sentimental verse, which was quite genuine and unaffected in its homespun way; all that remains is his song "The Old Oaken Bucket," although his ballad, "The Pride of the Valley," was a better poem.

Out of the postwar group, four younger poets showed signs of talent, but all of them lost themselves in imitation. William Clifton, a Philadelphia Quaker who was also a musician and painter, wrote both in the old tradition of neoclassical satire and in the newer strain of preromantic sensitivity. His attacks on the Jeffersonians were clever satires straight out of Pope, Butler, and Churchill; so too was his *Rhapsody of the Times,* a wry lament for the good old days before "the scrabbling knaves" who cheered Jefferson "began to claim more rights than God designed for man." On the other hand, Clifton knew Gray, Warton, and the whole meditative "graveyard" school and wrote numerous odes on "Fancy," flowers, lost friendships, and nature. The result was skilled imitation but nothing more.

John Blair Linn, who read law in Alexander Hamilton's office, abandoned it to join Charles Brockden Brown and the New York literati. He wrote a play, *Bourville Castle, or the Gallic Orphan* (1797), a number of Ossianic poems, some sentimental verse, and a three-part blank verse poem called *The Power of Genius* (1801), which went into a second edition. He died in 1804, however, leaving behind a long, wildly Gothic narrative, *Valerian,* published in 1804, which took place in a fanciful, exotic kingdom of magicians, knights, and robbers.

Robert Treat Paine (who changed his name from "Thomas" to avoid confusion) was one of Boston's most promising lads—class poet at Harvard, admired and praised by such men as Washington and Adams. Paine, however, fell in love with the theater, married a sixteen-year-old actress, and took up what his biographer tactfully referred to as "an unsettled mode of life" that apparently precluded serious poetic composition. A predecessor of Poe as the image of the rebellious, bohemian poet, Paine frittered away his considerable talent in verse of little consequence and died in his thirties.

Potentially the best of the younger generation, Edward Coote Pinkney, died in 1828 at the age of twenty-six. Son of a distinguished Maryland family, Pinkney served in the navy, read law, edited the Baltimore *Marylander* for a year, and at twenty-four became Professor of Rhetoric and Belles Lettres at the Univer-

sity of Maryland. He published a number of poems in the magazines, a Byronic-tinted fragment *Rudolph* (1823), and more of
his verse in *Poems* (1825). However, much of his poetry remained uncollected until 1926. Pinkney, widely read in English
and Continental literature, enthusiastically absorbed the new poetry of Wordsworth, but he was also deeply drawn to the seventeenth-century Cavaliers, to whom he felt temperamentally akin.
He handled his favorite themes of love and melancholy (antici-
pating Poe) without much originality but with skill and sensitivity. *The North American Review,* which tended to overlook
Southern poets, remarked on him favorably, while Poe later sin-
gled him out for praise in "The Poetic Principle." Pinkney un-
questionably possessed a powerful lyric talent that, had he lived
beyond his apprenticeship, might well have matured into first-
rank poetry.

"Knickerbockers" in New York

The problems of trying to be simultaneously artistic, American, and conventional were aptly illustrated by the
so-called "Knickerbocker" group in New York City, who hoped
to find the best way to use native American materials within the
boundaries of prevailing poetic fashion. After the turn of the
century, New York emerged as the focus of an energetic intellectual and social life, with theaters, bookshops, art galleries, musical organizations, and almost as many clubs as London. The
Knickerbockers included a number of writers who played a leading part in the city's cultural life over the years—N. P. Willis,
Gulian Verplanck, Charles Fenno Hoffman, Theodore Fay, later
William Cullen Bryant and Cooper—but its early impetus came
from the bright young men who gathered about Washington
Irving, James Kirke Paulding, Fitz-Green Halleck, and Joseph
Rodman Drake shortly after 1800. Halleck, born in Connec-
ticut, came to New York to serve as secretary to John Jacob
Astor and became one of the city's best known men-about-town.

Drake, who died at twenty-five, collaborated in 1819 with Halleck on the excellent "Croaker" essays and wrote a number of witty satires and "occasion" poems.

They all knew English and Continental literature thoroughly and set themselves the task of absorbing the English-European tradition instead of copying it. Halleck's spectacularly popular *Fanny* (1819) furnished a case in point. A satire on the adventures of a rich merchant and his daughter in New York society, Halleck chose Byron as his model and cast his poem in ottava rima; later he patterned his historical poem on Connecticut after Byron's *Beppo* and chose the same stanza. Drake's famous *Culprit Fay* (written in 1816 and not published until 1835) originated in an argument with Halleck and Cooper, who claimed that an American river, unlike European or English rivers, could never furnish the associations needed for great poetry. Drake, therefore, wrote a poem with the Hudson as his locale; it was patterned directly on Coleridge's *Christabel,* and was about a faery fay condemned to do penance for having loved a mortal maid. The result for both Drake and Halleck was sheer artistic disaster, as Poe pointed out in his review of the two.

Paulding, who collaborated with the Irvings on the *Salmagundi* series, wrote novels, satires, plays, poems, essays, and reviews. Strongly nationalistic, he used the American frontier for his long poem *The Backwoodsman* (1818) and in his essay "National Literature" (1820) emphasized the great opportunities their native land presented to American artists. Paulding wrote far too much for his limited gifts, however, and although he complained in middle age that "the world has not done me justice as an author," it probably had. His "whim whams," as he called them, were graceful and humorous but little more. With all their talent, not one of the Knickerbockers left a line that warrants recall. Yet though they failed in their attempt to create a viable urban literary culture, they provided the base for Washington Irving, who succeeded in naturalizing England and Europe to the American climate, as they could not.

Philip Freneau

The case of Philip Freneau, the first genuine poetic voice to be heard in the United States, is somewhat different. Like Paine, Jefferson, and Barlow, Freneau was a child of the American Enlightenment, and like them he threw himself into a variety of contemporary causes. He was a Princeton graduate in the same class with Madison, Burr, and Brackenridge; when they were students, in 1771, Freneau and Brackenridge collaborated on a long, aggressively patriotic commencement poem called "The Rising Glory of America."

Determined to be a poet, for, as he said

To write was my sad destiny,
The worst of trades, we all agree,

Freneau moved restlessly from job to job. He taught school, worked as a sailor, visited and dreamed in the West Indies, returned to enlist in the Revolutionary army, was captured and nearly died in a British prison ship, and shipped out as a captain in the coastal trade. After entering politics on the side of the Jeffersonians, he was appointed a government clerk of foreign languages and made out a precarious living as farmer, sea captain, and journalist. Much of his poetry was elicited by the Revolutionary War or by the political battles of the Federalist period, but this was not the kind of verse he was drawn to or the kind he wrote best. A large part of his energy was consumed in newspaper work and by writing some 600 essays on various topics published in the journals.

Freneau's poetry, issued in collected editions in 1786, 1788, 1809, and 1815, fell into fairly clear divisions. His wartime verse reflected the heated passions of the times and his hatred of the British, whose treatment on the prison ship he neither forgot nor forgave. His political satires, modeled on the English tradition of Dryden and Churchill and directed against the Federalists, were so effective that Washington called him "that rascal Freneau." An avowed radical, Freneau threw himself into a number of reform causes. He was proud of his service to the cause of liberalism and of his determination to be

Hostile to garter, ribbon, crown, and star;
Still on the people's, still on Freedom's side,
With full-determined aim, to baffle every claim,
Of well-born wights, that aim to mount and ride.

He lived until 1832, usually in poverty, writing poetry largely unread, an anachronism in an age dominated by Bryant, Cooper, and Irving.

Freneau's political verse, by far the larger part of his work, is less important than his poetry dealing with nature, beauty, transience, the past, and personal experience. His satire was so well known that the public and critics tended to overlook his real achievement; William Cullen Bryant later called him "a writer of inferior verse . . . distinguished by a coarse strength of sarcasm" (the most inaccurate critical judgment Bryant ever made). A restless, divided man, Freneau reflected his two worlds in his poetry—the snarling, savage satires of military and political conflict; the sensitive and delicate lyrics of solitude, nature, and intense personal emotion. Though he often echoed Gray, Collins, Akenside, and other English pre-Romantics of the "melancholy" school, there was in his better verse a freshness, originality, and haunting beauty unsurpassed in the American poetry of his times.

Freneau constructed his lyric verse about three themes, all familiar to the period. The first of these, and the one most frequent in his verse, was the concept of Nature as a reflection of the poet and as a key to the meaning of life and art. Like other pre-Romantics, Freneau approached Nature (which they tended to capitalize) meditatively as well as appreciatively, finding in it both philosophic and sensuous values. The wild honeysuckle, delicate and beautiful as it was, soon faded, and thereby taught the poet something about his own condition:

From morning suns and evening dews
At first thy little being came:

If nothing once, you nothing lose,
For when you die you are the same;
The space between, is but an hour,
The frail duration of a flower.

And the sky reflected at night on the sea taught him the vanity of existence:

In youth, gay scenes attract our eyes,
And not suspecting their decay
Life's flowery fields before us rise,
Regardless of its winter day.

But vain pursuits, and joys as vain,
Convince us life is but a dream.
Death is to wake, to rise again
To that true life you best esteem.

So nightly on some shallow tide,
Oft have I seen a splendid show;
Reflected stars on either side,
And glittering moons were seen below.

But when the tide had ebbed away,
The scene fantastic with it fled,
A bank of mud around me lay,
And sea-weed on the river's bed.

Freneau's second theme was that of transience and mutability, the "ubi sunt" theme of medieval poetry rediscovered by the English meditative poets and pervasive in the poetry of the times. Life is short, time is fleeting, or as Freneau wrote in *The House of Night,* all is change:

The towering Alps, the haughty Apennine,
The Andes, wrapt in everlasting snow,
The Appalachian and the Ararat
Sooner or later must to ruin go.

Hills sink to plains, and man returns to dust,
That dust supports a reptile or a flower;
Each changeful atom by some other nurs'd
Takes some new form, to perish in an hour.

His third theme, again a stock-in-trade of the pre-Romantics, concerned the power of the "fancy" or imagination to transform and transmute experience (a doctrine developed more fully by Wordsworth). In his own *Ode to Fancy* (1770), Freneau explored that "wakeful, vagrant, restless" power that, he wrote, could "lift me into immortality, depict new dreams, or draw the scenes of hell."

Freneau handled these three themes with a grace and insight unusual for the times; no poet in contemporary America, certainly, treated them better. But Freneau's importance lies instead in the fact that he began to explore new areas of subject matter and to strike out in new directions in how he used them. Some of his nature poetry was little more than warmed-over Thomson, but at other times he infused new energy into the generalized, traditional patterns of English-style, nature verse and brought it suddenly to life with a vivid metaphor or a flash of vision.

In a day when poets tended to look at Nature as an artificial abstraction, Freneau looked at it directly and saw it in its ordinary, American detail—buckwheat, pumpkins, honeysuckles and field daisies, katydids and squirrels, cornfields and mudflats—things neither British nor American poets of the times were likely to see and less likely to use in poetry. He reveled in the sensuous appeal of the exotic West Indies with Keats-like pleasure, recalling the taste of "cool acid limes" and "juicy lemons" and the glitter of the tropical fish that slid through the purple waters:

Some streaked with burnished gold, resplendent glare,
Some cleave the limpid deep, all silver'd o'er,
Some, clad in living green, delight the eye,
Some red, some blue, of mingled colors more.

Freneau knew the sea firsthand as a professional sailor—before Cooper or Melville—and unlike any of his poetic contemporaries found it a source of meaning and mystery. He observed on the one hand the order and discipline of naval life and on the other its constant danger. As "Hezekiah Salem," Freneau recounted the pleasures of life on "a vessel well-timbered and sound," where "a hamper of porter and plenty of grog . . . a coop that will always some poultry afford," gave the sailor "a treasure in store, that millions possess not who live on the shore." Yet the sea kills; Freneau knew that it was "a watery tomb of ocean-green" for the sailor, and that only "a frail plank" lay between him and death "beneath the glossy surface, calm and clear." He wrote only a few sea poems, but they opened a poetic door no other American poet entered for another generation.

After 1812, Freneau experimented with an unusual kind of rough, realistic, local-color verse, a surprising element to find in the poetry of that time and place—"The Jug of Rum," "The Drunkard's Apology," "The Drunken Soldier," "Jack Straw," "The Virtue of Tobacco," and so on—which, had he continued it, might have initiated a new American style. Then, too, in spite of the contradiction in terms, Freneau was a deist poet, who in a small body of excellent work put into verse such central deist doctrines as "The Uniformity and Perfection of Nature" and "The Religion of Nature." Freneau's importance lies in the fact that he broke out of the constrictions of neoclassical imitation to look at life directly, read it imaginatively, and record it sensitively. He was, despite his restlessness and lack of artistic discipline, the first major American poet.

"The Servile Habit" in American Verse

Where American poetry stood within the national literary effort during the latter decades of the eighteenth century and the early years of the nineteenth was aptly summarized by William Cullen Bryant in an essay-review done for *The North American Review* in 1818. Bryant, at twenty-four, belonged to the new generation of poets raised on Pope and Thomson, converted to Wordsworth and Coleridge, anxious to create not only a national but a worthy literature of their own. Asked to review Solyman Brown's *Essay on American Poetry,* he used the assignment not only to destroy Brown, who was not a very good poet or critic, but to reassess the accomplishments and direction of contemporary American verse.

Poetry should be judged for its excellence and for nothing else, Bryant wrote—by universal standards and not by the "swaggering and pompous pretensions" of the chauvinists. American poetry had accomplished little, he continued, not because the nation possessed no competent poets (he mentioned Hopkinson, Barlow, the Connecticut group, and his contemporaries Clifton, Alsop, and Paine); it was rather that none of them had broken out of the prison of imitation. Shackled by "the servile habit of copying," Americans of talent had failed both as poets and Americans. The poetry of his native land displayed too much rigidity and too little freedom, too much emulation and too little daring. If "the splendid talents" of American poets could be liberated, he concluded, their poetry would come of age.

The Theater Before the Revolution

Though the American Colonies were settled at the height of England's great age of dramatic writing, there was no colonial theater for nearly a hundred years afterward. Drama, a peculiarly social art, required a sophisticated, cohesive, group culture to support it—something that seventeenth-century America had little of. Actors and plays were viewed with distaste and suspicion by colonial churches, New England Calvinists, Pennsylvania Quakers, and Dutch New Yorkers alike. Even as late as 1750, Massachusetts authorities decried drama because of its tendency "generally to increase immorality, impiety, and a contempt for religion." In the eighteenth century, with the growth of cities and the establishment of a wealthy leisure class, opposition to the theater lessened. New York, Baltimore, Philadelphia, Charleston, and other cities developed a cultivated and urbane society that could not only support a theater, but hoped to emulate the fashions of British aristocracy by encouraging it.

In the opening years of the eighteenth century, itinerant English actors and companies made fairly regular tours of the Southern and Middle Colonies. Tony Aston, a comedian who advertised himself as "Gentleman, Lawyer, Poet, Actor, Soldier, Sailor, Exciseman, and Publican," made such a tour in 1702-1704, one of the very first to do so. Williamsburg built a theater in 1716, New York in 1732, Charleston in 1735 (or 1736), though plays were more often presented in ballrooms, taverns, barns, and assembly halls. Murray and Kean's company had great success in New York and Philadelphia in 1750, but the first professional company to play regularly to American audiences was Lewis Hallam's London company, which opened at Williamsburg in 1752 and moved later to New York and Philadelphia.

To accommodate the Hallams and other companies, new theaters sprang up in the 1760s (the Chapel Street and the John Street in New York City, the Southwark in Philadelphia), a sure sign of public acceptance. Except for the accident of location, these companies were no different from British companies in England; they drew their talent from the London stage and played Shakespeare, Gay, Otway, Addison, Cibber, Farquahar, Sheridan, and others from the standard English repertoire. The single play written by an American and presented by a professional company before the Revolution was Thomas Godfrey's *Prince of Parthia* (produced in Philadelphia in 1767), primarily an imitation of Restoration tragedy following the principles laid down by Dryden and Rowe.

For the two or three decades prior to the Revolution, dramatic activity centered in the colleges. "Dialogues," or exercises in public speaking and rhetorical training, were almost plays, sometimes (despite the name) involving several characters who discussed political, religious, and educational subjects. Princeton students in 1762, for example, presented a public dialogue on "The Military Glory of Great Britain"; many similar recitations were recorded elsewhere. John Smith of Dartmouth wrote a

comic dialogue between an Indian and an Englishman and a satire on feminine gossip called "A Little Teatable Chitchat." Colleges also encouraged students to produce plays, masques, and
classic tragedies for training in "oratory and correct speaking,"
as Provost William Smith of the College of Philadelphia advised
in 1757, while at Yale an observer complained that the students
had "turn'd the College into Drury Lane" to the detriment of
"the more solid parts of learning."

In 1774, Continental Congress asked for the suspension of
"horseracing, gambling, cockfighting, exhibitions of shows,
plays, and other expensive diversions and entertainments," a re-
quest fairly well respected throughout the war years. In the
cities, most of which were occupied by the British, there were
theatricals for the amusement of resident British and Loyalist
society—playwrights usually preferring to remain anonymous,
since the fortunes of war might change. Supporters of the Revolutionary cause managed to stage some plays of their own before
the ban and after, such as Jonathan Sewall's *Americans Roused*
(1774) and those of Mrs. Mercy Otis Warren, James Otis' sister
and wife of General Joseph Warren. She lampooned the British
in *The Adalateur* (1773) and *The Blockheads* (1775), and the
Loyalist "swarm of court sycophants, hungry harpies, and un-
principled danglers" in *The Group* (1775). Mrs. Warren was a
good hater, and her works crackled with animosity.

Theater After the War: Tyler and Dunlap

Nearly all the professional actors retired either to
London or to the West Indies during the war, flocking back
immediately afterward. A hastily organized company played the
1782–1783 season in Baltimore and New York, while Lewis
Hallam Junior arrived with another group in Philadelphia in
1784 and moved to New York in 1785. John Henry, a talented
Irish actor, later came to the United States to join Hallam and
formed "The Old American Company," which dominated the
American theater for the next decade. In 1794, Thomas Wignell
withdrew from this group to form a company of his own in

Philadelphia, leaving the Old American players, now owned by Hallam and William Dunlap, in control of the New York stage.

Theological opposition to the theater gradually disappeared after the Revolution, though prejudice remained. In 1785, for example, 700 Philadelphians signed a protest against the Old American Company. In 1790, Boston refused to grant a license to Hallam and Henry, and two years later Joseph Harper's "exhibitions" of Sheridan were turned out of town as tending to "fleece the giddy Youth of their money." Since it was still deemed tactful in smaller towns during the period to advertise plays as "moral lectures," managers billed *Richard III* as "The Fate of Tyranny," *Hamlet* as "Filial Piety," and *She Stoops to Conquer* as "Improper Education"; "Pleasure the means, the end virtue" the inscription read on the proscenium arch at a theater in Providence, Rhode Island.

On the other hand, George Washington's well-known liking for the theater gave it a measure of respectability. The President often attended plays, and during the war (the rumor ran) he approved a performance of Addison's *Cato* as beneficial to troop morale. Wealthy gentlemen in Boston, New York, Philadelphia, and Charleston, anxious to imitate London and Paris society, campaigned against restrictive legislation and succeeded in repealing much of it by 1795. A Boston group built the Federal Street Theater at almost the same time as Philadelphia's new Chestnut Street Theater was built. Charleston built its Church Street Theater in 1786, and New York's famous Park Theater was completed in 1798.

Ten years after Yorktown the American theater was in a rather sound state of health. At least two permanent companies, the Old American and Wignell's Philadelphia group, gave highly skilled professional performances probably equal to those of the better British troupes. The plays themselves were a different matter. While London continued to provide the majority of plays for the American stage after the war, a few Americans tried their skill at dramatic writing with indifferent success. David Humphreys of the "Connecticut Wits" group modeled his *Widow of Malabar* (1790) on French tragedy; Elihu Hubbard

Smith, a New York physician and poet, in 1796 wrote a romantic opera, *Edwin and Angelina,* about "robbers." Susannah Rowson, the novel-writing lady, used the war with the Barbary pirates as background for *Slaves in Algiers* (1794) and the Whiskey Rebellion for *The Volunteers* (1795). John Daly Burk, a bright young Irishman killed in a duel in 1808, wrote a number of popular plays, among them *Bunker Hill* (1797), which played almost continuously through the states for the next twenty years. The level of American dramatic achievement, however, was admittedly low.

There were, however, two notable exceptions, Royall Tyler and William Dunlap. Tyler, a Harvard graduate and army veteran who eventually became Chief Justice of Vermont's Supreme Court, wrote a delightful Sheridan-like comedy of manners, *The Contrast,* first performed in 1787. Built about the theme of native American worth versus foreign affectation, the play contrasted Colonel Manly, an upstanding, true-blue American, with Billy Dimple, an Anglicized fop (much to the latter's disadvantage). The hit of the play, however, was the character of the Yankee farmer Jonathan, who was the first of a long line of comic rustics in the American theater; he was played to the hilt by the famous comedian Thomas Wignell. Tyler also wrote poetry, essays, a novel, an opera, a translation of Molière, and three Biblical plays.

More important in the history of American drama was William Dunlap, who helped to organize and stabilize the theater during its most chaotic period. Dunlap, a talented painter who studied with Benjamin West in London, returned to New York with a play of his own modeled on Tyler's successful *Contrast.* His second play, a sentimental comedy called *The Father* (1788), started him on a theatrical career that lasted forty years. He eventually wrote about sixty-five plays and adapted a large number of foreign imports for American production. Between 1798 and 1803, he produced so many German plays that they made up nearly the majority of all recorded performances in New York. An amazingly energetic and versatile man, Dunlap wrote comedy, tragedy, farce, opera, melodrama, and historical

plays; he also produced, designed, directed (he hired and directed
Edgar Allan Poe's parents), and managed theatrical companies
and theaters. Of his own plays, the best and most successful was
André (1798), based on the capture and execution of the British spy.

Dunlap might have been a better dramatist had he not spent
so much of his energy in production and direction. He purchased
a share of Hallam and Hodgkinson's Old American Company in
1796, managed it until its bankruptcy in 1805, and also managed
New York's Park Theater for some time after 1798. In addition,
Dunlap helped to found the National Academy of Design,
taught painting, and wrote *The History of the American Theater* (1832), which, despite errors and personal bias, is still a
landmark in American theatrical history. He also propagandized
constantly for a sound, mature, artistic American drama. A great
nation, he reasoned, deserved a great theater—"The rise, progress, and cultivation of the drama mark the progress of refine-
ment and the state of manners at any given time in any country"
—and he did his best to create it in the United States. He wrote
and produced many bad and mediocre plays, yet Dunlap was not
afraid to experiment, encouraged originality, and was himself a
serious student of producing, acting, staging, and management.

Dunlap's collapse into bankruptcy pointed up the difficulties
of the American theater in the decade before the War of 1812.
Little hostility against the theater remained anywhere in the
United States, but drama needed something more than merely
absence of opposition to encourage its growth. Foreign competition was formidable; the Park Theater in New York, for
example, between 1810 and 1820, presented Shakespeare, Dryden, Otway, Sheridan, a great deal of London melodrama, drama-
tizations of Scott and Byron, musical plays, Italian opera, and
pantomime ballet. The play-going public was accustomed to
regular attendance and good playhouses, but the stage lacked
distinguished American playwrights—though plays about the
Revolution, the Algerian pirates, the War of 1812, sentimental
comedies, and romantic tragedies flooded the boards and drew
well.

Plays and Players in the Twenties

Of the dozens of authors who wrote for the stage before 1830, only James Nelson Barker, John Howard Payne, and Samuel Woodworth gained noticeable, though rather small, reputations. Barker, a Philadelphian, wrote *Tears and Smiles* (1807), a popular comedy patterned on Tyler's hit, and another very successful play, *The Indian Princess, or La Belle Sauvage* (1808), an operatic drama centered on the Indian-white conflict—a theme due to appear and reappear in the American theater. There were thirty-five Indian plays before 1850 (according to Richard Moody), among them John Augustus Stone's *Metamora,* which appeared in 1829 and starred the great Edwin Forrest; it ran over 200 performances over the next forty years. Barker continued to use American materials in his plays, the best of which was *Superstition* (1824), a powerful treatment of the regicide judges and the witchcraft delusions, one of the half-dozen or so good plays written during the period.

John Howard Payne, who was also a popular actor at London's Drury Lane Theatre, produced his first play at fifteen and wrote more than sixty others, nearly all adaptations of English and continental dramas; he wrote two in collaboration with Washington Irving. Payne's fame also came from the song "Home, Sweet Home," inserted in his opera *Clari* in 1823.

Woodworth wrote operas, melodramas, comedies, and almost everything else. His musical play *Forest Rose; or the American Farmer* (1825), which combined the stage Yankee with a love plot and numerous songs, was a great hit in England and the United States; it had 150 performances in London alone and was still on the boards in 1866 in Ireland.

Though most of the plays written and produced by Americans from 1800 to 1830 were undistinguished and derivative, an amazing number were written with a deliberate emphasis on American materials for American audiences. Authur Hobson Quinn counted 700 plays actually produced by Americans before 1860, perhaps one-third of them before 1832. In them appeared a number of themes and characters destined to become familiar in American drama, poetry, and fiction—Pocahontas, Rip Van Winkle, the Indian-white conflict, the raw frontiersman, the Plymouth settlers, the stage Yankee, the comedy Negro, the city dude, the blustering soldier, the Revolutionary soldier hero, and many others. If a mature and artistic native drama had not yet appeared by 1830, it was not for lack of effort by American playwrights.

The quality of acting on the American stage during the first third of the nineteenth century was far higher than the quality of its plays. Managers discovered the "star system" before 1800 and as a result usually emphasized individual popularity over excellence of vehicle. In 1810 Thomas Cooper of the Park Theater brought the famous English tragedian George Frederick Cooke to New York, where he made an immediate hit. But Cooke was an unpredictable alcoholic, and while his stay was a financial success, his popularity swiftly declined. However, Cooke opened the way for other touring British stars, and theater managers were quick to recognize the value of taking plays on the road.

Edmund Kean, who toured the United States for the first time in 1820, averaged $3,000 a night for nine nights in Boston. Charles Matthews, the famed London comedian, made highly lucrative tours in 1822, 1833, and 1835. William Charles Macready, whom Hazlitt thought the greatest Shakespearian actor of them all, traveled in the United States with tremendous success in 1826 and 1843, but his rivalry with the American actor Edwin Forrest in 1849 touched off bitter anti-foreign riots in New York. In addition to such tourists, some excellent foreign actors came to stay, among them Junius Brutus Booth, who played on the American stage for thirty-nine years and contributed three sons to it; and James Wallack, who also founded a theatrical dynasty. New York-born James Henry Hackett was judged the equal of Matthews; his Kentucky rustic, "Solomon Swap," entertained generations of theatergoers. Towering over them all was Edwin Forrest, American-born and American-trained—a moody, arrogant genius who dominated American acting style for nearly fifty years.

Prospects for the Drama

Between 1776 and 1830, then, the American stage showed encouraging signs of strength and independence. After 1815, traveling companies carried plays inland, down the Ohio and Mississippi, and into the hinterlands to remote hamlets; amateur "Thespian" or "Aeolian" societies proliferated in colleges and cities. The increasing popularity of the theater was reflected by the boom in building between 1820 and 1830—the Bowery, Chatham, Lafayette, and New Park Street in New York, Boston's Tremont, the New Chestnut Street and Arch Street in Philadelphia, among others.

The American stage supported several skilled groups of professional actors (a growing percentage of them native-trained), a corps of experienced managers, and a number of knowledgeable producers. Still, few theaters or companies could be called prosperous. Actors were badly paid, and managers were forced to hold "third nights" and "farewell tours" to augment stars' pay. Pay for playwrights was equally small; $500 for an original play was unusual, $100 for an adaptation generous.

The most serious defect of the American stage was the paucity of good plays. No dramatist appeared before the Civil War to equal the achievements of American poets, novelists, or essayists, though in justice it should be pointed out that contemporary British dramatic writing was hardly more distinguished. The American stage had not yet outgrown its dependence on England and Europe. Americans were no better than "mental colonists" insofar as the drama was concerned, wrote James Nelson Barker, who found it advisable himself to spread the rumor in 1808 that his play *Marmion* really came from London. The American stage was still subordinate to the powerful British dramatic tradition and hesitant to compete with it.

Fiction, Morality, and Art

The American novel in the later eighteenth century still faced lingering public hostility. Timothy Dwight and

Noah Webster, who were barely willing to tolerate fiction, probably represented the majority in their conviction that the novel was not really a form of literary art worthy of serious effort. Clerics and critics cautioned that novels "lead onto a path of vice . . . inflame the passions and corrupt the heart . . . pollute the imaginations of young women and likewise give them false ideas of life." Nevertheless, the demand for fiction increased rapidly, magazine editors printed more and more novels and tales, and circulating libraries stocked greater numbers of books each year. Despite the warnings, there was a profitable market for fiction by the 1790's, which American authors hoped to supply. In response to accusations of "immorality" and "falseness to life," novelists claimed that their stories were really "moral lessons" and usually appended a subtitle or preface to point out that their plots were "founded on fact" or were "truthful representations of human passions."

The American public maintained this ambivalent attitude toward fiction deep into the nineteenth century. Writers found the novel an attractive and useful form of expression—not only did it seem flexible, free, and less demanding than other forms, but it gave the author opportunities for description, character analysis, opinions, and messages. It was agreed that excessive addiction to novels could be bad, and that at least some novels presented a false and delusive picture of life. On the other hand, *Pamela, Tom Jones, Roderick Random,* and *Tristram Shandy* (all of which appeared before 1770) seemed not to have corrupted England, and Americans read them as avidly as Englishmen.

The problem was, then, to separate good from bad novels, to read and write those which served the right purposes. Novelists therefore drew their stories from "real life" to show the consequences of irrationality, immorality, "mis-education," or bad judgment, placing them in the long and honorable American tradition of art and morality. Matthew Carey, a shrewd judge of public taste, thus endorsed such novels in his *American Museum* magazine because they were "true stories," which taught "moral lessons."

*The Early Novel: Sentimentalism
and Mrs. Rowson*

There were four major strains in the early American novel: the sentimental, the satiric, the Gothic, and the historical romance. All were closely imitative of the eighteenth- and early nineteenth-century British novel. The first of these, derived from Samuel Richardson and the British sentimentalists, was by far the most popular variety until displaced by the historical romances of Scott. It was natural for American writers to select Richardson as their model from among the great British novelists, not only because of his great popularity, but because his didacticism satisfied the American belief that fiction should teach and elevate. American audiences, too, were prepared for the Richardsonian manner by long familiarity with the journal, of which Richardson's epistolary style was a sophisticated extension.

After 1770, Richardsonian sentimentalism covered America with a rainstorm of tears, deluging the public with sad tales of seduction, suicide, and sentiment. Women read Richardson's *Pamela, Clarissa,* or *Sir Richard Grandison* voraciously and slept with the books under their pillows. Goethe's *Sorrows of Werther* (1794), soaked in even more excessive sentimentalism, made such a strong appeal in combination with Richardson that at least five novels were written against it; *The Slave of Passion* (1802), for example, had as its explanatory subtitle "The Fruits of Werther." Though a widely reprinted article of 1791 argued "Novel Reading as a Cause of Depravity," Richardson's defenders claimed that such novels really "cultivated the Principles of Virtue and Religion in the Minds of Youth of Both Sexes" by truthfully presenting the wages of sin.

Hundreds of Richardsonian imitations appeared in America, built to the master's formula, decorated with alluring subtitles such as "Female Frailty," "Delicate Embarrassments," or "Venial Trespasses." There was even a journal, *The American Moral and Sentimental Magazine,* founded in 1797. William Hill Brown's novel *The Power of Sympathy* (1789, long attributed to Sarah

Morton) was "founded in truth" and, according to its preface, intended "to expose the dangerous consequences of Seduction and to set forth the advantages of Female Education," which it did with a spectacular plot compounded of seduction, near incest, kidnapping, attempted rape, and suicide.

Mrs. Susannah Rowson's *Charlotte Temple* (1791) was the queen of them all. Susannah Haswell, the daughter of a British naval officer, was born in England and came to America with her family shortly before the Revolution. After the war, the Haswells returned to England, where Susannah in 1786 married William Rowson, a hardware merchant who was also a trumpeter in the Horse Guards. When his business failed, Rowson and his wife went on the stage with moderate success and came to Philadelphia in 1793 for an engagement at the Chestnut Street Theater in Philadelphia. They remained in Philadelphia until 1797, when Mrs. Rowson opened a girls' school in Boston. Thereafter she pursued a successful career as a Boston school mistress, editor and contributor to magazines, poet, and playwright. She also translated Horace and Vergil, compiled a dictionary, wrote an opera, and published textbooks.

Mrs. Rowson wrote several novels before coming to America. *Charlotte Temple: A Tale of Truth,* based upon an actual experience in her family, appeared in London in 1791 and in an American edition in 1794. It began slowly, with three editions before the turn of the century, and then its popularity grew— 50,000 copies sold before 1810, and ultimately over 200 editions appeared in the next century. She continued to write novels, such as *Trials of the Human Heart, Reuben and Rachel,* and *Lucy Temple, or The Three Orphans* (the story of Charlotte's daughter), none of which approached *Charlotte's* sales.

Mrs. Rowson had an inventive mind and more skill than most of her fellow practitioners. She had a knack for keeping her narrative moving despite the rigidity imposed on her by the sentimental conventions, and the ability to endow unbelievable coincidences with a kind of spurious authenticity. *Charlotte* she told simply and directly. The daughter of respectable upper-middle-class parents and a student at Madame Du Pont's School for Girls in England, Charlotte met Montraville, a young officer, shortly before his departure for the American wars. With the help of a devilish brother officer, Belcour, and a depraved Frenchwoman, Madamoiselle La Rue, the well-meaning but weak Montraville persuaded Charlotte to elope with him to New York on promise of marriage. There he became enamored of Julia Franklin, a young American girl; through the machinations of Belcour, who wanted Charlotte for himself, Montraville abandoned Charlotte and her illegitimate child. Belcour immediately lost interest, and the dying Charlotte sank deeper into virtuous poverty until she found refuge at the hut of a poor servant family. Here her true friend, Mrs. Beauchamp, her grieving father, and Montraville found her, but it was too late.

Charlotte opened the floodgates. The novels that inundated the market in the early decades of the nineteenth century followed Mrs. Rowson's pattern to the letter, and authors searched for ways to work ingenious changes into her formula without violating it. In their plots, young women had to distinguish between "false" and "true" love; lovers had to surmount scandal, parental objection, and misunderstandings of heroic proportions. Good people were deluded by false principles such as atheism, emotionalism, or irrationality; heroes had to choose between love and duty, honor and affection, selflessness and humanity.

Mrs. Sally Wood's *Julia and the Illuminated Baron* (1802), whose curious title came from the fact that the suitor for Julia's hand was a member of the Free Society of the Illuminati; Carolyn Warren's *The Gamesters* (1805) which dealt with gambling, duels, and seduction; Isaac Mitchell's *Alonzo and Melissa* (1811), a sentimental Gothic novel; Rebecca Rush's *Kelroy* (1812), a grim tale of a jealous and protective mother— the tide of sentimental novels never stopped. Conventional as their plots were, these novels reflected in their formalized, abstract fashion real problems in contemporary society; whatever their awkwardnesses and ineptitudes, they provide invaluable insights into the inward life of the era. The sentimental, didactic novel continued as an undercurrent in the mainstream of nineteenth-century fiction—running beneath the novels of Brown,

Cooper, Hawthorne, Harriet Stowe, Melville, and a host of others.

The Early Novel: Modern Chivalry and the Satiric Strain

The satiric novel, never so popular as the sentimental, stemmed from Swift, Cervantes, Fielding, and Smollett. Royall Tyler's *Algerine Captive* (1797) poked jabs at New England, contemporary politics, sentimentalism, slavery, and kindred targets. More important, however, was Hugh Henry Brackenridge's massive *Modern Chivalry.*

Born in Scotland, Brackenridge was brought by his parents to the Pennsylvania frontier in 1753. He entered the College of New Jersey (later Princeton) in 1768, where his interest in literature brought him to friendship with James Madison and Philip Freneau, with whom he formed a political and literary club called the Whig Literary Society, which combined the two interests that dominated his later career. With Freneau he wrote an early piece of prose fiction called *Father Bombo's Pilgrimage to Mecca* (1770), and for their commencement the two collaborated on a prophetic poem, *The Rising Glory of America* (1771).

After college, Brackenridge taught school for a time, became an army chaplain (1776–1778), and at last began the study of law, moving in 1781 to Pittsburgh, where he lived for twenty years. Elected to the State Assembly (1786), he was soon ousted and did not run again for office until 1798, when he was once more defeated in a bitter campaign. For his service in organizing and leading the Republicans in Western Pennsylvania, however, he was made a justice of the Pennsylvania Supreme Court (1799) and spent much of the remainder of his life as a defender of the judiciary and the common law, both of which were under vigorous attack.

Brackenridge's personal experience in the economic, legal, and political turmoil following the Revolution was not, for the most part, pleasant. Not satisfied to vent his personal pique and disillusionment directly upon his antagonists, he fortunately put on the satiric mask he had discovered in Cervantes, Samuel Butler, Swift, Smollett, and Fielding. The result was the most popular piece of prose fiction to come out of the region west of the Alleghenies before the nineteenth century. *Modern Chivalry* began as a Hudibrastic satire on Brackenridge's political opponents in the Pennsylvania legislature (1787), expanded into a long Hudibrastic poem called *The Modern Chevalier* (1788–1789), and by 1790 turned into prose, which Brackenridge thought "was a more humble and might be a safer walk."

The first two volumes, published in 1792, introduced the Quixotic characters of Captain John Farrago and his troublesome Irish servant Teague O'Regan, who encountered a series of adventures closely paralleling Brackenridge's own political interests—elections, tax collecting, the Whiskey Rebellion, frontier pretensions to learning, the French Revolution, the scurrility of the American press, and the Federal Constitution. Six more volumes of their adventures, interspersed with brief essays, had appeared by 1805. The entire work was issued in an enlarged, complete edition in 1815, a year before Brackenridge died.

Brackenridge kept no consistent plan throughout the book. "The term *novel*," Alexander Cowie remarks, "must be stretched considerably to accommodate it," for it is a stringing together in casual confusion of essays, character sketches, anecdotes, dialogues, and incidents. The controlling theme of the book—that the misconception and misuse of democracy may destroy it—holds the early portions of the narrative together, but its cohesion tends to disappear in later sections. For the most part, the story simply puts into thinly disguised fictional form Brackenridge's view of contemporary society, about which he held many strong opinions. He intended his book to amuse and instruct his countrymen, he said, feeling that such was "the duty of every man who possessed the facility of drawing such images as will arouse his neighbor to lend a hand, and do something."

Brackenridge's book stands in the early history of fiction as a kind of aboriginal classic whose rugged, rowdy, frontier quality is strictly American. Teague is the first fully developed comic fig-

ure in the American novel, whose adventures as lover, philosopher, socialite, politician, soldier, and in sundry other roles provide a sweeping panorama of life in the decades 1790–1810.
Modern Chivalry fixes in its pages the language, habits, characters, issues, and style of the new Republic as seen through the
eyes of an intelligent, slightly eccentric Scottish lawyer, whose
grasp of the vernacular, sense of rough humor, and insight into
his age anticipates something of Mark Twain.

The Early Novel: Charles Brockden Brown's American Gothic

The Gothic novel of terror, suspense, and mystery, which in the hands of Walpole, "Monk" Lewis, Mrs. Rad-
cliffe, and William Godwin swept over England, found a gifted
American practitioner in Charles Brockden Brown of Philadelphia. Born in 1771 and educated at the Quaker Latin School of
Robert Proud, Brown turned to the study of law but found himself much more attracted to literature. Fascinated by poetry—before he was sixteen he had planned several long epics—he met
the physician-poet Dr. Elihu Hubbard Smith, who introduced
him to Timothy Dwight among other Connecticut Wits and, in
New York, to William Dunlap and the literary society known as
the Friendly Club. But surrendering poetry for the essay and
fiction (he considered himself a "story-telling moralist"), Brown
published *Alcuin,* a defense of women's rights, in 1798; he spent
the next four years producing the six novels on which his fame
rests—*Wieland* (1798), *Edgar Huntly* (1799), *Ormond*
(1799), *Arthur Mervyn* (1799–1800), *Clara Howard* (1801),
and *Jane Talbot* (1801). He then returned to Philadelphia, kept
store, edited periodicals, and died of tuberculosis at thirty-nine.

Wieland, his best novel, brought praise from such men as
Keats, Thomas Hood, Godwin, Shelley, and Hazlitt, who found it
something more than merely another Gothic imitation. Strongly
attracted by contemporary reforms, Brown managed to insert in
his novels discussions of the status of women, morality, divorce,
deistic religion, and other issues. A strong nationalist, Brown

believed that the artist should "examine objects with his own eyes . . . employ the European models solely for the improvement of his taste, and adapt his fiction to all that is genuine and peculiar in the scene before him."

Brown is usually called "America's first professional man of letters," though he was not able to make his living by his pen as he wished. He was, however, a dedicated artist. Excited by ideas, he wanted to do everything—write an epic, edit magazines, write poetry, learn medicine, write a trilogy, reform society, and (his grand project) organize and classify all human knowledge for convenient reference. Never able to concentrate his talents, he scattered his energies into a dozen fields and was so anxious to get on to the next project that he published four novels in less than a year and three more within the next two.

Brown's major novels, *Wieland, Edgar Huntly, Ormond,* and *Arthur Mervyn,* were both brilliant and amateurish. His style could be incredibly overblown and inept (one of his characters, for example, says, "My habitation was a wooden edifice") and at other times swift, concrete, highly charged with meaning. He was unable to keep his plots straight, tried to cram two or three novels into one, and usually wrote dialogue badly. But he had a gift for description, an ability to probe character, and the art of maintaining a suspenseful narrative pace.

Wieland, a study of a group of young intellectuals caught up in a disturbing chain of events that constantly test their reason, is a complex psychological novel—something more than a combination of seduction story and Gothic tale with a moral. *Wieland* maintains a constant tension between the believable and unbelievable, the rational and irrational, and carries with it broad implications about the nature of ethical judgment. *Edgar Huntly,* a study of murder and guilt in which the narrator moves into insanity and returns, is an unusual combination of Gothic, historical, and psychological novel. It introduces the Indian-white conflict into American fiction and for the first time uses American nature as a functional element of the novel. Brown recognized the potential of the Indian for American literature and in his preface attacked the "puerile superstitions and exploded manners, Gothic castles and chimeras" of European fiction, proposing instead that novelists use "the incidents of Indian hostility and the perils of the Western wilderness."

Ormond pits an "enlightened" heroine, Constantia Dudley, against the amoral, dangerously handsome villain Ormond in a battle for her virtue; the story has tragic implications that Brown never fully realized and contains some powerfully written passages with surprisingly sexual undertones. *Arthur Mervyn,* a two part novel, is an "initiation" story of a young man learning about life in the city and is laid against the background of Philadelphia's yellow fever epidemic. A realistic and complicated novel, *Arthur Mervyn* is also the first American urban novel in which Brown recorded the feel of late eighteenth-century life with great fidelity—the Indian wandering in the street, the hawker of broadsides, the dancing teacher with his violin, the Quaker tradesman and overdressed dandy, the tumultuous taverns, muddy streets, noise, and confusion.

Brown wove Gothic mystery, sentimental romance, adventure, psychology, nature, and current issues into novels that, despite their obvious flaws, still retain compelling power. He was quite willing to introduce murder, rape, insanity, epidemics, somnambulism, ventriloquism, and other sensational elements into his fiction for public appeal. Yet his novels had serious artistic and intellectual purposes; they were in a broad sense "problem" novels, which probed human emotions and motivations.

Beginning with an idea, Brown then used incidents and characters to see what might happen if it were put into practice. In *Wieland* he asked, in effect, "What is real? How can one be sure of what he sees, thinks, feels?" and made the novel an examination of credibility—a theme developed later by Poe, who knew Brown's work well. *Huntly* studies the perversities of irrationality and the boundaries between sanity and insanity, other themes Poe found provocative. *Ormond* investigates the relationships between intellectuality and morality, *Arthur Mervyn* the process of maturation.

Unfortunately for Brown, he chose to write in two styles already obsolescent—the sentimental and the Gothic—hoping to infuse new life into forms no longer artistically viable. He wanted to retain the appeal of the Gothic (its ability to "excite and baffle curiosity," he said, "without shocking belief") and the moral involvement of the sentimental, while at the same time using both as tools for the exploration of new ideas. Neither fictional style possessed the vitality or flexibility he needed; their conventions were already frozen into place, and Brown could never loosen them.

Brown's place in the history of the American novel depends not on his success or lack of it, but rather on the themes he introduced, which were to appear later in Poe, Hawthorne, Cooper, Melville, and others—the settler, the forest, and the Indian; the conflict of reason and emotion; the dialectic between certainty and impossibility; the nature of sin and guilt; the interaction of sanity and madness; the complexities of human motivation. As Donald Ringe has pointed out, by questioning the value of reason as a moral guide, Brown implicitly brought into question the Enlightenment itself and forecast the Romantics' rejection of it. Certainly, whatever Charles Brockden Brown's flaws, no novelist of his stature appeared in America for another generation.

The Early Novel: Scott and American Romance

The fourth strand of American fiction, the historical romance, emerged directly from the work of Sir Walter Scott, whose novels of history, legend, adventure, scenery, love, and patriotism took the early nineteenth century by storm. His popularity in the United States was immense. His verse was memorized by thousands of school children and read aloud in countless family circles; in 1842 Dickens even discovered a Choctaw Indian who could recite whole sections of *The Lady of the Lake.* Announcement of a new Scott novel, according to bookseller Samuel Goodrich, caused "a greater sensation in the United States than some of the battles of Napoleon," while Fitz-

Greene Halleck believed that Scott's American popularity was "probably never equalled in the history of literature."

Americans bought Scott novels by the thousands (a half million volumes before 1823), adapted, summarized, dramatized, and imitated them. Though a stubborn minority of critics maintained that his liking for feudalism and ceremony encouraged "a diseased and perverted taste for the luxurious and aristocratic," few of his admirers cared. In the South, where Scott's chivalric apparatus found an especially responsive audience, there were thirty-five towns named Waverly, hundreds of little girls named Rowena, and side-wheel steamers named *Rob Roy* and *Marmion*.

Scott's fervent Scottish nationalism and his skillful use of historical materials were precisely what American authors hoped to emulate; why could they not, using their past as Scott used his, create an art of equal value? Rufus Choate's oration at Salem in 1810, titled *The Importance of Illustrating New England History by a Series of Romances Like the Waverly Novels,* summarized popular opinion exactly; every week, critic John Neal grumbled, seemed to see a new novel "after the Scottish fashion" with "native Rodericks and Rob Roys" by the dozen. James Kirke Paulding, Catherine Sedgwick, John Pendleton Kennedy, William Gilmore Simms, Daniel Thompson, and Neal himself tried to fit the Scott formula to American materials without notable success. But James Fenimore Cooper, after trying his hand at a Jane Austen-like novel of manners, wrote *The Spy* in 1821, *The Pioneers* in 1823, *The Last of the Mohicans* in 1826, and thirty more. When Natty Bumppo walked into American fiction and leaned on his long rifle, the American novel came of age.

The Development of the Tale

The short fictional narrative, or tale, developed naturally out of the character sketches and the essays of the eighteenth century, which contained most of the elements needed to make them into stories. At the same time, the folk tale and the anecdote, both hardy favorites, remained as staples-in-trade of the almanacs. Late in the century, for that matter, it became difficult to separate the essay from the anecdote and the rudimentary short story. Francis Hopkinson's "Old Bachelor" essay series, for example, could easily pass as fiction, since it was composed of essays built around a single assumed character involved in a series of situations. After 1800, American, English, and Continental magazines were filled with these half-essay, half-story contributions, leading Irving to complain of the quantity of sketches "now littering the presses" at home and abroad. The anonymous minister who wrote "A Narrative of the Unpardonable Sin" in *The Theological Magazine* in 1796 anticipated Hawthorne; "The Child of the Storm," published in *The Massachusetts Magazine* for 1792, adapted an old folk tale to fiction; "The Yankee Wedding," a comic anecdote published in the same journal in 1794, was virtually a local color story.

Hundreds of such pieces appeared in the magazines after 1790, for the market used up material swiftly, and editors were always in search of brief, saleable, narrative items. To make a short story, one needed only to take the components at hand and put them together. The short story or tale, then, did not spring suddenly into existence with Irving's *Sketch Book;* what Irving did was to add a dash of plot, a great deal of description, and a rudimentary structure to the kind of popular sketch that had been written for the previous twenty years. He did not, in fact, add much. An examination of either *Rip Van Winkle* or *The Legend of Sleepy Hollow,* the first true American short stories, will reveal how many of the characteristics of the essay and the character sketch they retain.

The Sketch Book itself included almost all the popular types of pre-fiction that went into the making of the short tale after 1790—character studies, anecdotes, incidents, travel pieces, folk legends, romantic essays ("Westminster Abbey"), even a *Charlotte Temple* in miniature ("The Pride of the Village")—colored with Irving's own gentle, sentimental imagination. Irving's tales lay only a step away from the indeterminate, fictional essays which flooded the magazines. When Poe added structure and design to the tale, and Hawthorne depth and density, the short story emerged as an American literary form in its own right. By the 1840s, in the hands of popular practitioners such as N. P. Willis (who received a hundred-dollar-a-month retainer from each of four magazines), it dominated the mass reading market.

Washington Irving: "Who Reads an American Book?"

Washington Irving, born in 1783 into a wealthy New York City merchant family, was educated for the law. He preferred to write essays for two newspapers edited by his brother Peter, however, and from 1802 to 1803 wrote a series of delightfully impudent satires on city society under the pseudonym of "Jonathan Oldstyle, Gent." The Irving family sent young Washington to Europe for two years, 1804–1806, and although he was admitted to the bar on his return and taken into the family firm, he showed little interest in either law or business. Instead he joined his brother William, James Kirke Paulding, and several other young men who called themselves "The Nine Worthies of Cockloft Hall" in the pleasant life of men-about-town. From 1807 to 1808 they published a series of Addison-style essays, *Salmagundi,* which enjoyed great popularity and showed also a great deal of promise. In 1809 Irving's fiancée, Mathilda Hoffman, died, and he threw himself into the completion of his *History of New York* by "Diedrich Knickerbocker," which gave him an immediate reputation as a burlesque humorist.

By this time Irving had learned a charming, pliable style, mastered the art of narrative, and developed a personal point of view that was soon to create a literary identity for him—the sauntering, meditative, gently antiquarian storyteller, whatever pseudonym he might choose to mask it. In 1815 Irving went to England on business, unaware that he was to make his literary reputation abroad and to remain there for seventeen years. When the family firm failed not long after, Irving was more or less thrown on his own resources. His friendship with Sir Walter Scott, publisher John Murray, and the London literary circle stood him in good stead, for it resulted in Murray's publication of *The Sketch Book* (1819–1820), which catapulted him to fame on both sides of the Atlantic. He became, a friend said, "the most fashionable fellow of the day" and certainly the best known American author of his generation.

In *The Sketch Book*, Irving brought to maturity his own distinct manner and mood. A great deal of the material in the collection concerned England, not America; of the thirty-two pieces in the collection (excluding the introduction), twenty-six are on English topics. The reader is likely to forget (as he is told in the prefatory "Author's Account of Himself") that there is an assumed narrator, "Geoffrey Crayon, Gent.," a sentimental, sensitive, American traveler who is trying to understand the character of English life, and who hopes to find in England "the storied and poetical associations" that his own country lacks. *The Sketch Book*, then, is essentially a book about an American in England, whose purpose is cultural discovery and self-analysis.

After *Bracebridge Hall* (1822), a continuation of the *Sketch Book* style, Irving lived in Germany for a year, published *Tales of a Traveller* (1824), spent some time in Paris, and went to Madrid to serve in the American legation. The appeal of Spain to his imagination produced *The Life of Columbus* (1828) and *The Companions of Columbus* (1831); two historical studies, *The Conquest of Granada* (1829) and *The Conquest of Spain* (1835); and his last volume of tales, *The Alhambra* (1832). After *The Alhambra*, Irving turned to history, biography, and travel; his work lost much of the imaginativeness and vitality that marked his Hudson Valley, German, English, and Spanish sketches and stories, though it may have gained in prestige. A conservative in his literary tastes, he preferred to remain in the tradition of Addison, Sterne, and Goldsmith, and (except for Scott) drew little from Coleridge, Wordsworth, Byron, and other writers of the new generation.

Irving returned to the United States in 1832 to find its social, political, and economic complexion drastically changed. This was Jacksonian America in the full flush of ebullient nationalism, and there seemed to be little place in it for an aristocratic Knickerbocker gentleman. In time, Irving made partial adjustment to the new society; he discovered the American frontier, took an extended tour into the prairies, and wrote three books about the new West—*Astoria* (1834), an account of John Jacob Astor's fur empire; *A Tour of the Prairies* (1835), an expansion of his travel journal; and *The Adventures of Captain Bonneville* (1837), who was a Rocky Mountain scout and explorer. Finally, in 1842, he accepted the post of Minister to Spain for three years, after which he returned to Sunnyside, his gracious country home at Tarrytown, New York, near Sleepy Hollow, where he completed his *Life of Mahomet* and a five-volume *Life of Washington.* Here he died, a much-loved and greatly respected figure, in 1859.

Although Irving wrote burlesque, biography, history, travel, and essays, his fame rests on his tales. Excluding character sketches and amorphous essay-like narratives, Irving wrote no more than forty-nine pieces that can be classified as tales; of those, only seven were laid in Hudson country. Yet two of these, *Rip Van Winkle* and *The Legend of Sleepy Hollow* (both from *The Sketch Book*) opened a whole new vista to American writers, set a style, created a manner, and became an integral part of the American cultural heritage. In these seven American stories, Irving succeeded in doing what Geoffrey Crayon hoped to do— that is, to discover in America the literary ambiance that England and Europe seemed to possess, and America did not. His aim, Irving wrote, was "to clothe home scenes and places and familiar names with those imaginative and whimsical associations so seldom met with in this country, but which lie like charms and spells about the cities of the Old World."

What Irving began in *The Sketch Book* and continued in later collections was to make short fiction artistically respectable by investing it with style, depth, and craftsmanship. After Irving, no man dared to write short fiction badly; he took his art seriously, and his skill and success gave the form a literary status it had hitherto lacked. By showing Americans the potential of American materials, he stirred dozens of young men to an interest in American themes and a new consciousness of the American scene. Almost every aspiring American writer over the next generation began by imitating Irving in one way or another; Longfellow, Bryant, Whittier, Thoreau, Hawthorne, even Bret Harte learned something from him.

Irving stripped the tale of its moralizing. He did not like "those barefaced tales," he said, "which carry their moral on the surface." "I have preferred addressing myself to the feeling and fancy of the reader more than to his judgment," he told his friend Brevoort in 1824. "I have attempted no lofty theme, nor sought to look wise and learned." As William Prescott noted in his review of *The Sketch Book* in 1822, it had "no direct moral purpose, but is founded on sentiment and deep feeling."

For this reason, *The Sketch Book* marks a shift away from eighteenth-century literary values toward American Romanticism. The book's point was not, in Addisonian terms, to "expose and reform the follies of the age" (as in *Salmagundi* or *New-York*) but, as Irving wrote, "to wander . . . to meditate . . . to escape. . . ."—in other terms, to alter reality into believable unreality. Much of Irving's genius lies in his ability to shift from real to unreal by imperceptible degrees and to release the reader from the palpable. *Rip Van Winkle,* for example, begins at a definite time in a definite place, but soon the "magical hues and shapes" of the "fairy mountains" work their spell, and as Rip moves from sunlight into the shadows of the mountain glen, so the story moves with him into Irving's special world of dream. The voice of the strange old Dutchman calling Rip's name makes the transition final. This synthesis of believable and marvelous is the unique trademark of Irving's art, as operative in Moorish Spain or the Rhineland as in Sleepy Hollow.

Irving's romanticism was very much a part of his temperament. He wrote, he said, out of "literary excitement." "An author's right time to work is when the mind is aglow, when his imagination is kindled. These are his precious moments. Let him wait until they come. . . ." As Henry Pochmann has noted, Irving's imagination was not strong, and he always needed some stimulus (the Hudson, Scott, Moorish Spain, Rhine castles) to stir it to activity. He was sensitive rather than creative; his tales were transcriptions of feeling and impression rather than conceptions. As he had little structural sense, he knew himself incapable of a novel, preferring, he said, to write in shorter units, "a line of writing peculiar to myself." To him plot was secondary, mood primary. He told Brevoort:

For my part I consider a story merely as a frame on which to stretch my materials. It is the play of thought, and sentiment and language; the weaving in of characters, lightly yet expressively delineated; the familiar and faithful exhibition of scenes in common life; and the half-concealed vein of humor that is often playing through the whole—these are among what I am at.

Irving's greatest asset, of course, was his style, which placed him among the major prose writers of his (or any) age. For years, selections from his writings were used in European and Asian schools as models of graceful English. A cursory analysis of any Irving story will reveal how little actually happens, and how much the tale's effectiveness depends on his mastery of the language.

Irving's major theme was that of change, flux, mutability—the familiar theme of Romanticism, but also one which fitted his own view of life, and one which he handled with unusual skill. Acutely conscious of the mutations of his own society, Irving, like "Geoffrey Crayon," hoped to escape "the common place realities of the present" by reconstructing "the shadowy grandeurs of the past." In Jacksonian America, Irving saw the old values swiftly flitting away into a disappearing past; he was, he confessed, given to a "foolish fondness for old and obsolete things" no longer valued by his times. The recurring figure of the nostalgic traveler in Irving's tales is almost an overt symbol of loss and estrangement. Intensely aware of the brevity of things, Irving created in Rip—with his pathetic cry, "Does nobody know Rip Van Winkle?"—the classic example of what time and change may do to us all.

Not a man of ideas but of feeling, Irving gave his readers no guide to action or any "philosophy" of life. He made no commitments (except to the past), and he was capable of no deep convictions. Artists, he wrote, were "mere chameleons, fed with air, changing color with anything with which we come into contact." A man of sentiment to his fingertips, Irving's artistic problem was to keep his sentimentality under control lest it sink into bathos, as it occasionally did in stories such as "The Broken Heart" or "The Widow and her Son."

Yet this sensitivity to the emotional overtones of experience was one of Irving's great strengths. He liked the pageant of life, even though he knew that it soon passed—the taste, color, and feel of experience, whether it be at Westminster Abbey, the Alhambra, or a glen in the Catskills. One might tread through all of Irving without stumbling against an idea, though certainly few readers of Irving ever cared, as Irving did not. "I have always been of the opinion," he wrote in *Bracebridge Hall,* "that much good might be done by keeping mankind in good humour with one another," adding that he liked "to see the world in as pleasant a light as circumstance will permit," which is perhaps the best summary of his art.,

Washington Irving became the first American classic. He was the first to compel European recognition of an American author as a major literary figure—not as an imitator of a British author or style, but as an artist in his own right with a mind and an art of his own. *The Sketch Book* was a swift, decisive answer to Sidney Smith's famous sneer of 1820, "Who reads an American book?" In addition, Irving served his generation as a sort of literary ambassador-at-large to Europe from America and to America from Europe. In the midst of a rancorous war between American and British critics, which often degenerated into name-calling, Irving had much to do with restoring good manners and common sense to the argument. He was American; yet he knew Europe well, revered its past and its traditions, and at the same time felt deep pride in his own native land and its potentialities. Eventually, by his pen and his example, he helped bring American literature another step toward critical maturity.

# Postscript

The American of the early nineteenth century looked at the years ahead with magnificent self-assurance. He no longer said, as his grandfather had, "the United States are," nor did he think of England, as occasionally his father had, as "home." When he stepped on the soil his forefathers had left, Irving felt that "he was a stranger in the land." Instead the American knew who he was, where he had come from, and what he intended to do with the future. Daniel Webster saw the beginnings of "a wonderful advancement of the country in all its interests," especially in "the progress and success of the cause of letters." William Ellery Channing observed "a tendency and a power to exalt the people" founded on "devotion to the progress of the whole human race." The Shaker seeress, Paulina Bates, welcomed "the present age as commencing the most extraordinary and momentous era that ever took place on earth." Ralph Waldo Emerson, who represented the new generation, opened the Golden Day of the American Renaissance when he told the young men at Harvard that the years of uncertainty and trial for their nation's culture were over. His assertion in *The American Scholar* in 1837 that "We will walk on our own feet; we will work with our own hands; we will speak our own minds" rang with confidence. Thus was the American point of view established, the American style made a reality.

BIBLIOGRAPHY

The following list, although it is by no means exhaustive, should serve as a guide to the sources used in this study and as a reference list for additional readings in the history and literature of the Colonial and early national periods.

General Reference

HART, JAMES D. *The Oxford Companion to American Literature.* 4th ed. New York, 1965.

HERZBERG, MAX. *The Reader's Encyclopaedia of American Literature.* New York, 1962.

KUNITZ, STANLEY, and HOWARD HAYCRAFT. *American Authors, 1600–1900.* New York, 1944.

SPILLER, ROBERT, *et al.,* eds. *The Literary History of the United States.* 8 vols. New York, 1948.

Literary and Cultural History

BLAIR, WALTER, THEODORE HORNBERGER, and RANDALL STEWART. *American Literature, a Brief History.* Chicago, 1964.

BOORSTIN, DANIEL. *The Lost World of Thomas Jefferson.* New York, 1948.

———. *The Americans: The Colonial Experience.* New York, 1958.

———. *The Americans: The National Experience.* New York, 1965.

BROWN, HERBERT. *The Sentimental Novel in America.* Durham, 1957.

BURBANK, REX, and JACK MOORE, eds. *The Literature of Early America*. Columbus, 1967.

CAIRNS, WILLIAM T. *Early American Writings*. New York, 1909.

CASH, WILBUR J. *The Mind of the South*. New York, 1951.

CLARK, HARRY H., ed. *Transitions in American Literary History*. Durham, 1953.

CLOUGH, WILSON O., ed. *The Intellectual Origins of American Thought*. Rev. ed. New York, 1961.

DORSON, RICHARD. *American Folklore*. Chicago, 1959.

EATON, CLEMENT. *The Growth of Southern Civilization*. New York, 1961.

FORBES, JAMES D., ed. *The Indian in America's Past*. Englewood Cliffs, 1964.

HALLINE, ALLAN, ed. *American Plays*. New York, 1935.

HEIMERT, ALAN. *Religion and the American Mind*. Cambridge, 1966.

HOWARD, LEON. *Literature and the American Tradition*. Garden City, 1960.

HUBBELL, JAY B. *The South in American Literature*. Durham, 1954.

JANTZ, HAROLD. *The First Century of New England Verse*. New York, 1962.

KURTZ, PAUL, ed. *American Thought Before 1900*. New York, 1966.

LOSHE, LILY. *The Early American Novel*. New York, 1907.

MOODY, RICHARD, ed. *Dramas from the American Theater: 1762–1909*. Bloomington, 1967.

MOORE, FRANK, ed. *Songs and Ballads of the American Revolution*. New York, 1856.

MORISON, SAMUEL E. *Intellectual Life in Early New England*. Cambridge, 1956.

———. *Builders of the Bay Colony*. Boston, 1930.

NYE, RUSSEL B. *The Cultural Life of the New Nation*. New York, 1960.

———, and NORMAN GRABO, eds. *American Thought and Writing*. 2 vols. New York, 1965.

OLMSTED, CLIFTON. *Religion in America, Past and Present.* Englewood Cliffs, 1961.

PEARCE, ROY H. *The Savages of North America.* Baltimore, 1953.

————. *The Continuity of American Poetry.* Baltimore, 1961.

QUINN, ARTHUR H. *A History of American Drama.* 2 vols., rev. New York, 1943.

————. *American Fiction.* New York, 1936.

ROBSON, ERIC. *The American Revolution: Its Political and Military Aspects.* New York, 1966.

SCHNEIDER, HERBERT. *A History of American Philosophy.* New York, 1946.

SMITH, JAMES W., and A. LELAND JAMISON, eds. *The Shaping of American Religion.* Princeton, 1961.

TYLER, MOSES COIT. *A History of American Literature During the Colonial Period.* 2 vols., rev. New York, 1897.

————. *The Literary History of the American Revolution.* 2 vols. New York, 1897.

WERTENBAKER, THOMAS J. *The Golden Age of Colonial Culture.* Ithaca, 1959.

WHITTEMORE, ROBERT, ed. *Makers of the American Mind.* New York, 1964.

WISH, HARVEY. *Society and Thought in Early America.* New York, 1950.

WRIGHT, LOUIS. *The Atlantic Frontier: Colonial American Civilization.* New York, 1948.

————. *The Cultural Life of the American Colonies.* New York, 1957.

WRIGHT, LYLE H. *American Fiction 1774–1850.* San Marino, 1948.

Biography, Criticism

ALDRIDGE, ALFRED O. *Benjamin Franklin, Philosopher and Man.* Philadelphia, 1965.

————. *Man of Reason: The Life of Thomas Paine.* Philadelphia, 1959.

————. *Jonathan Edwards.* Philadelphia, 1964.

BALDWIN, ALICE. *The New England Clergy in the American Revolution.* Durham, 1928.

BARBOUR, PHILIP L. *The Three Worlds of Captain John Smith.* Boston, 1964.

BEATTY, RICHARD. *William Byrd of Westover.* Boston, 1932.

BORDEN, MORTON, ed. *The Antifederalist Papers.* East Lansing, 1965.

BROOKS, VAN WYCK. *The World of Washington Irving.* New York, 1944.

BROWN, ARTHUR. *Always Young for Liberty: William Ellery Channing.* Syracuse, 1956.

CADY, EDWIN. *John Woolman.* New York, 1965.

CHARVAT, WILLIAM. *The Origins of American Criticism 1810–1831.* Philadelphia, 1936.

COWIE, ALEXANDER. *John Trumbull, Connecticut Wit.* Chapel Hill, 1936.

CROWDER, RICHARD. *No Featherbed to Heaven: A Biography of Michael Wigglesworth.* East Lansing, 1962.

CUNINGHAM, CHARLES. *Timothy Dwight.* Boston, 1942.

DAVIDSON, PHILIP. *Propaganda and the American Revolution 1763–1783.* Chapel Hill, 1941.

DAVIS, RICHARD BEALE. *Intellectual Life in Jefferson's Virginia.* Chapel Hill, 1964.

————. *William Fitzhugh and His Chesapeake World.* Chapel Hill, 1963.

DORSON, RICHARD. *America Begins.* New York, 1950.

————. *American Rebels.* New York, 1953.

DUNN, RICHARD S. *Puritans and Yankees: The Winthrop Dynasty of New England, 1630–1717.* Princeton, 1962.

EARNEST, ERNEST. *John and William Bartram, Botanists and Explorers.* Philadelphia, 1940.

EMERSON, EVERETT. *John Cotton.* New York, 1965.

FAGIN, NATHAN B. *William Bartram, Interpreter of the American Landscape.* Baltimore, 1933.

GRABO, NORMAN. *Edward Taylor*. New York, 1962.

HEDGES, WILLIAM L. *Washington Irving*. Baltimore, 1965.

HEIMERT, ALAN, ed. *Barrett Wendell, Cotton Mather, Puritan Priest*. Chicago, 1962.

HENSLEY, JEANNINE. *The Works of Anne Bradstreet*. Cambridge, 1967.

HINDLE, BROOKE. *The Pursuit of Science in Revolutionary America*. Chapel Hill, 1956.

HOWARD, LEON. *The Connecticut Wits*. Chicago, 1943.

KENYON, CELIA, ed. *The Antifederalists*. Indianapolis, 1966.

LEARY, LEWIS. *That Rascal Freneau*. New Brunswick, 1941.

LEMAY, J. A. LEO. "Richard Lewis and Augustan American Poetry," *PMLA* 83 (March 1968): 80–88.

MALONE, DUMAS. *Jefferson the Virginian*. Boston, 1948.

———. *Jefferson and the Rights of Man*. Boston, 1951.

———. *Jefferson and the Ordeal of Liberty*. Boston, 1962.

MARDER, DANIEL. *Hugh Henry Brackenridge*. New York, 1967.

MARSH, PHILIP. *Philip Freneau, Poet and Journalist*. Minneapolis, 1967.

MESEROLE, HARRISON, ed. *Seventeenth-Century American Poetry*. Garden City, 1968.

MILLER, JOHN C. *The First Frontier: Life in Colonial America*. New York, 1966.

MILLER, PERRY. *Jonathan Edwards*. New York, 1949.

———. *The New England Mind: The Seventeenth Century*. Cambridge, 1939.

———. *The New England Mind: From Colony to Province*. Cambridge, 1953.

MITCHELL, JULIA. *St. Jean de Crèvecoeur*. New York, 1916.

MORGAN, EDMUND S. *The Puritan Dilemma: The Story of John Winthrop*. Boston, 1958.

MURDOCK, KENNETH. *Literature and Theology in Colonial New England*. Cambridge, 1949.

NEWLIN, CLAUDE. *The Life and Writings of Hugh Henry Brackenridge*. Princeton, 1932.

NYE, RUSSEL B., ed. *Franklin's Autobiography*. Boston, 1962.

PEARE, CATHERINE O. *John Woolman: Child of Light*. New York, 1954.

PIERCY, JOSEPHINE. *Anne Bradstreet*. New York, 1965.

———. *Studies in Literary Types in Seventeenth Century America*. New Haven, 1939.

RICE, MADELEINE. *Federal Street Pastor: William Ellery Channing*. New York, 1961.

RINGE, DONALD. *Charles Brockden Brown*. New York, 1966.

ROSSITER, CLINTON, ed. *The Federalist Papers*. New York, 1961.

RUTMAN, DARRET B. *Winthrop's Boston*. Chapel Hill, 1965.

SMITH, BERNARD. *Bradford of Plymouth*. New York, 1951.

SMITH, BRADFORD. *Captain John Smith: His Life and Legend*. Philadelphia, 1963.

STANFORD, DONALD. *The Poems of Edward Taylor*. New Haven, 1960.

STRANDNESS, BEN. *Samuel Sewall*. East Lansing, 1968.

THOMPSON, IRA M. *The Religious Beliefs of Thomas Paine*. New York, 1965.

WAGENKNECHT, EDWARD. *Washington Irving*. Oxford, 1962.

WAGGONER, HYATT H. *American Poets, from the Puritans to the Present*. New York, 1968.

WILLISON, GEORGE F. *Saints and Strangers*. Boston, 1945.

WINSLOW, OLA E. *Jonathan Edwards*. New York, 1940.

———. *Samuel Sewall of Boston*. New York, 1964.

WOODRESS, JAMES. *A Yankee's Odyssey: The Life of Joel Barlow*. Philadelphia, 1958.

WRIGHT, BENJAMIN F., ed. *The Federalist Papers*. Cambridge, 1961.

WRIGHT, LOUIS. *The First Gentlemen of Virginia*. San Marino, 1940.

VAN DOREN, CARL. *Benjamin Franklin*. New York, 1938.

Index

263

A NOTE ON THE TYPE

The text of this book was set on the Linotype in Garamond, a modern rendering of the type first cut by Claude Garamond (1510–1561). Garamond was a pupil of Geoffroy Troy and is believed to have based his letters on the Venetian models, although he introduced a number of important differences, and it is to him we owe the letter which we know as old-style. He gave to his letters a certain elegance and a feeling of movement that won for their creator an immediate reputation and the patronage of Francis I of France.

Composed by H. Wolff Book Manufacturing Co., Inc., New York, N.Y. Printed and bound by Halliday Lithograph Corp., West Hanover, Mass.

Typography by Jack Ribik.